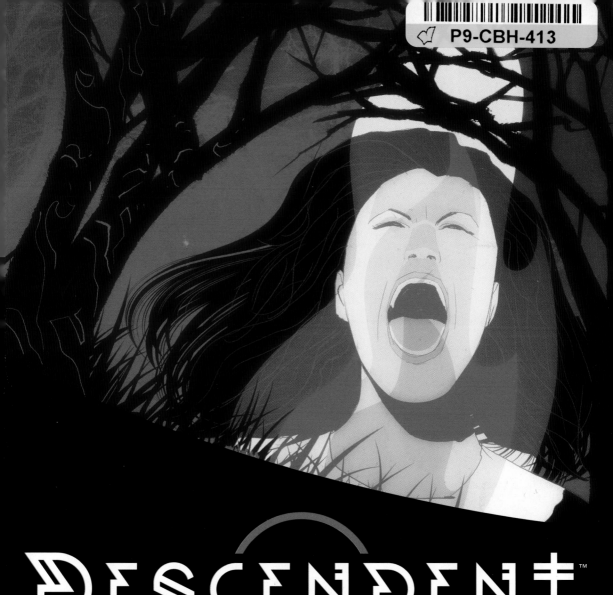

DESCENDENT

STEPHANIE PHILLIPS

EVGENIY BORNYAKOV

LAUREN AFFE

TROY PETERI

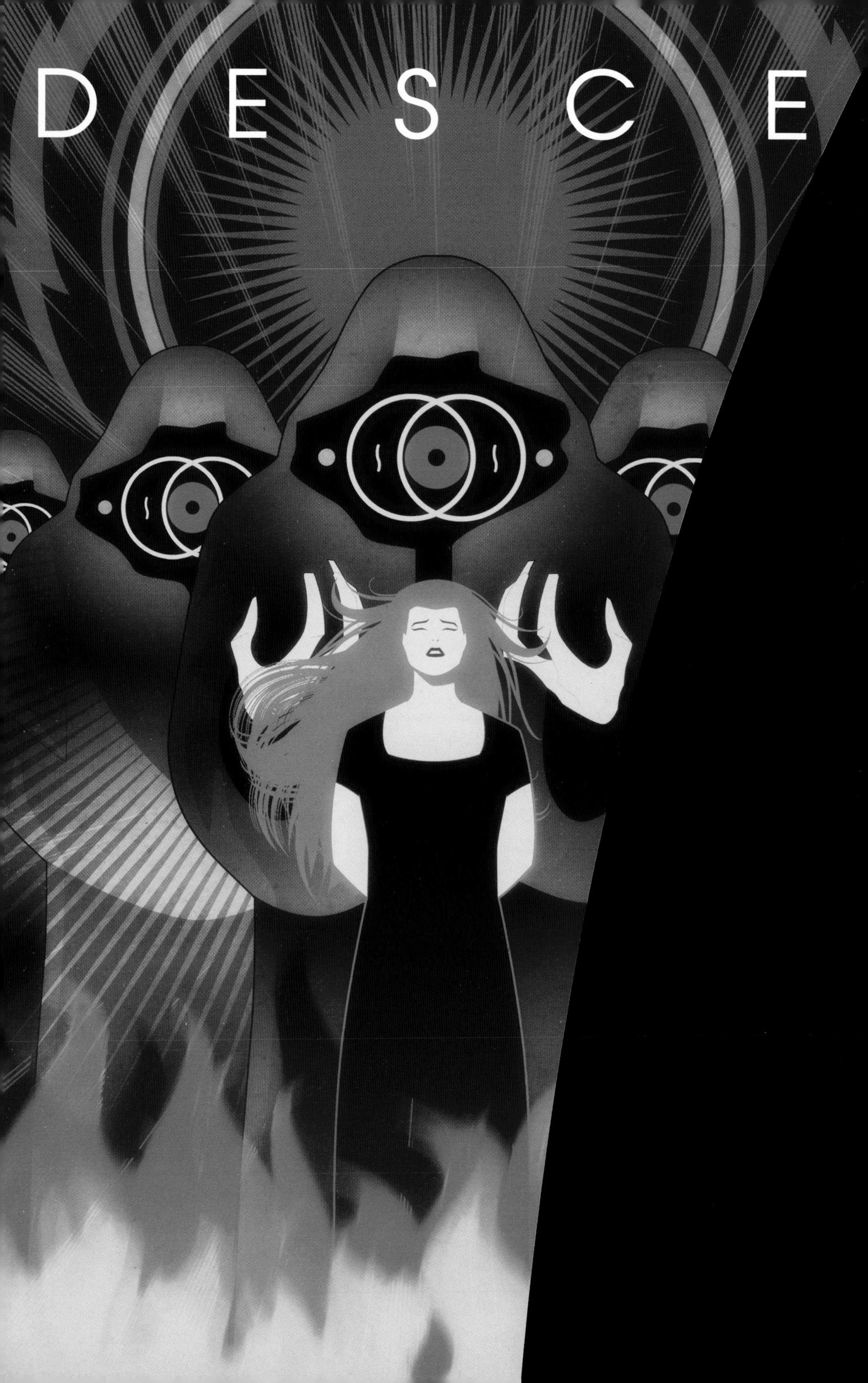
D E S C E

N D E N T ™

STEPHANIE PHILLIPS creator & writer

EVGENIY BORNYAKOV artist

LAUREN AFFE colorist

TROY PETERI letterer

JUAN DOE front & original covers

ANDREI BRESSAN w/ **ADRIANO LUCAS** variant cover

JARED K. FLETCHER logo designer

COREY BREEN book designer

MIKE MARTS editor

AFTERSHOCK™

MIKE MARTS - Editor-in-Chief • **JOE PRUETT** - Publisher/CCO • **LEE KRAMER** - President • **JON KRAMER** - Chief Executive Officer
STEVE ROTTERDAM - SVP, Sales & Marketing • **DAN SHIRES** - VP, Film & Television UK • **CHRISTINA HARRINGTON** - Managing Editor
MARC HAMMOND - Sr. Retail Sales Development Manager • **RUTHANN THOMPSON** - Sr. Retailer Relations Manager • **KATHERINE JAMISON** - Marketing Manager
BLAKE STOCKER - Director of Finance • **AARON MARION** - Publicist • **LISA MOODY** - Finance • **RYAN CARROLL** - Development Coordinator
JAWAD QURESHI - Technology Advisor/Strategist • **CHARLES PRITCHETT** - Comics Production • **COREY BREEN** - Collections Production
TEDDY LEO - Editorial Assistant • **STEPHANIE CASEBIER & SARAH PRUETT** - Publishing Assistants

AfterShock Logo Design by **COMICRAFT**
Publicity: contact **AARON MARION** (aaron@publichausagency.com) & **RYAN CROY** (ryan@publichausagency.com) at **PUBLICHAUS**
Special thanks to: **IRA KURGAN, MARINE KSADZHIKYAN, ANTONIA LIANOS & STEPHAN NILSON**

AFTERSHOCKCOMICS.COM Follow us on social media 🐦 📷 f

I N T R O D U C T I O N

As a kid, my parents gave me a little notepad that I used to try to solve mysteries around the house. I would beg my mom to give me cases to solve. I don't want to brag or anything, but I really cracked "the case of the missing lipstick" wide open. I was a real mystery-solving sleuth and in no way a hindrance to my mother trying to make dinner.

Whether it's missing lipstick or the unknown location to ancient buried treasure, I've always felt a deep-rooted pull towards the *unsolvable*. Rising to the occasion of solving something seemingly unsolvable always creates the best action and the best heroes.

The idea behind DESCENDENT started with one such unsolvable mystery: the unknown icon on the bottom of the ransom note left at the scene of Charles Lindbergh Jr.'s kidnapping in 1932. As prolific as the Internet can be when it comes to weird and obscure theories, there are surprisingly few out there about this unknown symbol. Couple this bizarre mystery with plenty of other odd and unsolved occurrences throughout U.S. history, and DESCENDENT was born.

While reading, I hope you will allow a little mystery into your own life and perhaps even feel that same drive to answer the ever-alluring call of the unknown and the unsolvable.

STEPHANIE PHILLIPS
November 2019

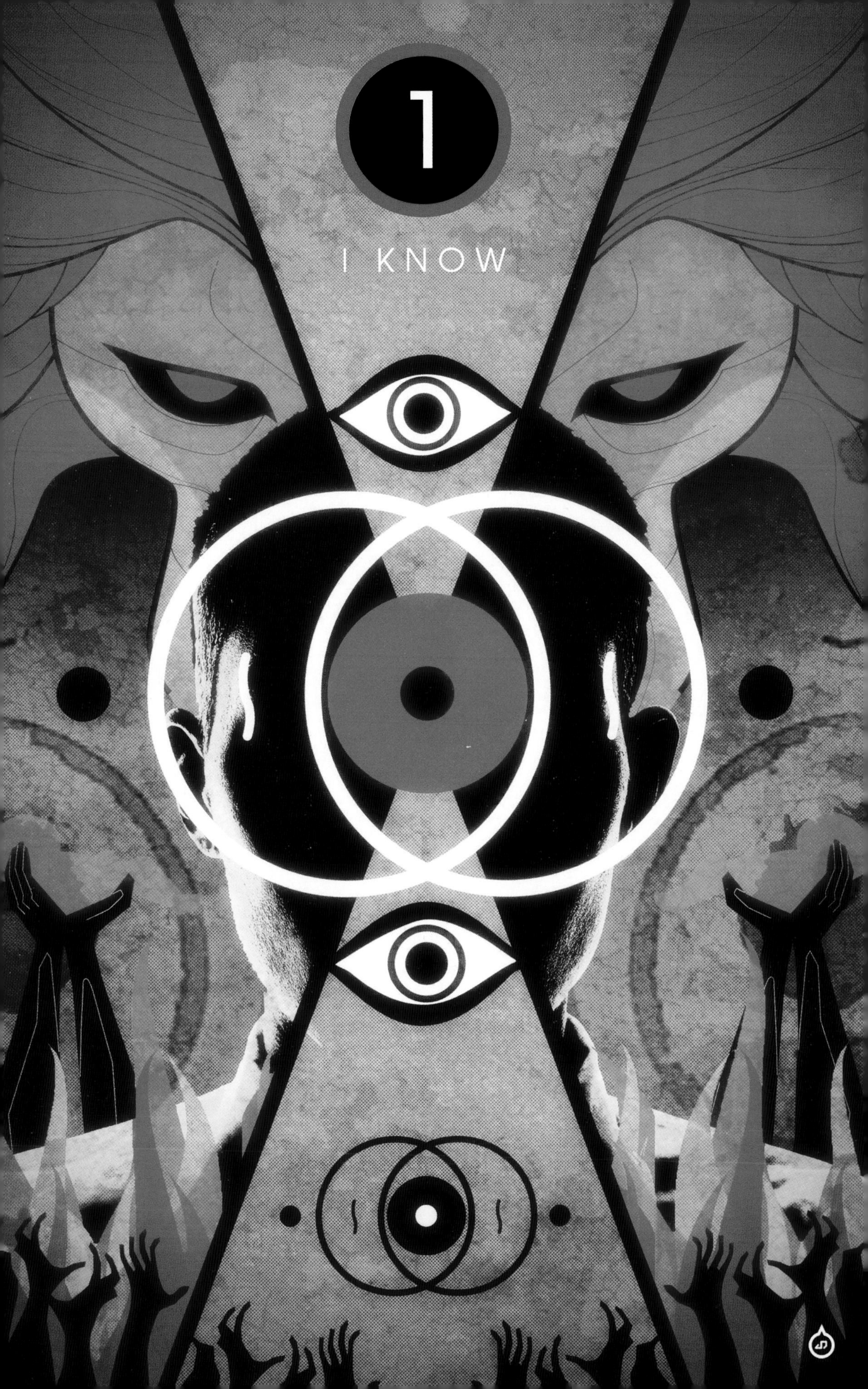
1
I KNOW

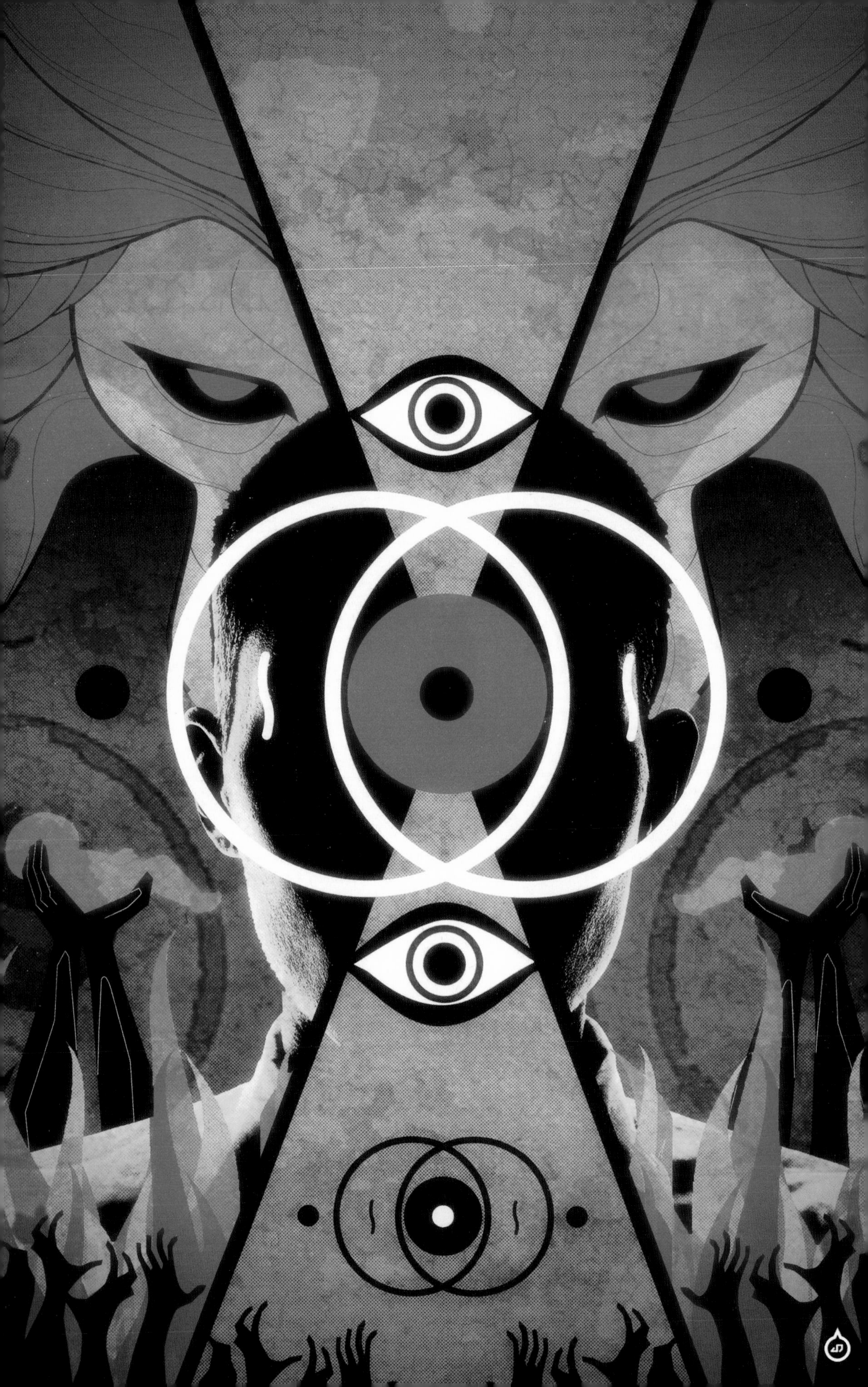

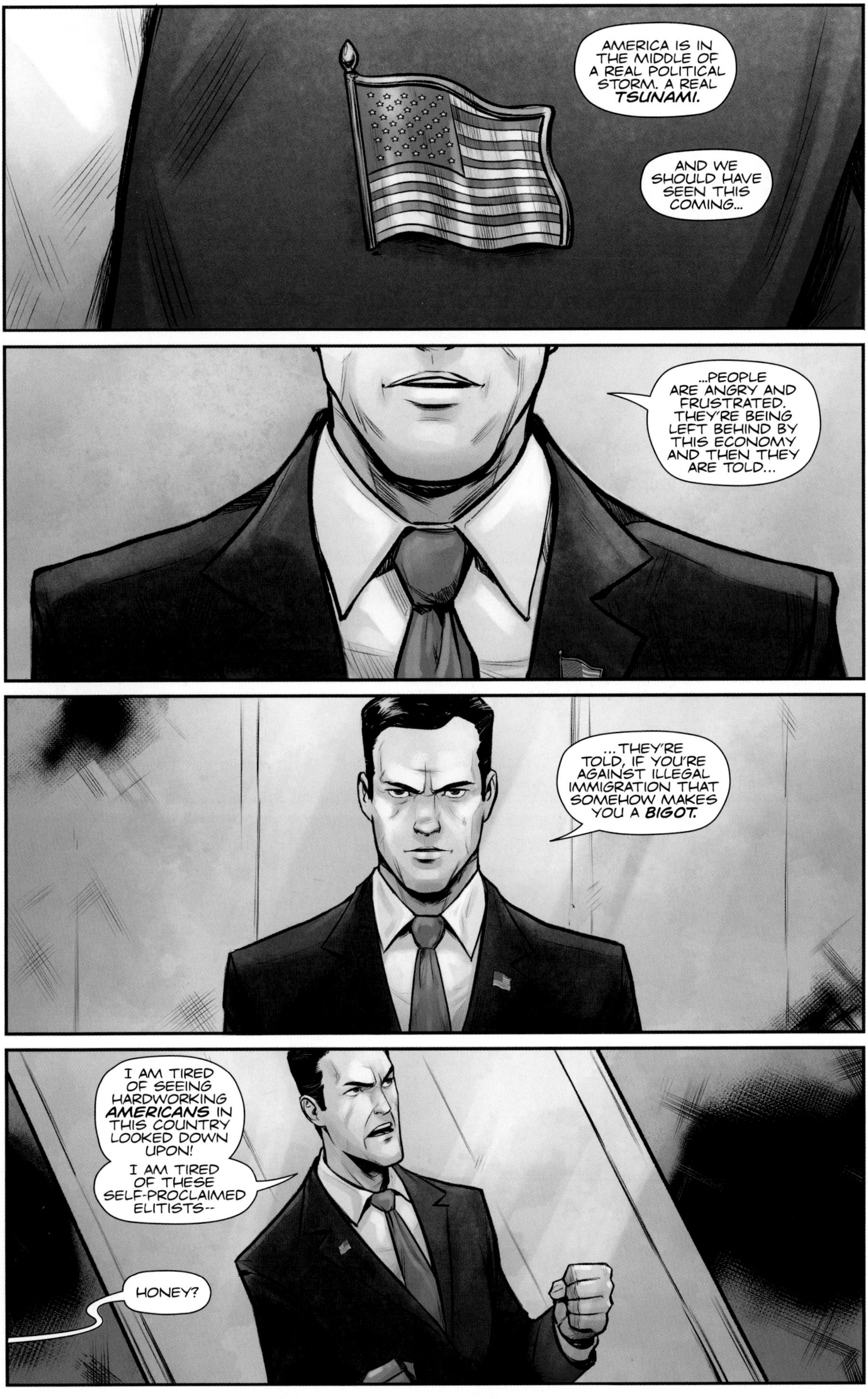
AMERICA IS IN THE MIDDLE OF A REAL POLITICAL STORM. A REAL **TSUNAMI.**
AND WE SHOULD HAVE SEEN THIS COMING...
...PEOPLE ARE ANGRY AND FRUSTRATED. THEY'RE BEING LEFT BEHIND BY THIS ECONOMY AND THEN THEY ARE TOLD...
...THEY'RE TOLD, IF YOU'RE AGAINST ILLEGAL IMMIGRATION THAT SOMEHOW MAKES YOU A **BIGOT.**
I AM TIRED OF SEEING HARDWORKING **AMERICANS** IN THIS COUNTRY LOOKED DOWN UPON!
I AM TIRED OF THESE SELF-PROCLAIMED ELITISTS--
HONEY?

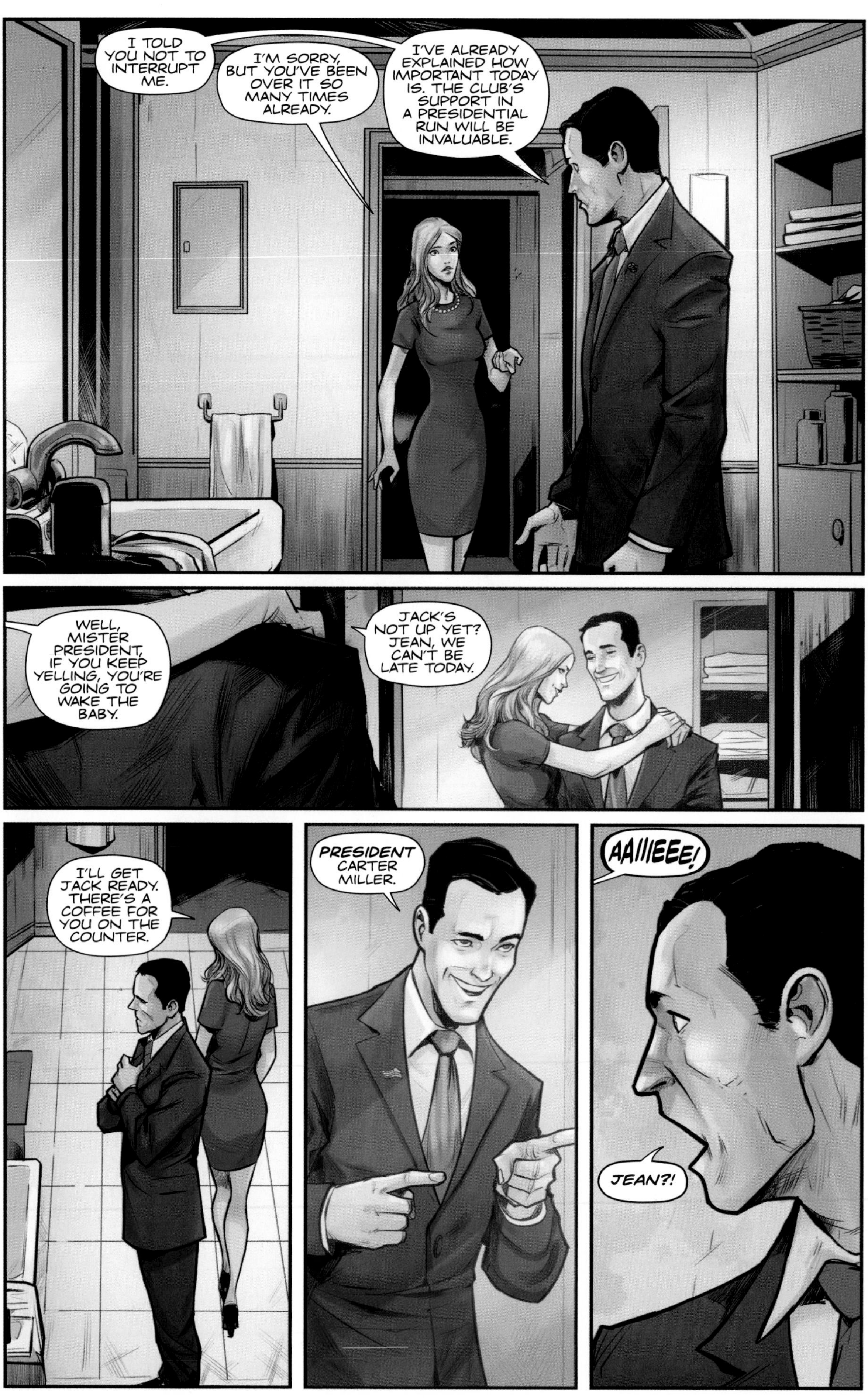
I TOLD YOU NOT TO INTERRUPT ME.
I'M SORRY, BUT YOU'VE BEEN OVER IT SO MANY TIMES ALREADY.
I'VE ALREADY EXPLAINED HOW IMPORTANT TODAY IS. THE CLUB'S SUPPORT IN A PRESIDENTIAL RUN WILL BE INVALUABLE.
WELL, MISTER PRESIDENT, IF YOU KEEP YELLING, YOU'RE GOING TO WAKE THE BABY.
JACK'S NOT UP YET? JEAN, WE CAN'T BE LATE TODAY.
I'LL GET JACK READY. THERE'S A COFFEE FOR YOU ON THE COUNTER.
PRESIDENT CARTER MILLER.
AAIIIEEE!
JEAN?!

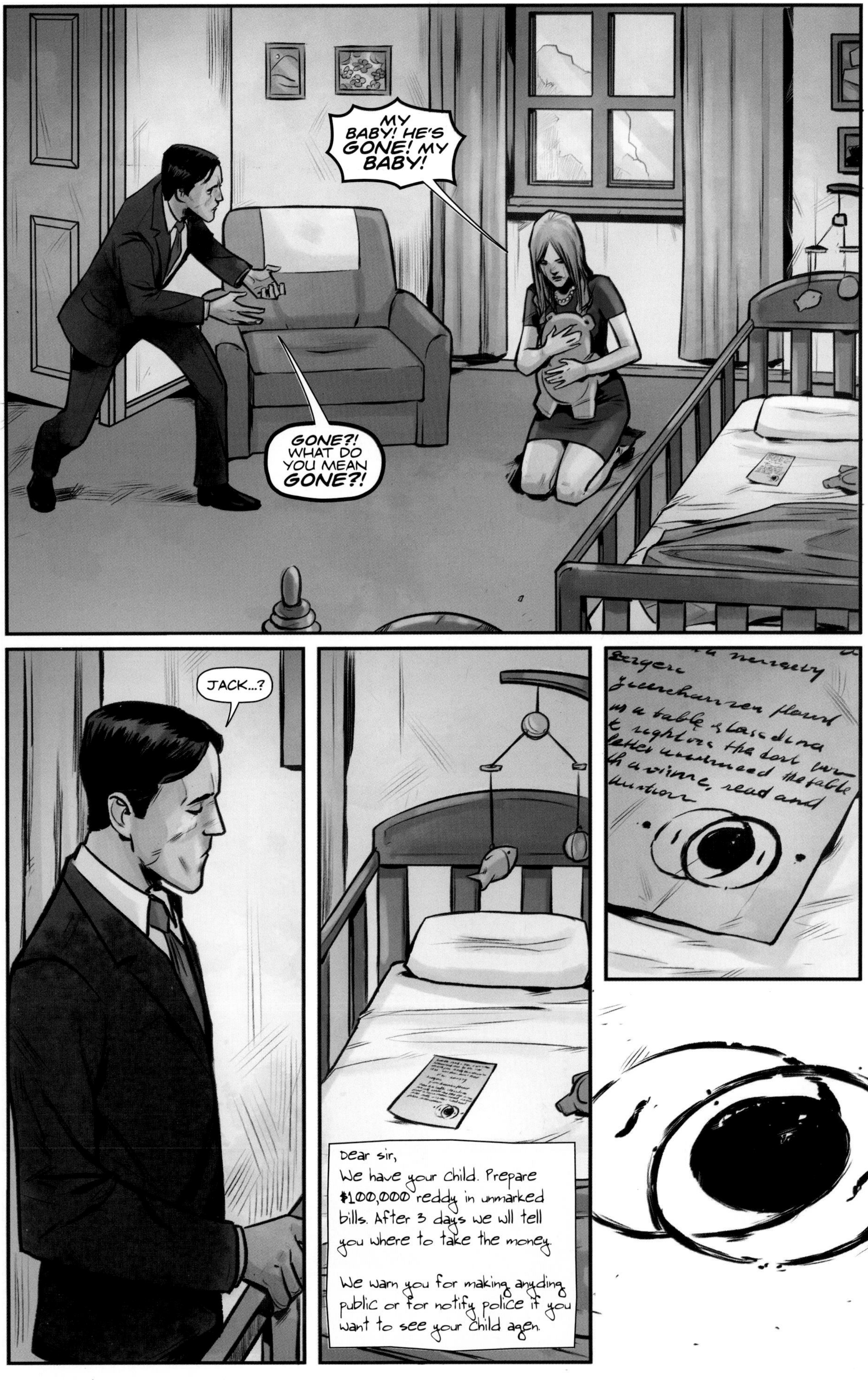
MY BABY! HE'S GONE! MY BABY!
GONE?! WHAT DO YOU MEAN GONE?!
JACK...?
Dear sir,
We have your Child. Prepare $100,000 reddy in unmarked bills. After 3 days we wll tell you where to take the money.
We warn you for making anyding public or for notify police if you want to see your Child agen.

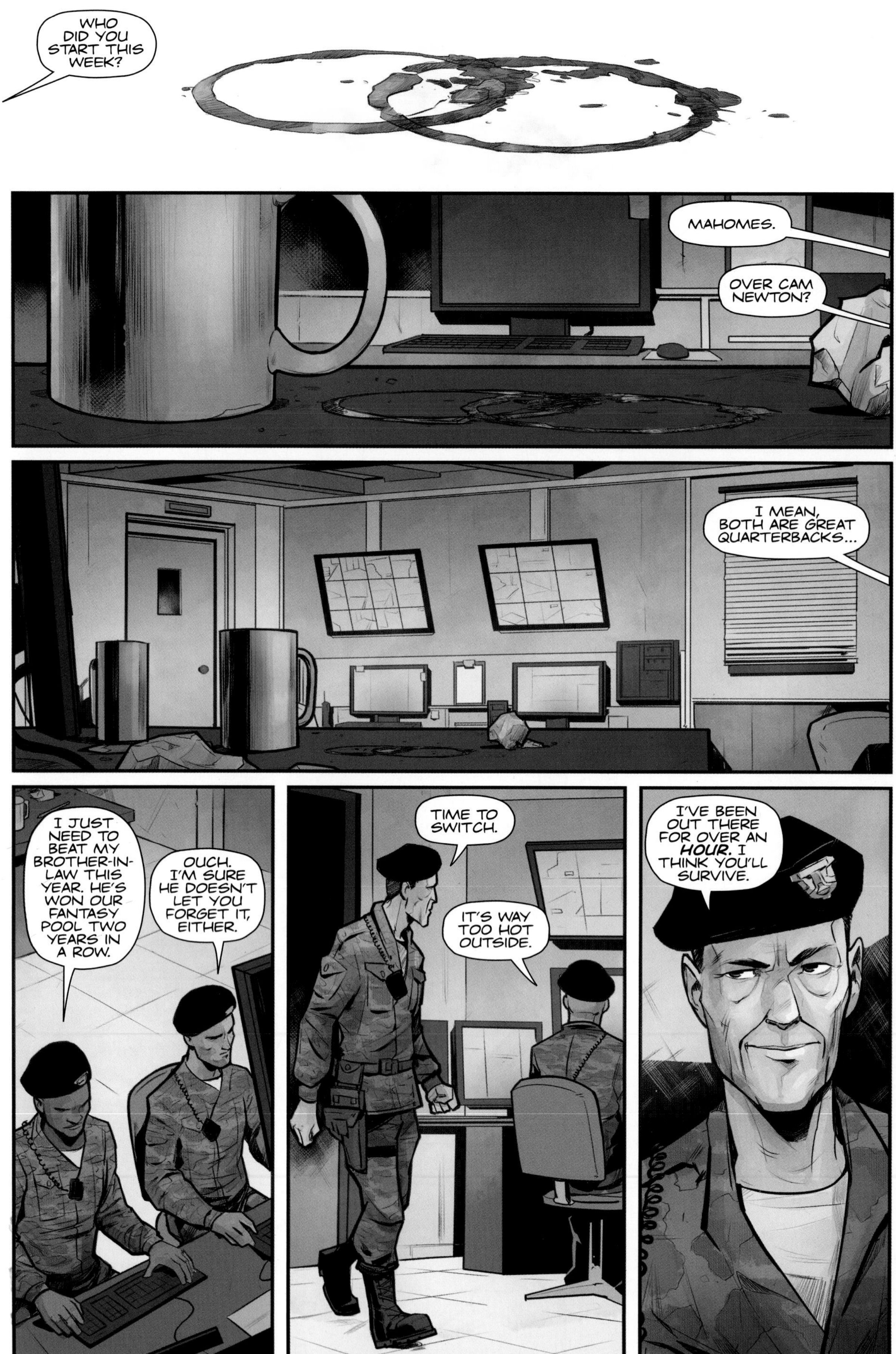
WHO DID YOU START THIS WEEK?
MAHOMES.
OVER CAM NEWTON?
I MEAN, BOTH ARE GREAT QUARTERBACKS...
I JUST NEED TO BEAT MY BROTHER-IN-LAW THIS YEAR. HE'S WON OUR FANTASY POOL TWO YEARS IN A ROW.
OUCH. I'M SURE HE DOESN'T LET YOU FORGET IT, EITHER.
TIME TO SWITCH.
IT'S WAY TOO HOT OUTSIDE.
I'VE BEEN OUT THERE FOR OVER AN HOUR. I THINK YOU'LL SURVIVE.

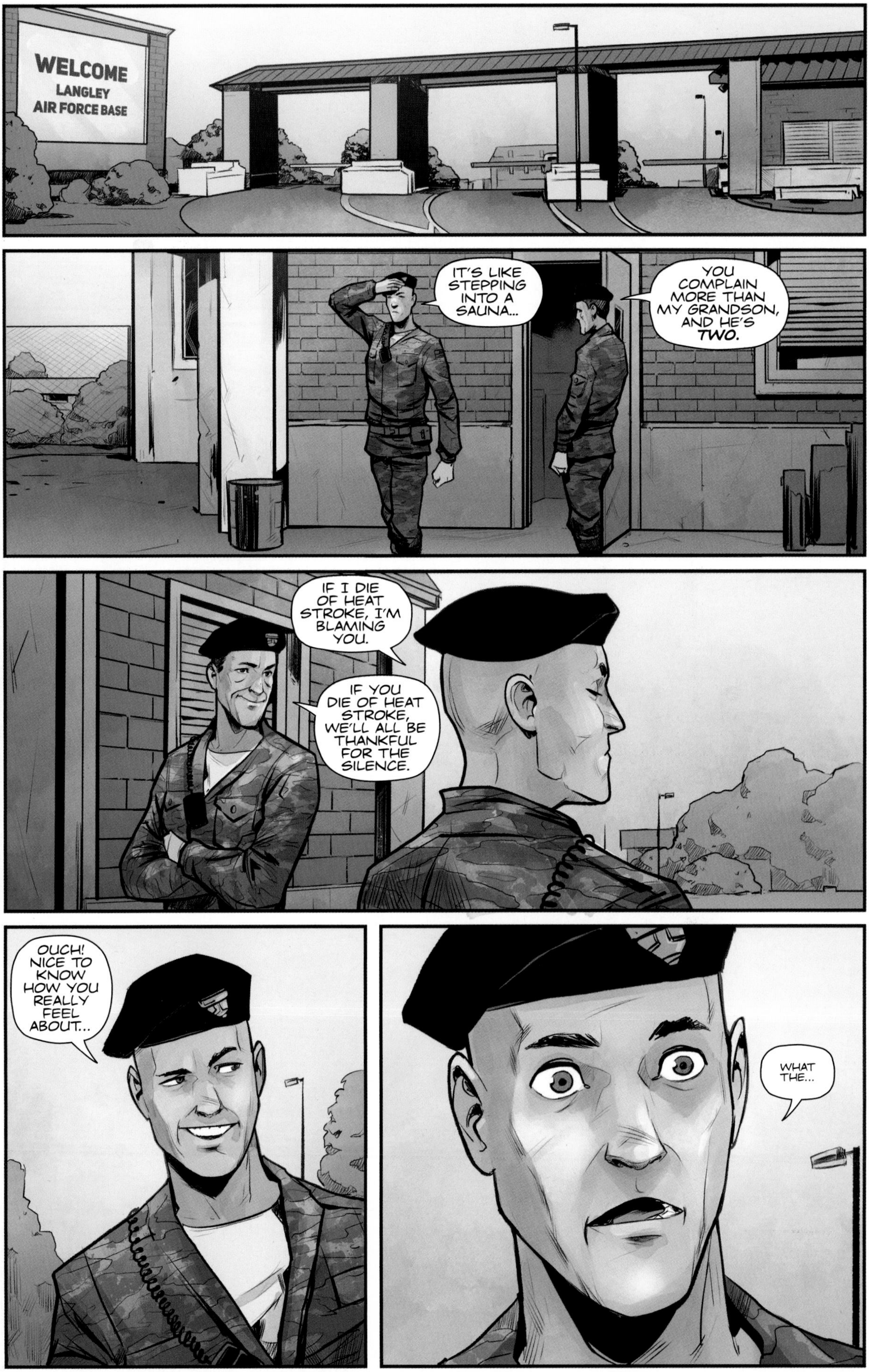
WELCOME
LANGLEY
AIR FORCE BASE
IT'S LIKE STEPPING INTO A SAUNA...
YOU COMPLAIN MORE THAN MY GRANDSON, AND HE'S **TWO.**
IF I DIE OF HEAT STROKE, I'M BLAMING YOU.
IF YOU DIE OF HEAT STROKE, WE'LL ALL BE THANKFUL FOR THE SILENCE.
OUCH! NICE TO KNOW HOW YOU REALLY FEEL ABOUT...
WHAT THE...

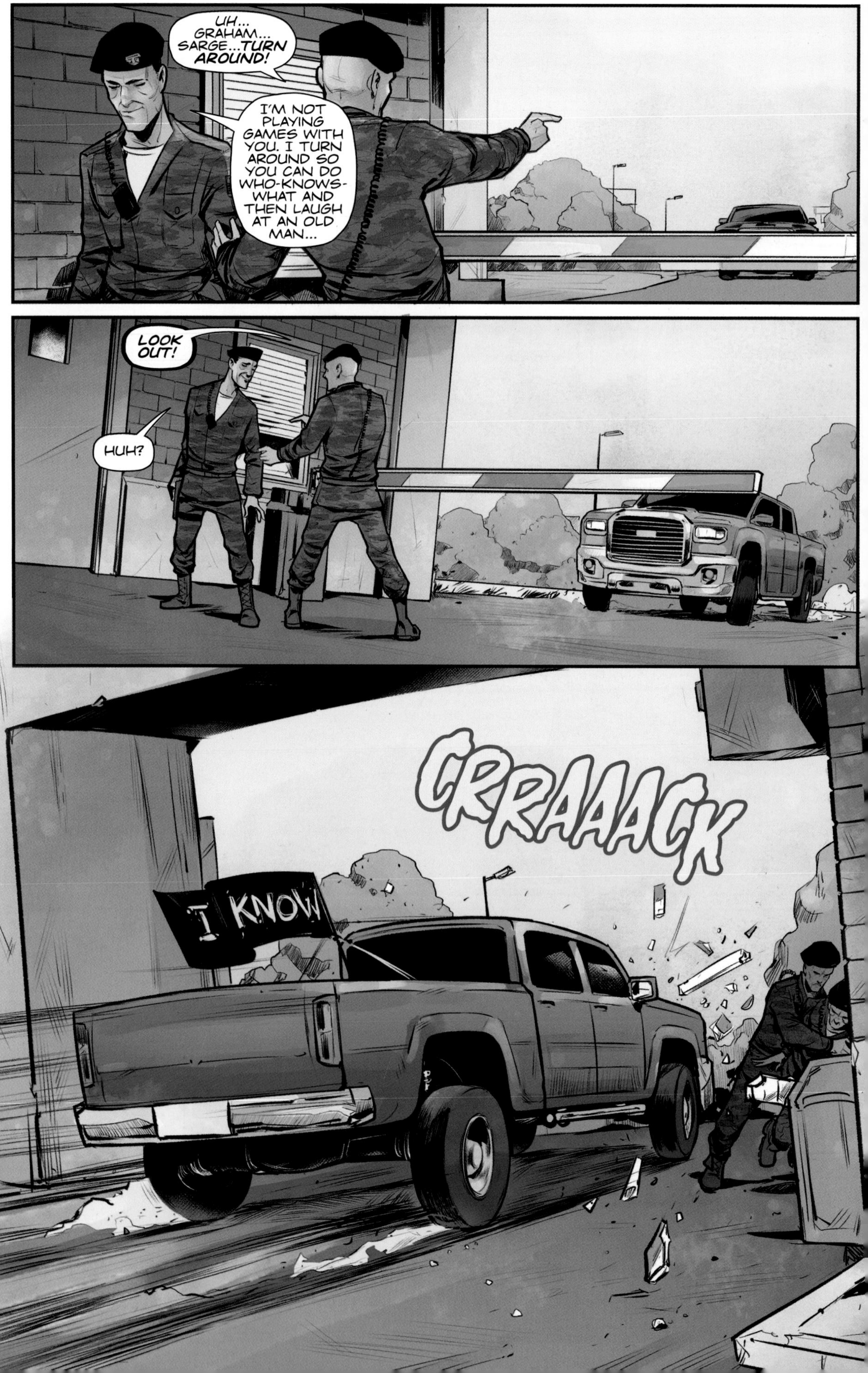
UH... GRAHAM... SARGE...TURN AROUND!
I'M NOT PLAYING GAMES WITH YOU. I TURN AROUND SO YOU CAN DO WHO-KNOWS-WHAT AND THEN LAUGH AT AN OLD MAN...
LOOK OUT!
HUH?
CRRAAACK
I KNOW

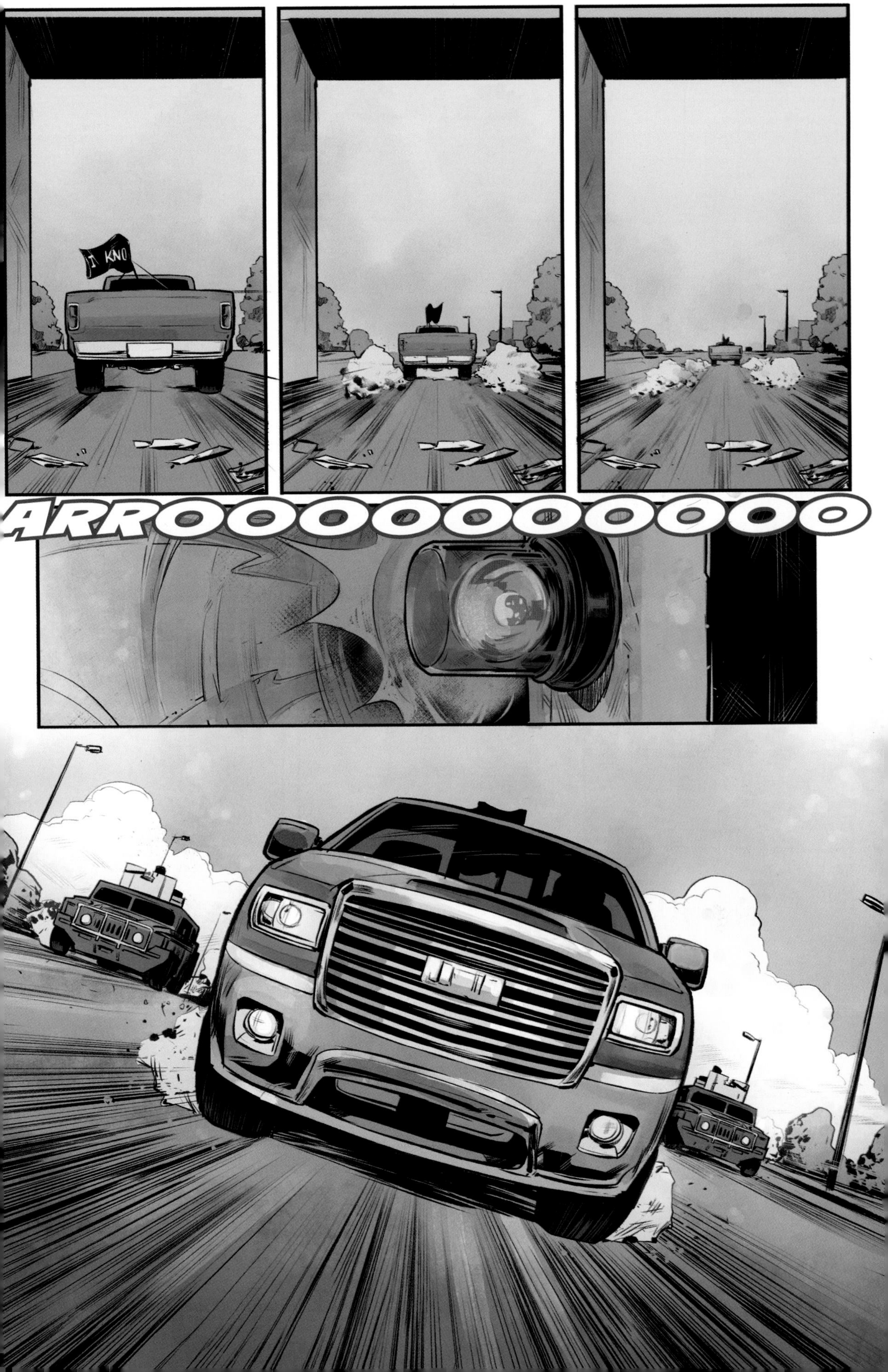
I KNO
ARROOOOOOOOOO

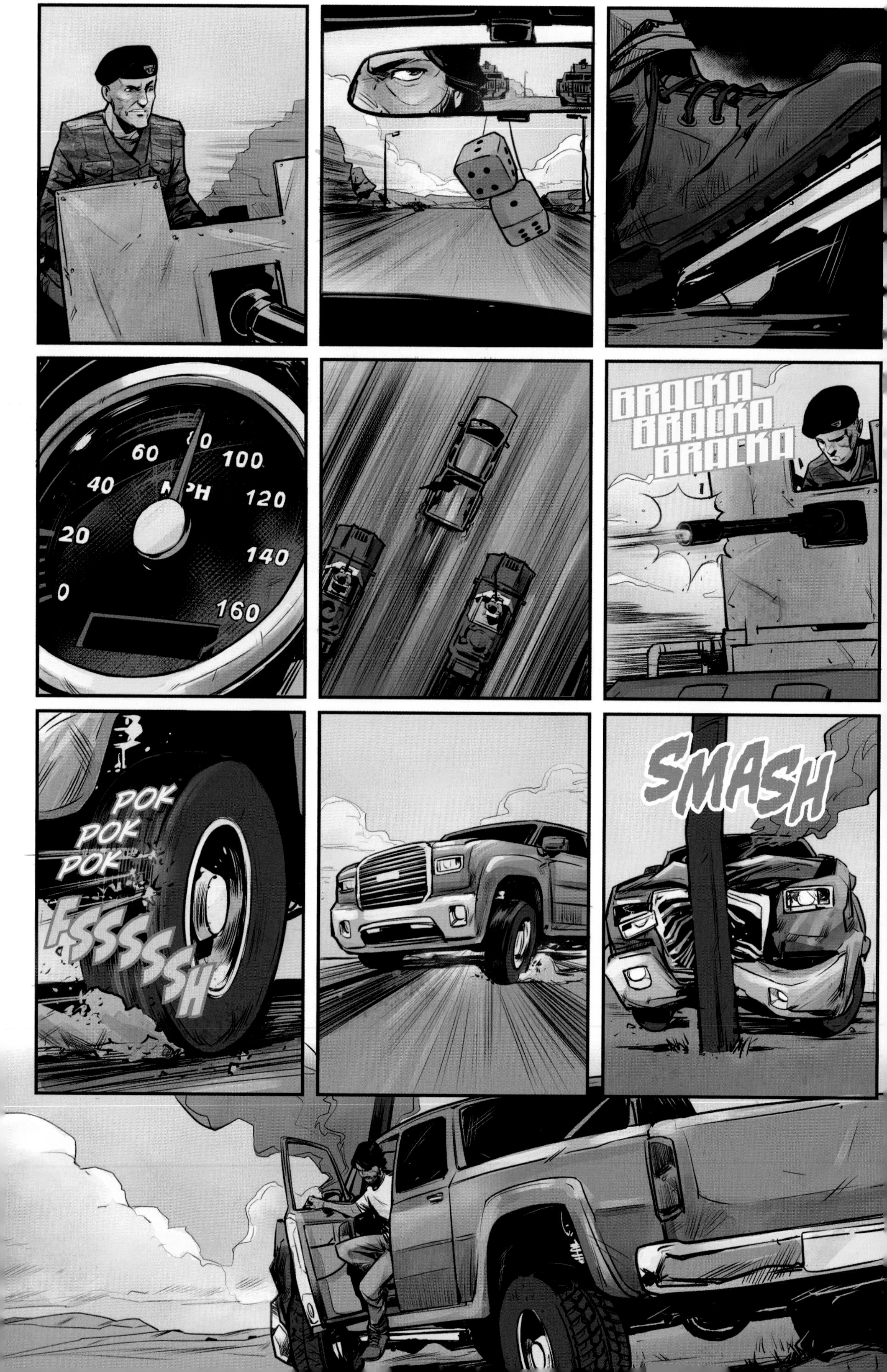

60
80
100
40
MPH
120
20
140
0
160
BRACKA
BRACKA
BRACKA
POK
POK
POK
FSSSSSH
SMASH

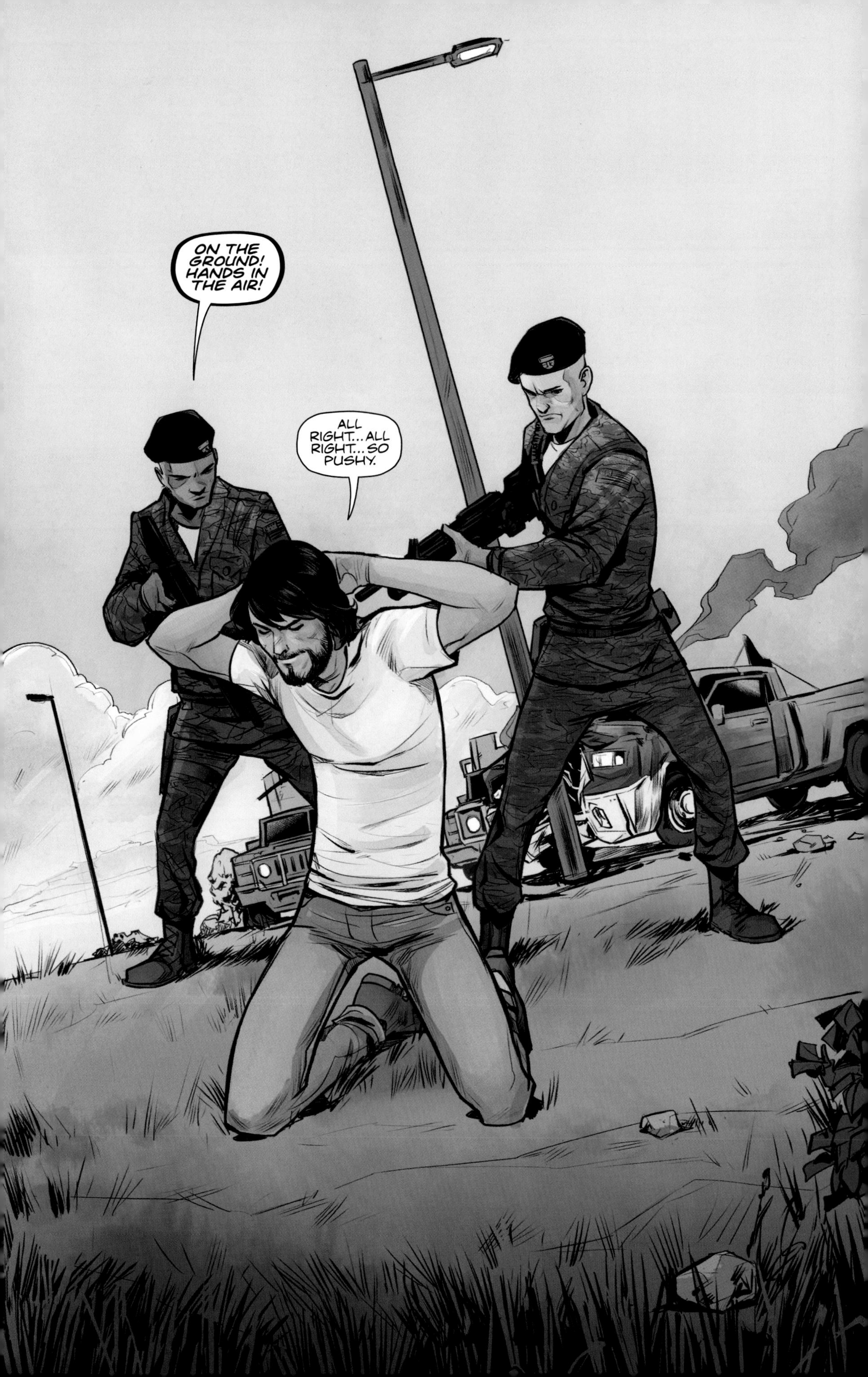
ON THE GROUND! HANDS IN THE AIR!
ALL RIGHT... ALL RIGHT... SO PUSHY.

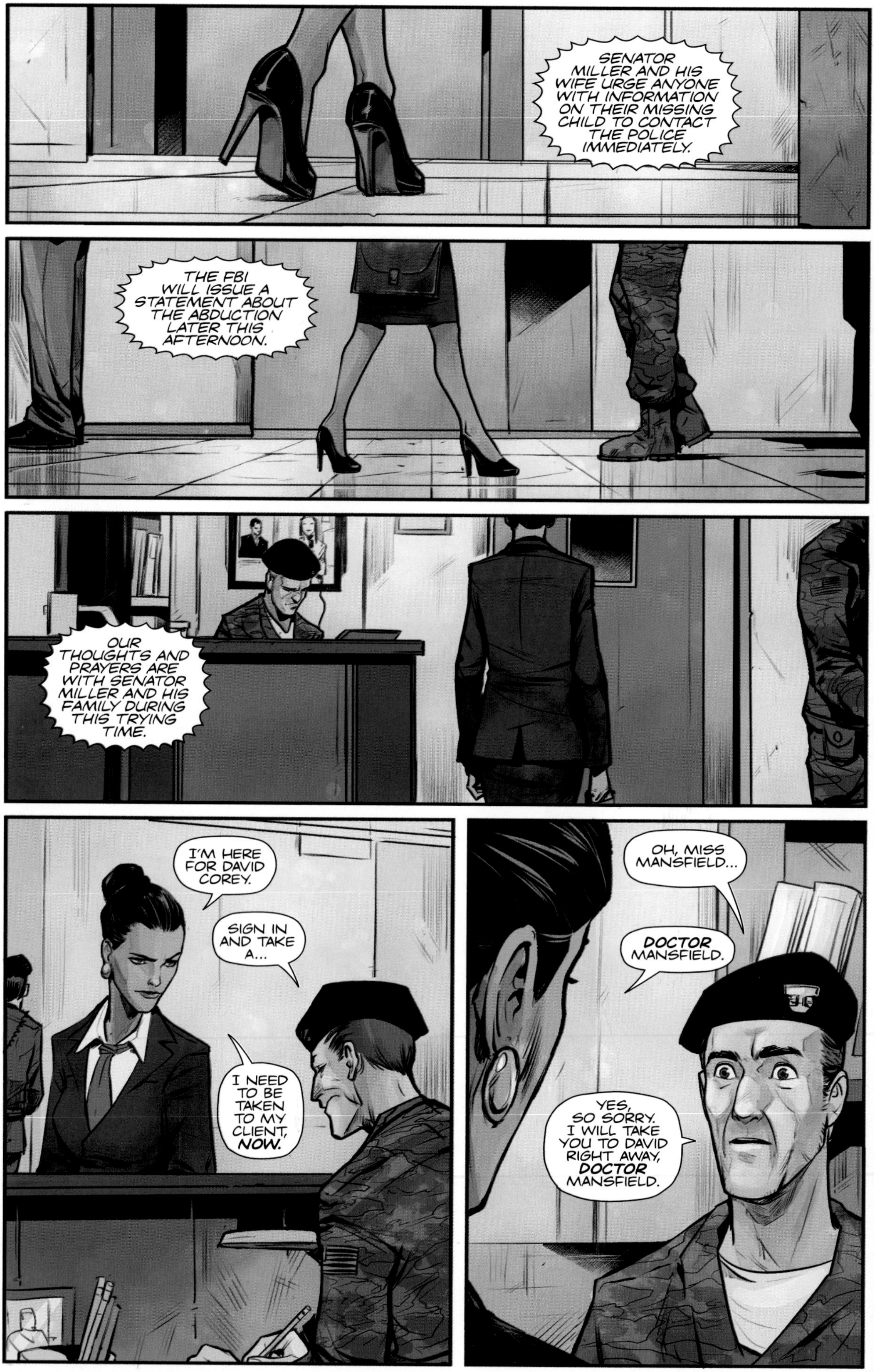
SENATOR MILLER AND HIS WIFE URGE ANYONE WITH INFORMATION ON THEIR MISSING CHILD TO CONTACT THE POLICE IMMEDIATELY.
THE FBI WILL ISSUE A STATEMENT ABOUT THE ABDUCTION LATER THIS AFTERNOON.
OUR THOUGHTS AND PRAYERS ARE WITH SENATOR MILLER AND HIS FAMILY DURING THIS TRYING TIME.
I'M HERE FOR DAVID COREY.
SIGN IN AND TAKE A...
I NEED TO BE TAKEN TO MY CLIENT, **NOW.**
OH, MISS MANSFIELD...
DOCTOR MANSFIELD.
YES, SO SORRY. I WILL TAKE YOU TO DAVID RIGHT AWAY, **DOCTOR** MANSFIELD.

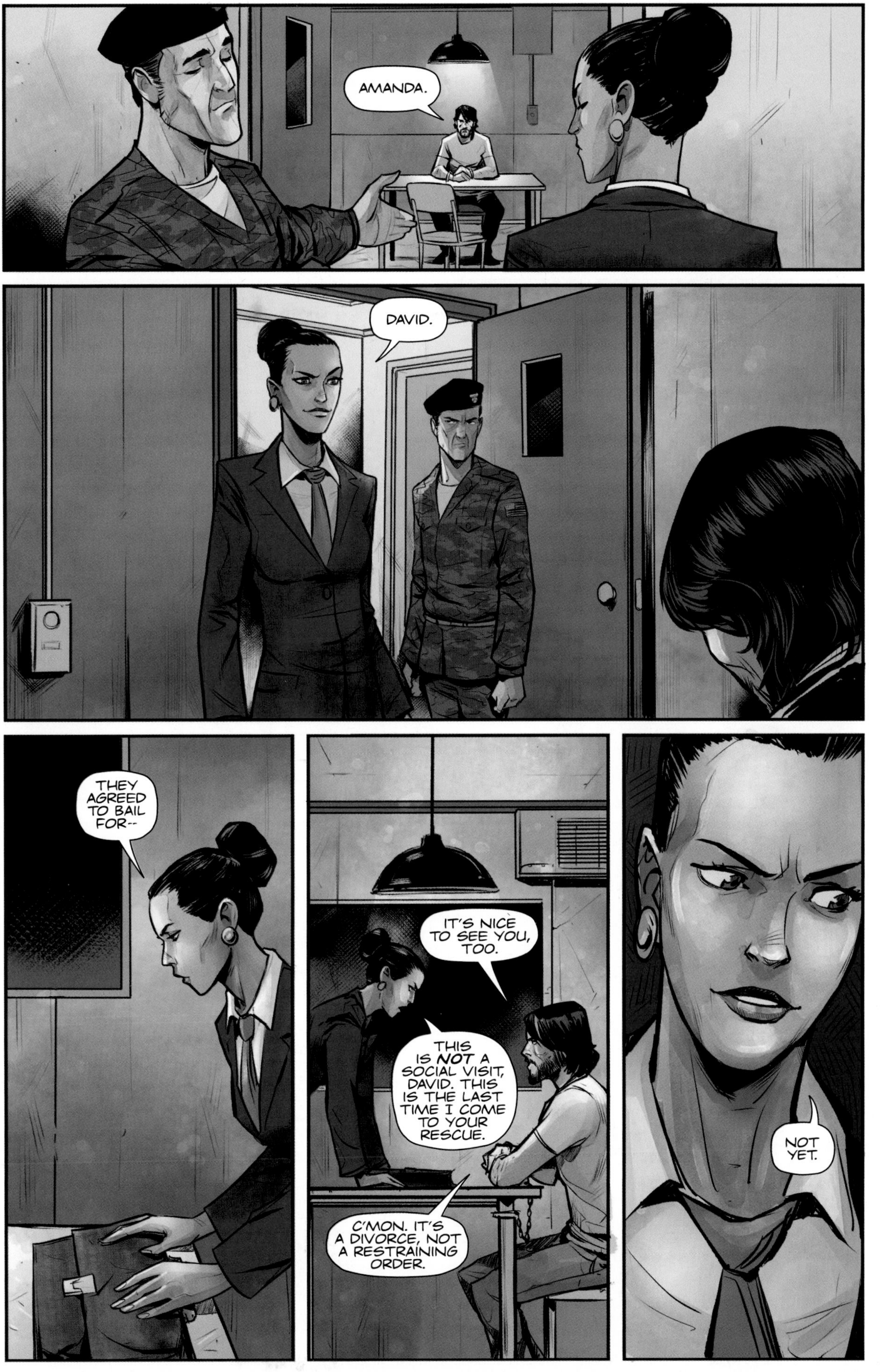
AMANDA.
DAVID.
THEY AGREED TO BAIL FOR--
IT'S NICE TO SEE YOU, TOO.
THIS IS **NOT** A SOCIAL VISIT, DAVID. THIS IS THE LAST TIME I COME TO YOUR RESCUE.
C'MON. IT'S A DIVORCE, NOT A RESTRAINING ORDER.
NOT YET.

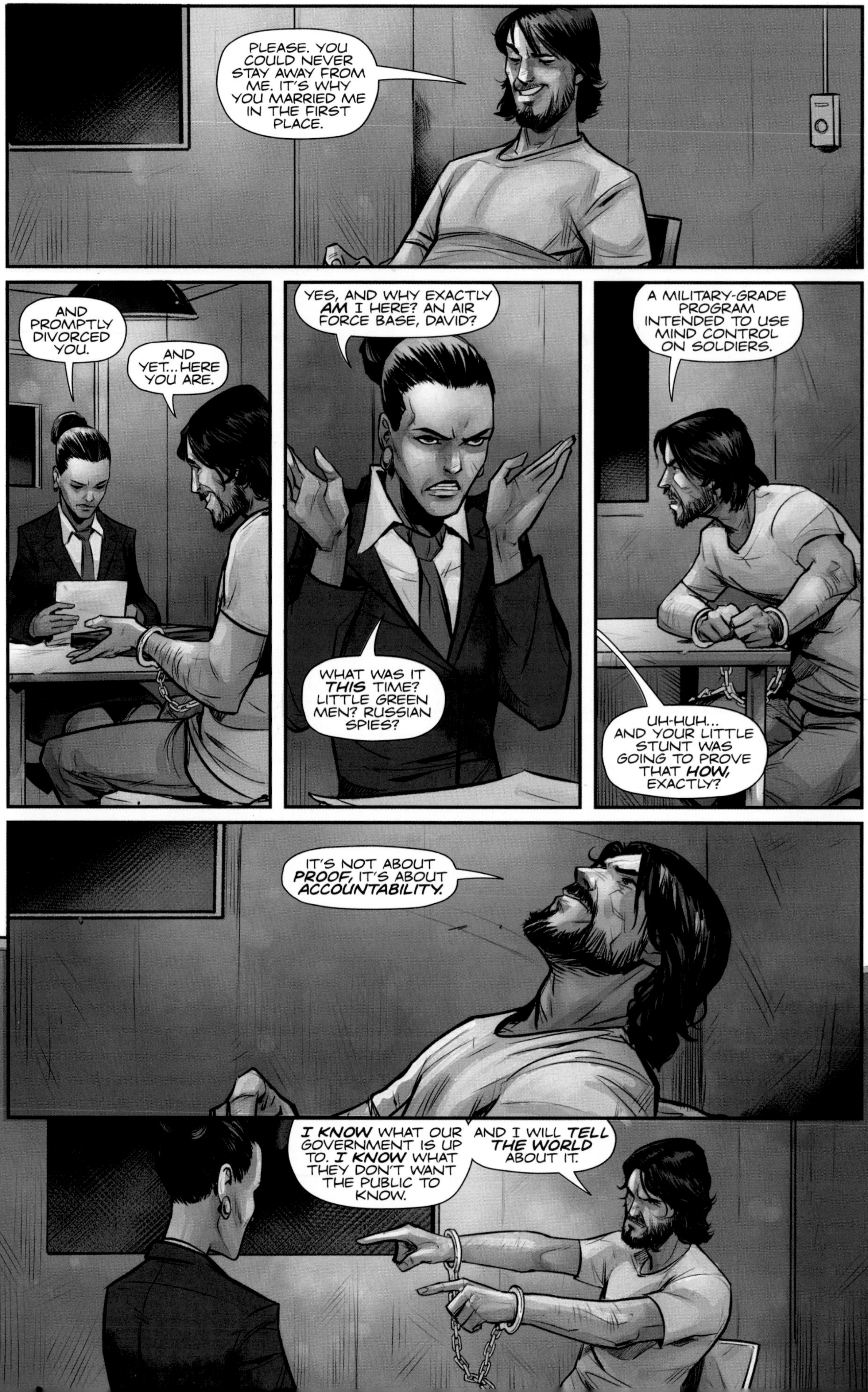
PLEASE. YOU COULD NEVER STAY AWAY FROM ME. IT'S WHY YOU MARRIED ME IN THE FIRST PLACE.
AND PROMPTLY DIVORCED YOU.
AND YET...HERE YOU ARE.
YES, AND WHY EXACTLY AM I HERE? AN AIR FORCE BASE, DAVID?
WHAT WAS IT THIS TIME? LITTLE GREEN MEN? RUSSIAN SPIES?
A MILITARY-GRADE PROGRAM INTENDED TO USE MIND CONTROL ON SOLDIERS.
UH-HUH... AND YOUR LITTLE STUNT WAS GOING TO PROVE THAT HOW, EXACTLY?
IT'S NOT ABOUT PROOF, IT'S ABOUT ACCOUNTABILITY.
I KNOW WHAT OUR GOVERNMENT IS UP TO. I KNOW WHAT THEY DON'T WANT THE PUBLIC TO KNOW.
AND I WILL TELL THE WORLD ABOUT IT.

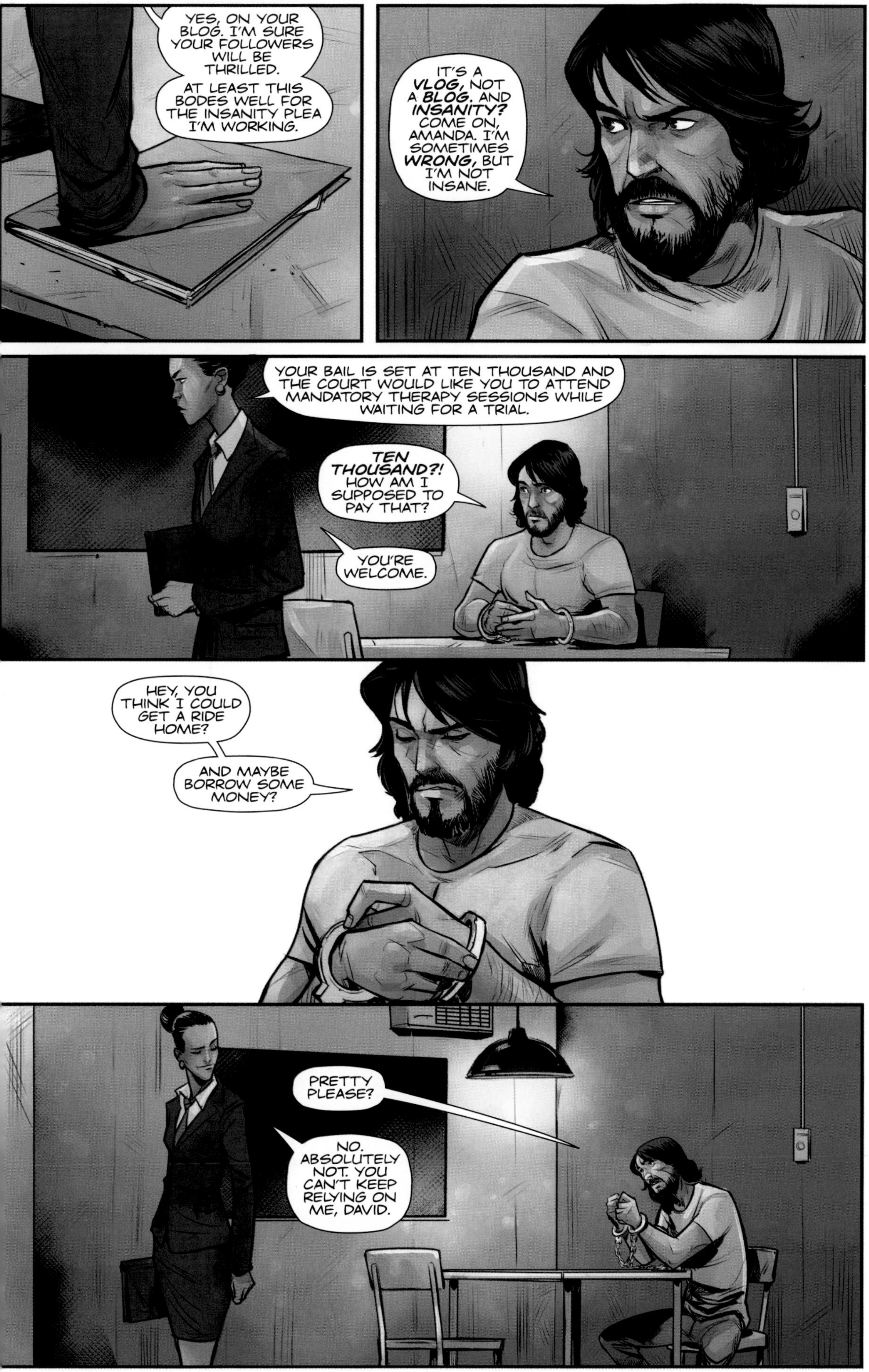
YES, ON YOUR BLOG. I'M SURE YOUR FOLLOWERS WILL BE THRILLED.
AT LEAST THIS BODES WELL FOR THE INSANITY PLEA I'M WORKING.
IT'S A VLOG, NOT A BLOG. AND INSANITY? COME ON, AMANDA. I'M SOMETIMES WRONG, BUT I'M NOT INSANE.
YOUR BAIL IS SET AT TEN THOUSAND AND THE COURT WOULD LIKE YOU TO ATTEND MANDATORY THERAPY SESSIONS WHILE WAITING FOR A TRIAL.
TEN THOUSAND?! HOW AM I SUPPOSED TO PAY THAT?
YOU'RE WELCOME.
HEY, YOU THINK I COULD GET A RIDE HOME?
AND MAYBE BORROW SOME MONEY?
PRETTY PLEASE?
NO. ABSOLUTELY NOT. YOU CAN'T KEEP RELYING ON ME, DAVID.

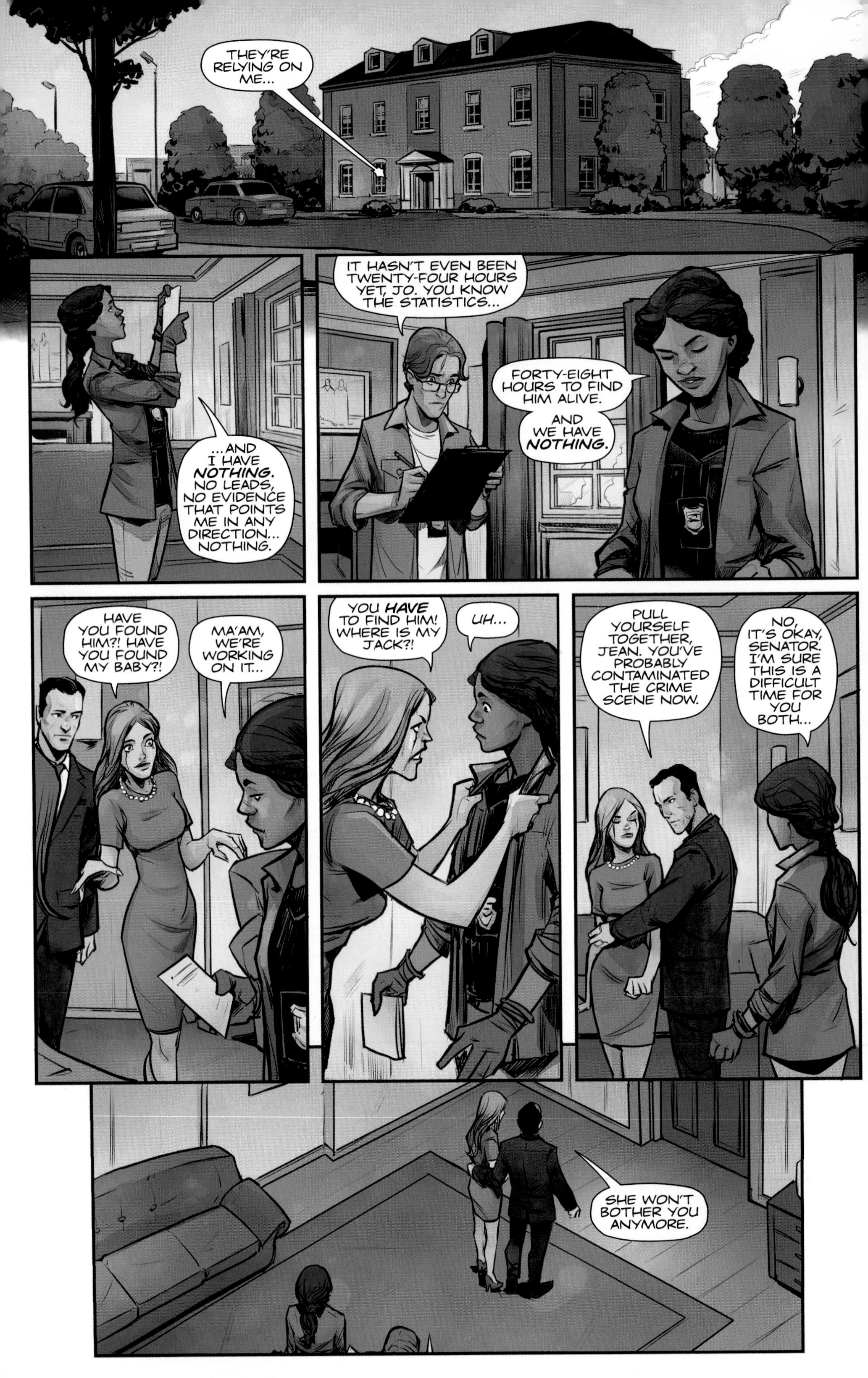
THEY'RE RELYING ON ME...
...AND I HAVE NOTHING. NO LEADS, NO EVIDENCE THAT POINTS ME IN ANY DIRECTION... NOTHING.
IT HASN'T EVEN BEEN TWENTY-FOUR HOURS YET, JO. YOU KNOW THE STATISTICS...
FORTY-EIGHT HOURS TO FIND HIM ALIVE.
AND WE HAVE NOTHING.
HAVE YOU FOUND HIM?! HAVE YOU FOUND MY BABY?!
MA'AM, WE'RE WORKING ON IT...
YOU HAVE TO FIND HIM! WHERE IS MY JACK?!
UH...
PULL YOURSELF TOGETHER, JEAN. YOU'VE PROBABLY CONTAMINATED THE CRIME SCENE NOW.
NO, IT'S OKAY, SENATOR. I'M SURE THIS IS A DIFFICULT TIME FOR YOU BOTH...
SHE WON'T BOTHER YOU ANYMORE.

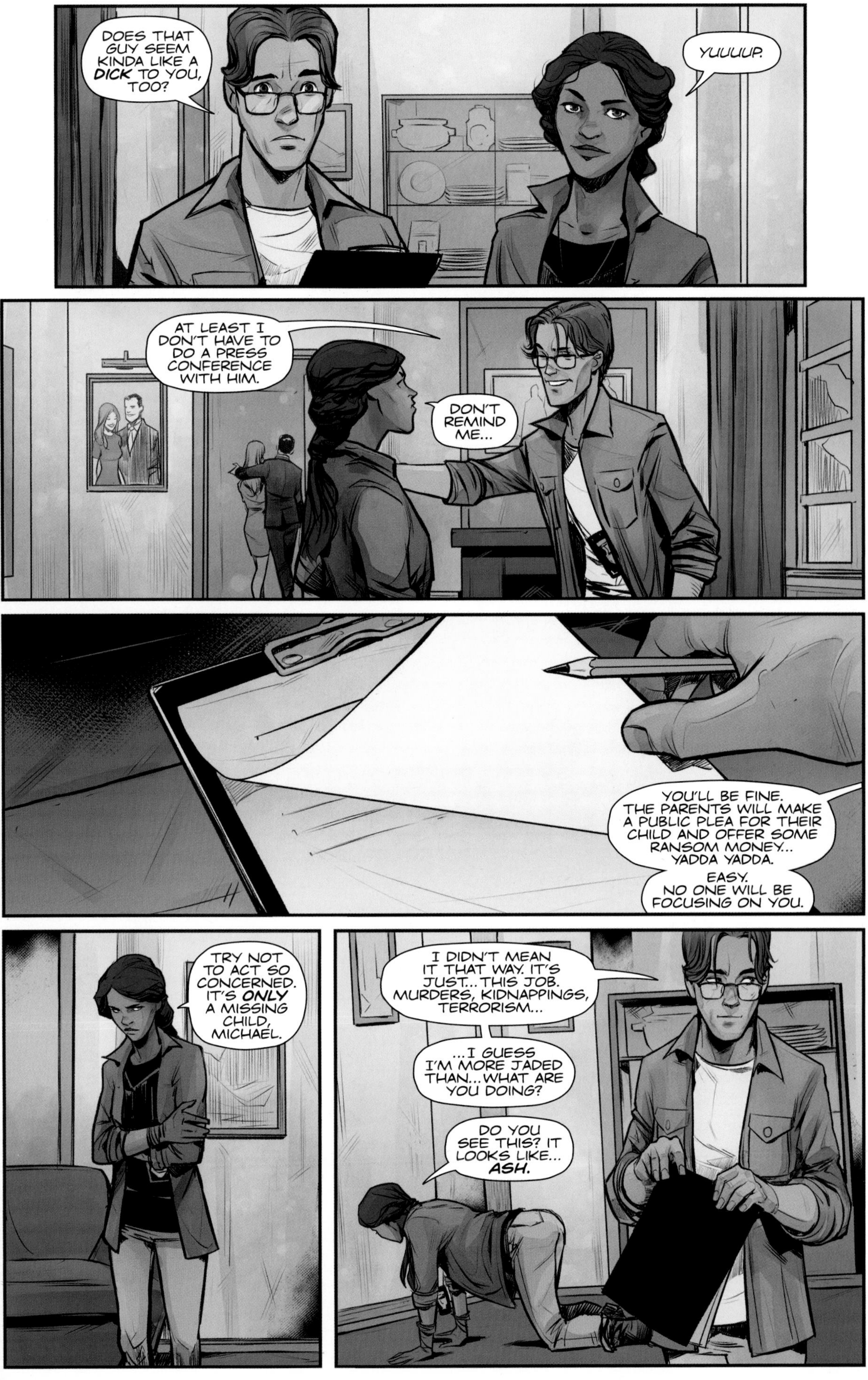
DOES THAT GUY SEEM KINDA LIKE A DICK TO YOU, TOO?
YUUUUP.
AT LEAST I DON'T HAVE TO DO A PRESS CONFERENCE WITH HIM.
DON'T REMIND ME...
YOU'LL BE FINE. THE PARENTS WILL MAKE A PUBLIC PLEA FOR THEIR CHILD AND OFFER SOME RANSOM MONEY... YADDA YADDA.
EASY. NO ONE WILL BE FOCUSING ON YOU.
TRY NOT TO ACT SO CONCERNED. IT'S ONLY A MISSING CHILD, MICHAEL.
I DIDN'T MEAN IT THAT WAY. IT'S JUST... THIS JOB. MURDERS, KIDNAPPINGS, TERRORISM...
...I GUESS I'M MORE JADED THAN... WHAT ARE YOU DOING?
DO YOU SEE THIS? IT LOOKS LIKE... ASH.

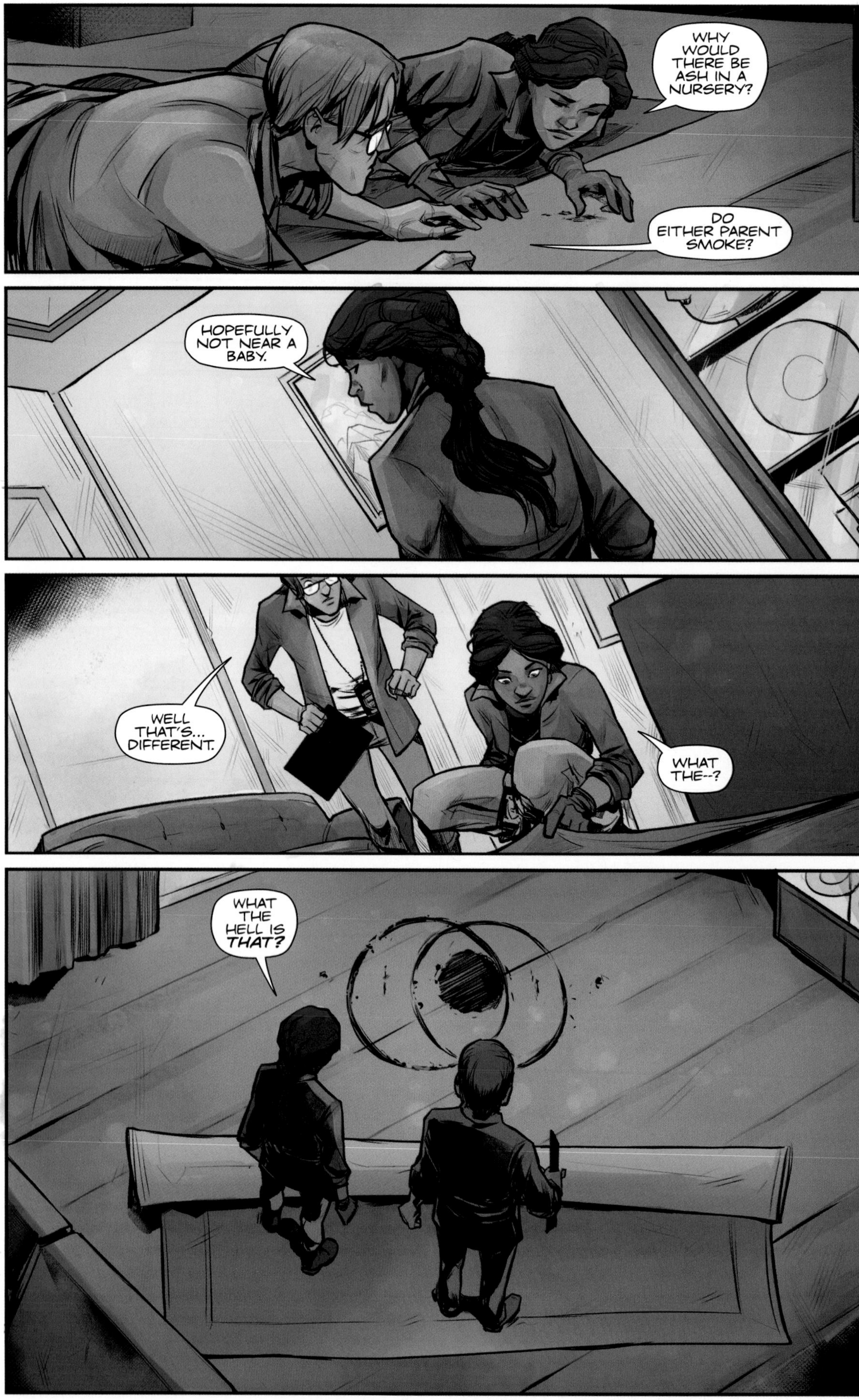
WHY WOULD THERE BE ASH IN A NURSERY?
DO EITHER PARENT SMOKE?
HOPEFULLY NOT NEAR A BABY.
WELL THAT'S... DIFFERENT.
WHAT THE--?
WHAT THE HELL IS *THAT?*

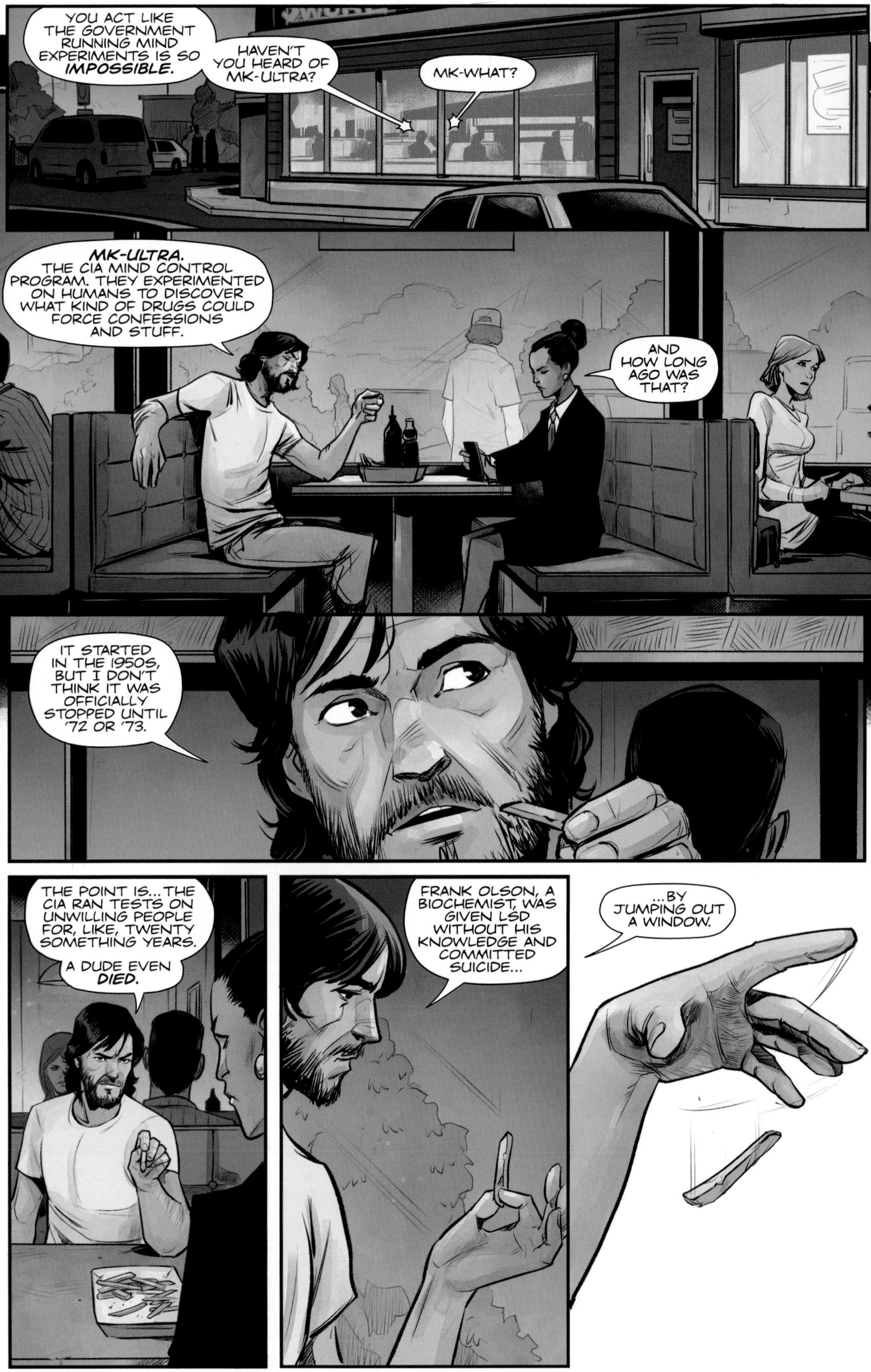
YOU ACT LIKE THE GOVERNMENT RUNNING MIND EXPERIMENTS IS SO **IMPOSSIBLE**.
HAVEN'T YOU HEARD OF MK-ULTRA?
MK-WHAT?
MK-ULTRA. THE CIA MIND CONTROL PROGRAM. THEY EXPERIMENTED ON HUMANS TO DISCOVER WHAT KIND OF DRUGS COULD FORCE CONFESSIONS AND STUFF.
AND HOW LONG AGO WAS THAT?
IT STARTED IN THE 1950S, BUT I DON'T THINK IT WAS OFFICIALLY STOPPED UNTIL '72 OR '73.
THE POINT IS... THE CIA RAN TESTS ON UNWILLING PEOPLE FOR, LIKE, TWENTY SOMETHING YEARS.
A DUDE EVEN **DIED.**
FRANK OLSON, A BIOCHEMIST, WAS GIVEN LSD WITHOUT HIS KNOWLEDGE AND COMMITTED SUICIDE...
...BY JUMPING OUT A WINDOW.

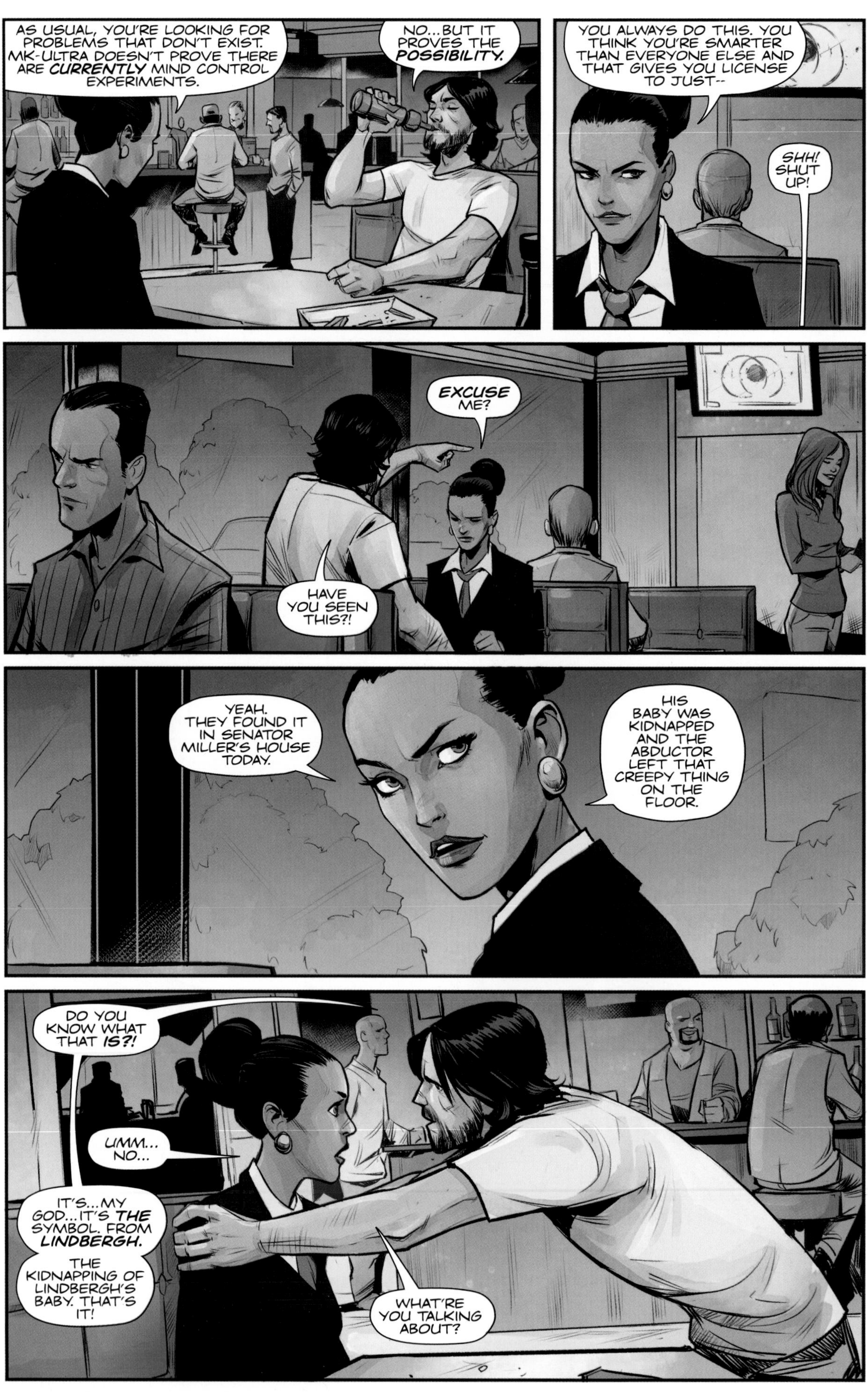

AS USUAL, YOU'RE LOOKING FOR PROBLEMS THAT DON'T EXIST. MK-ULTRA DOESN'T PROVE THERE ARE CURRENTLY MIND CONTROL EXPERIMENTS.
NO...BUT IT PROVES THE POSSIBILITY.
YOU ALWAYS DO THIS. YOU THINK YOU'RE SMARTER THAN EVERYONE ELSE AND THAT GIVES YOU LICENSE TO JUST--
SHH! SHUT UP!
EXCUSE ME?
HAVE YOU SEEN THIS?!
YEAH. THEY FOUND IT IN SENATOR MILLER'S HOUSE TODAY.
HIS BABY WAS KIDNAPPED AND THE ABDUCTOR LEFT THAT CREEPY THING ON THE FLOOR.
DO YOU KNOW WHAT THAT IS?!
UMM... NO...
IT'S...MY GOD...IT'S THE SYMBOL. FROM LINDBERGH.
THE KIDNAPPING OF LINDBERGH'S BABY. THAT'S IT!
WHAT'RE YOU TALKING ABOUT?

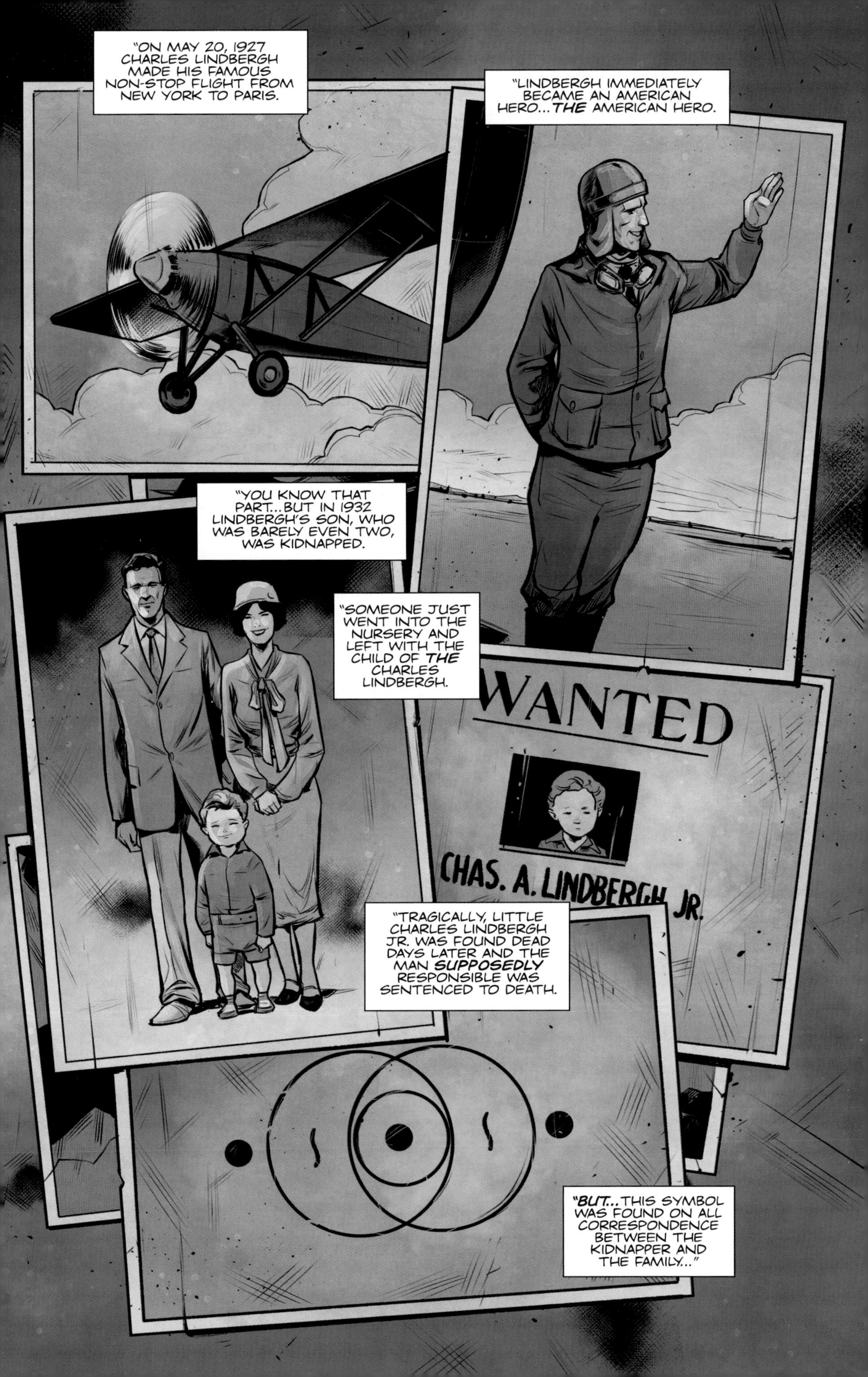
"ON MAY 20, 1927 CHARLES LINDBERGH MADE HIS FAMOUS NON-STOP FLIGHT FROM NEW YORK TO PARIS.
"LINDBERGH IMMEDIATELY BECAME AN AMERICAN HERO... THE AMERICAN HERO.
"YOU KNOW THAT PART... BUT IN 1932 LINDBERGH'S SON, WHO WAS BARELY EVEN TWO, WAS KIDNAPPED.
"SOMEONE JUST WENT INTO THE NURSERY AND LEFT WITH THE CHILD OF THE CHARLES LINDBERGH.
WANTED
CHAS. A. LINDBERGH JR.
"TRAGICALLY, LITTLE CHARLES LINDBERGH JR. WAS FOUND DEAD DAYS LATER AND THE MAN SUPPOSEDLY RESPONSIBLE WAS SENTENCED TO DEATH.
"BUT... THIS SYMBOL WAS FOUND ON ALL CORRESPONDENCE BETWEEN THE KIDNAPPER AND THE FAMILY..."

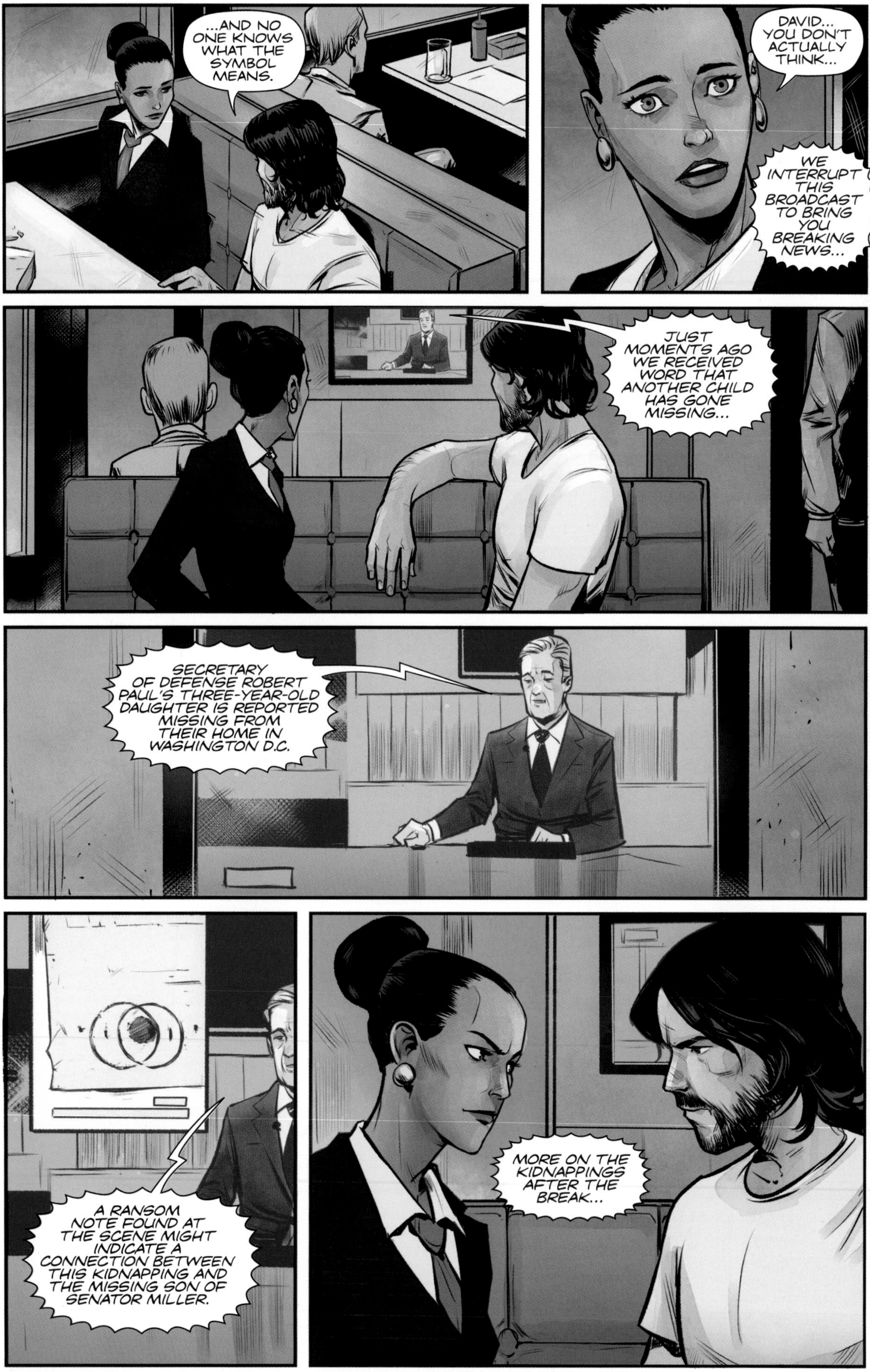
...AND NO ONE KNOWS WHAT THE SYMBOL MEANS.
DAVID... YOU DON'T ACTUALLY THINK...
WE INTERRUPT THIS BROADCAST TO BRING YOU BREAKING NEWS...
JUST MOMENTS AGO WE RECEIVED WORD THAT ANOTHER CHILD HAS GONE MISSING...
SECRETARY OF DEFENSE ROBERT PAUL'S THREE-YEAR-OLD DAUGHTER IS REPORTED MISSING FROM THEIR HOME IN WASHINGTON D.C.
A RANSOM NOTE FOUND AT THE SCENE MIGHT INDICATE A CONNECTION BETWEEN THIS KIDNAPPING AND THE MISSING SON OF SENATOR MILLER.
MORE ON THE KIDNAPPINGS AFTER THE BREAK...

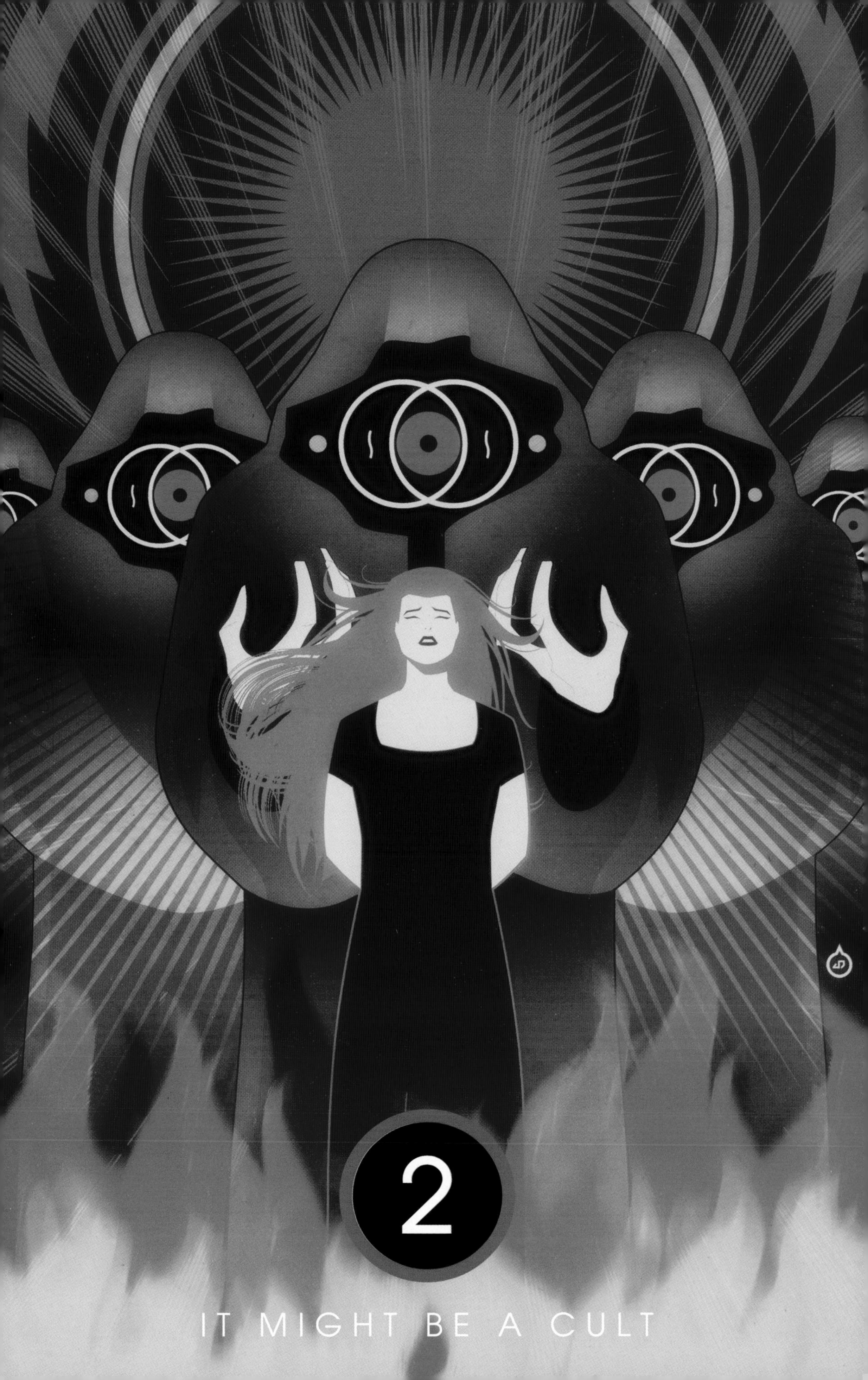

2

IT MIGHT BE A CULT

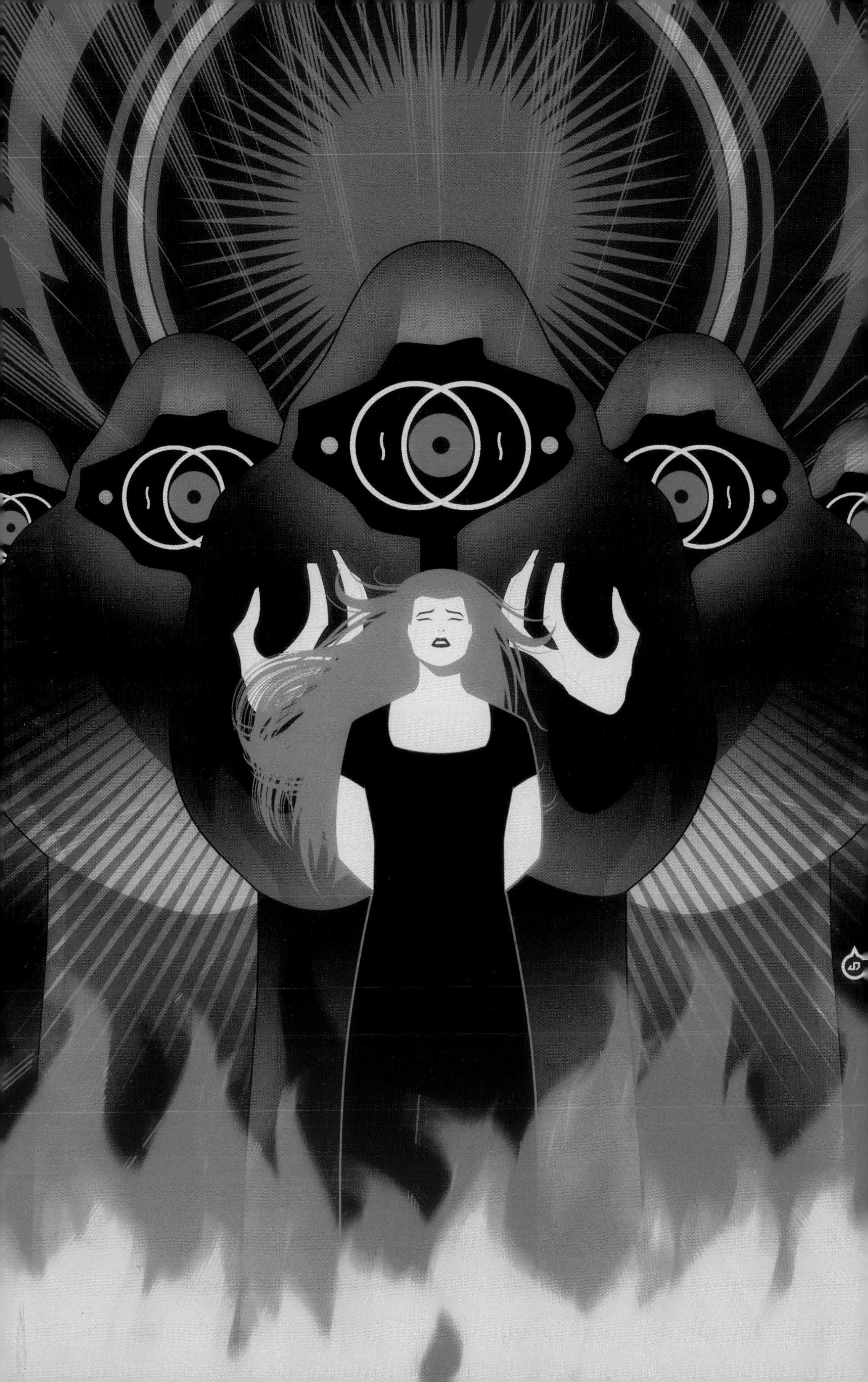

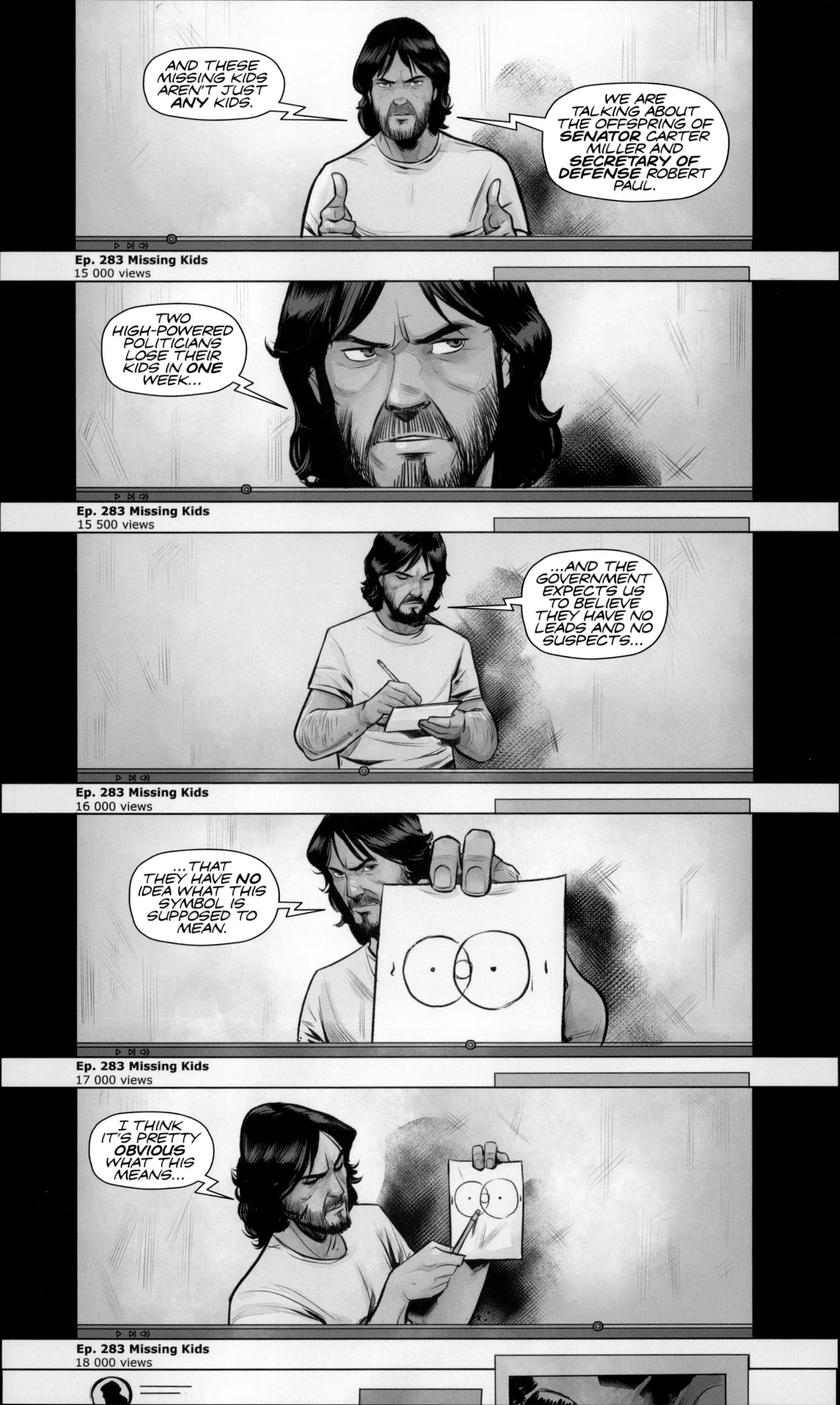

AND THESE MISSING KIDS AREN'T JUST **ANY** KIDS.
WE ARE TALKING ABOUT THE OFFSPRING OF **SENATOR** CARTER MILLER AND **SECRETARY OF DEFENSE** ROBERT PAUL.
Ep. 283 Missing Kids
15 000 views
TWO HIGH-POWERED POLITICIANS LOSE THEIR KIDS IN **ONE** WEEK...
Ep. 283 Missing Kids
15 500 views
...AND THE GOVERNMENT EXPECTS US TO BELIEVE THEY HAVE NO LEADS AND NO SUSPECTS...
Ep. 283 Missing Kids
16 000 views
...THAT THEY HAVE **NO** IDEA WHAT THIS SYMBOL IS SUPPOSED TO MEAN.
Ep. 283 Missing Kids
17 000 views
I THINK IT'S PRETTY **OBVIOUS** WHAT THIS MEANS...
Ep. 283 Missing Kids
18 000 views

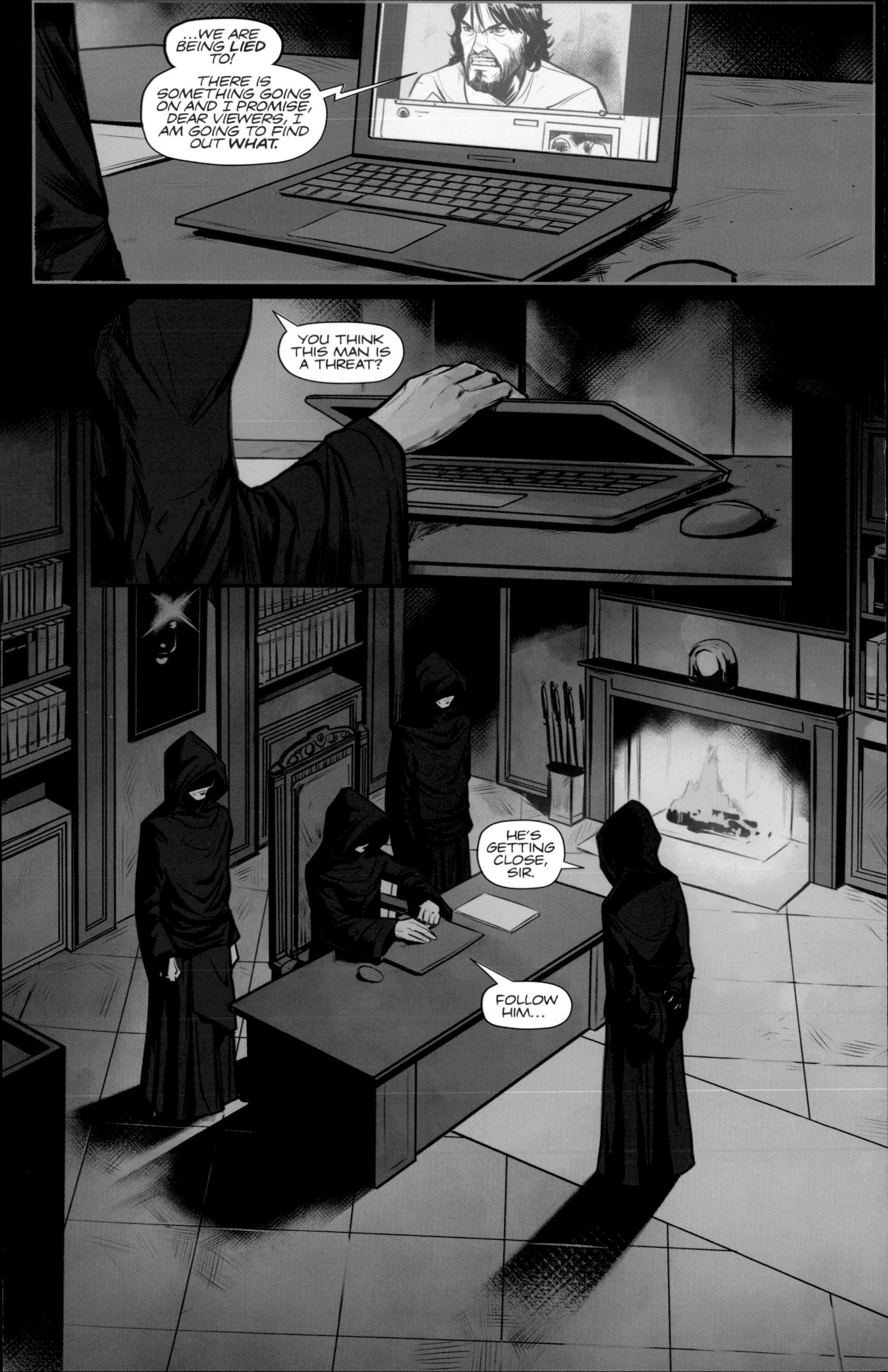
...WE ARE BEING LIED TO!
THERE IS SOMETHING GOING ON AND I PROMISE, DEAR VIEWERS, I AM GOING TO FIND OUT WHAT.
YOU THINK THIS MAN IS A THREAT?
HE'S GETTING CLOSE, SIR.
FOLLOW HIM...

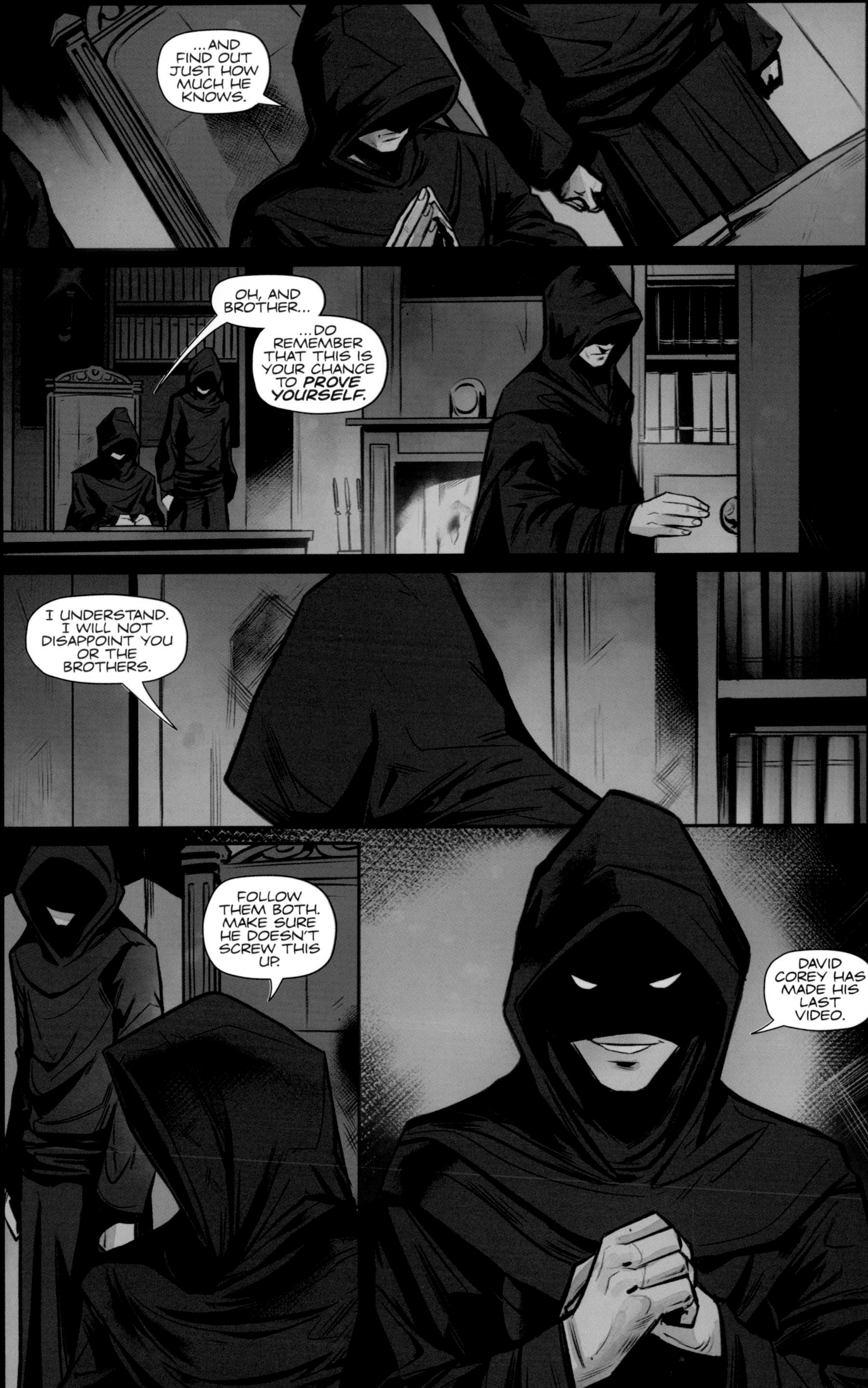
...AND FIND OUT JUST HOW MUCH HE KNOWS.
OH, AND BROTHER...
...DO REMEMBER THAT THIS IS YOUR CHANCE TO **PROVE YOURSELF.**
I UNDERSTAND. I WILL NOT DISAPPOINT YOU OR THE BROTHERS.
FOLLOW THEM BOTH. MAKE SURE HE DOESN'T SCREW THIS UP.
DAVID COREY HAS MADE HIS LAST VIDEO.

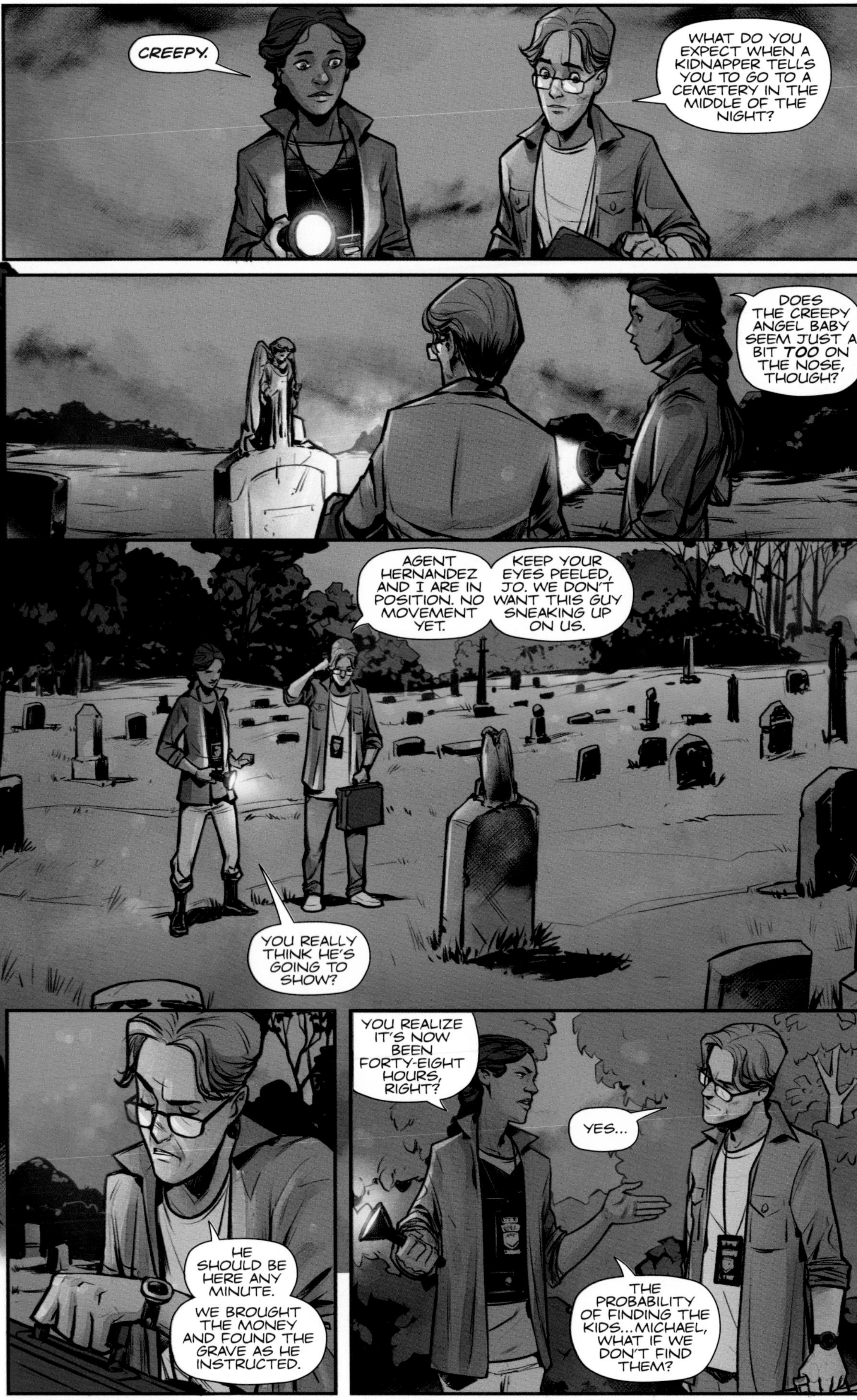
CREEPY.
WHAT DO YOU EXPECT WHEN A KIDNAPPER TELLS YOU TO GO TO A CEMETERY IN THE MIDDLE OF THE NIGHT?
DOES THE CREEPY ANGEL BABY SEEM JUST A BIT TOO ON THE NOSE, THOUGH?
AGENT HERNANDEZ AND I ARE IN POSITION. NO MOVEMENT YET.
KEEP YOUR EYES PEELED, JO. WE DON'T WANT THIS GUY SNEAKING UP ON US.
YOU REALLY THINK HE'S GOING TO SHOW?
HE SHOULD BE HERE ANY MINUTE.
WE BROUGHT THE MONEY AND FOUND THE GRAVE AS HE INSTRUCTED.
YOU REALIZE IT'S NOW BEEN FORTY-EIGHT HOURS, RIGHT?
YES...
THE PROBABILITY OF FINDING THE KIDS...MICHAEL, WHAT IF WE DON'T FIND THEM?

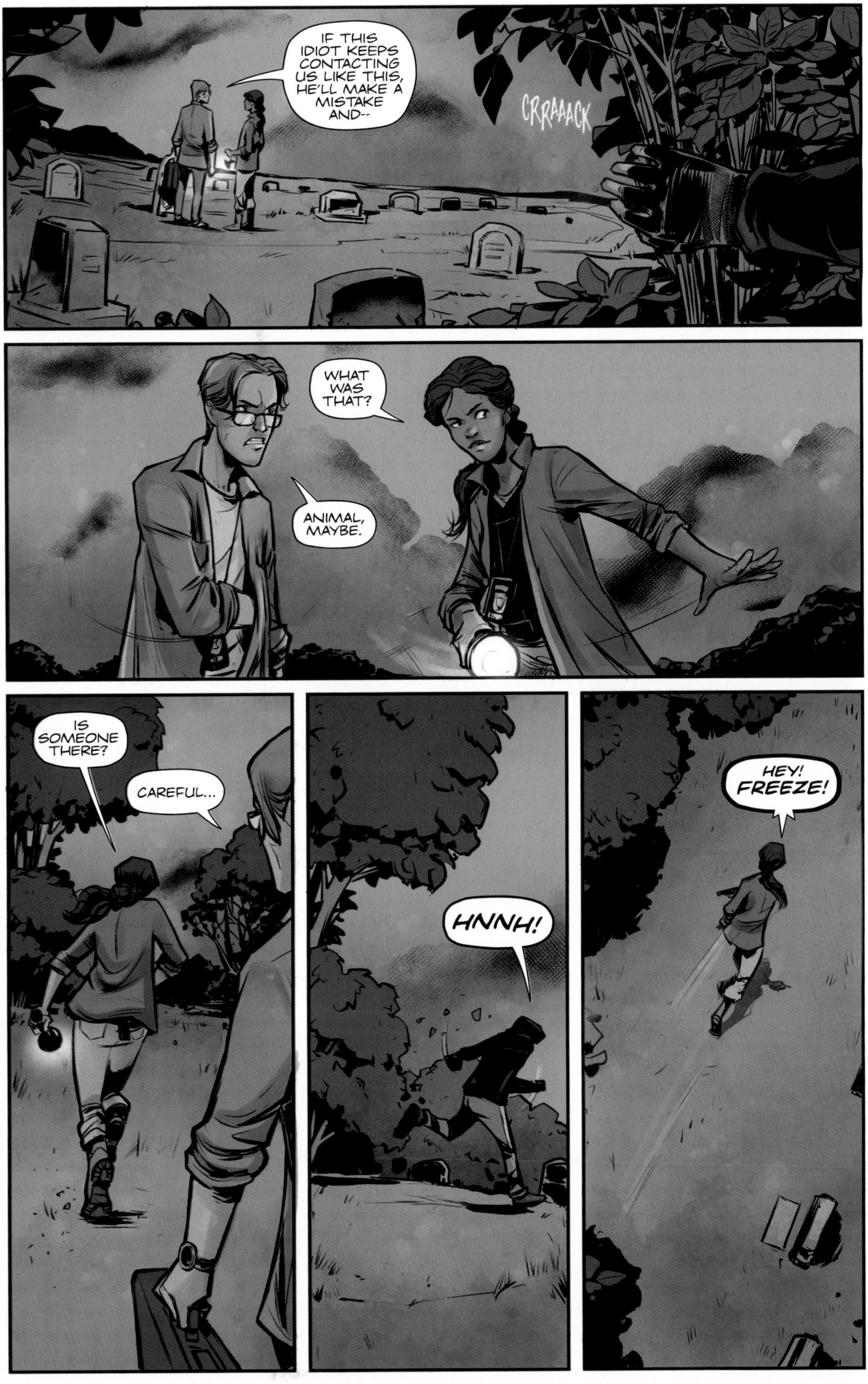
IF THIS IDIOT KEEPS CONTACTING US LIKE THIS, HE'LL MAKE A MISTAKE AND--
CRRAAACK
WHAT WAS THAT?
ANIMAL, MAYBE.
IS SOMEONE THERE?
CAREFUL...
HNNH!
HEY! FREEZE!

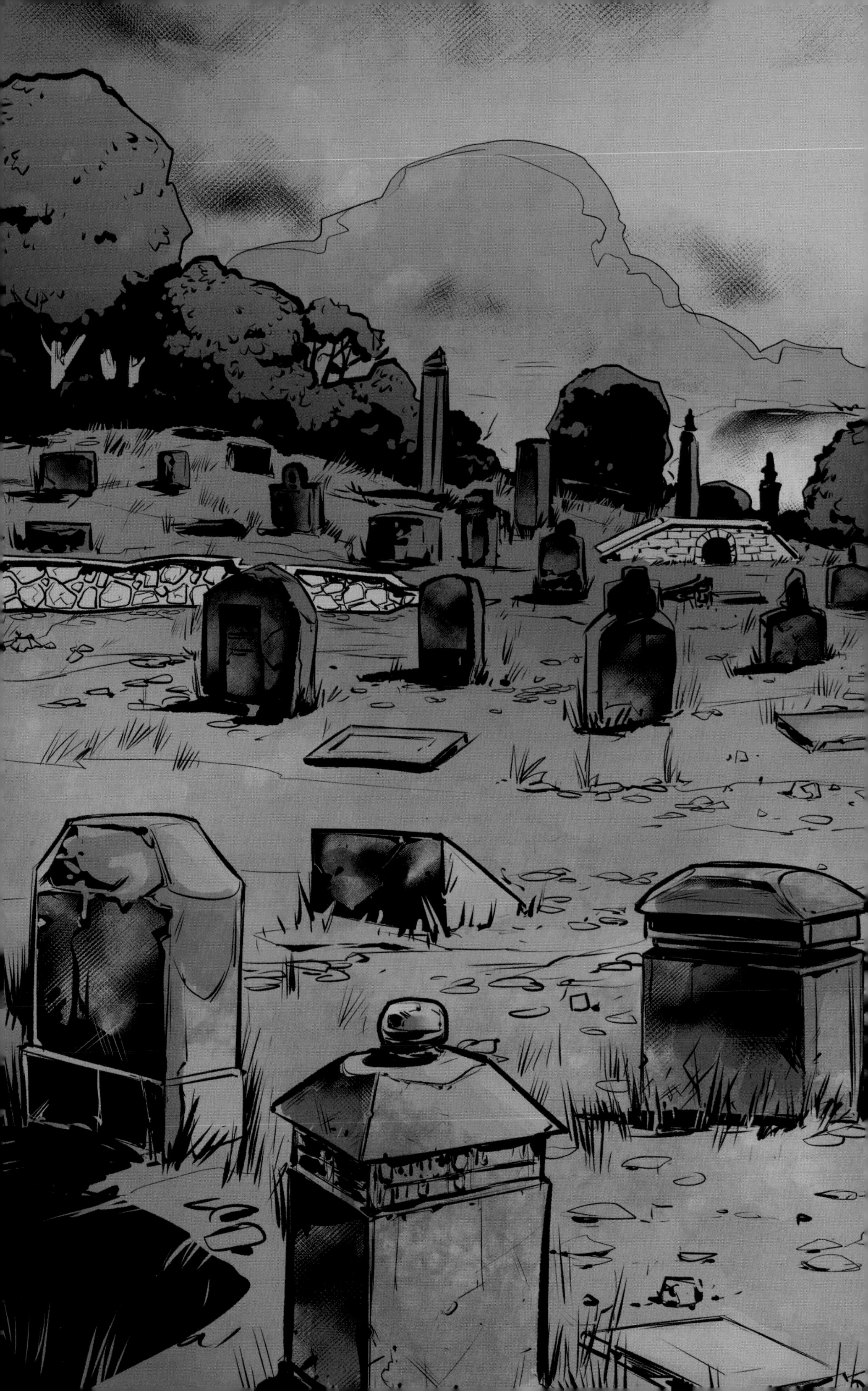

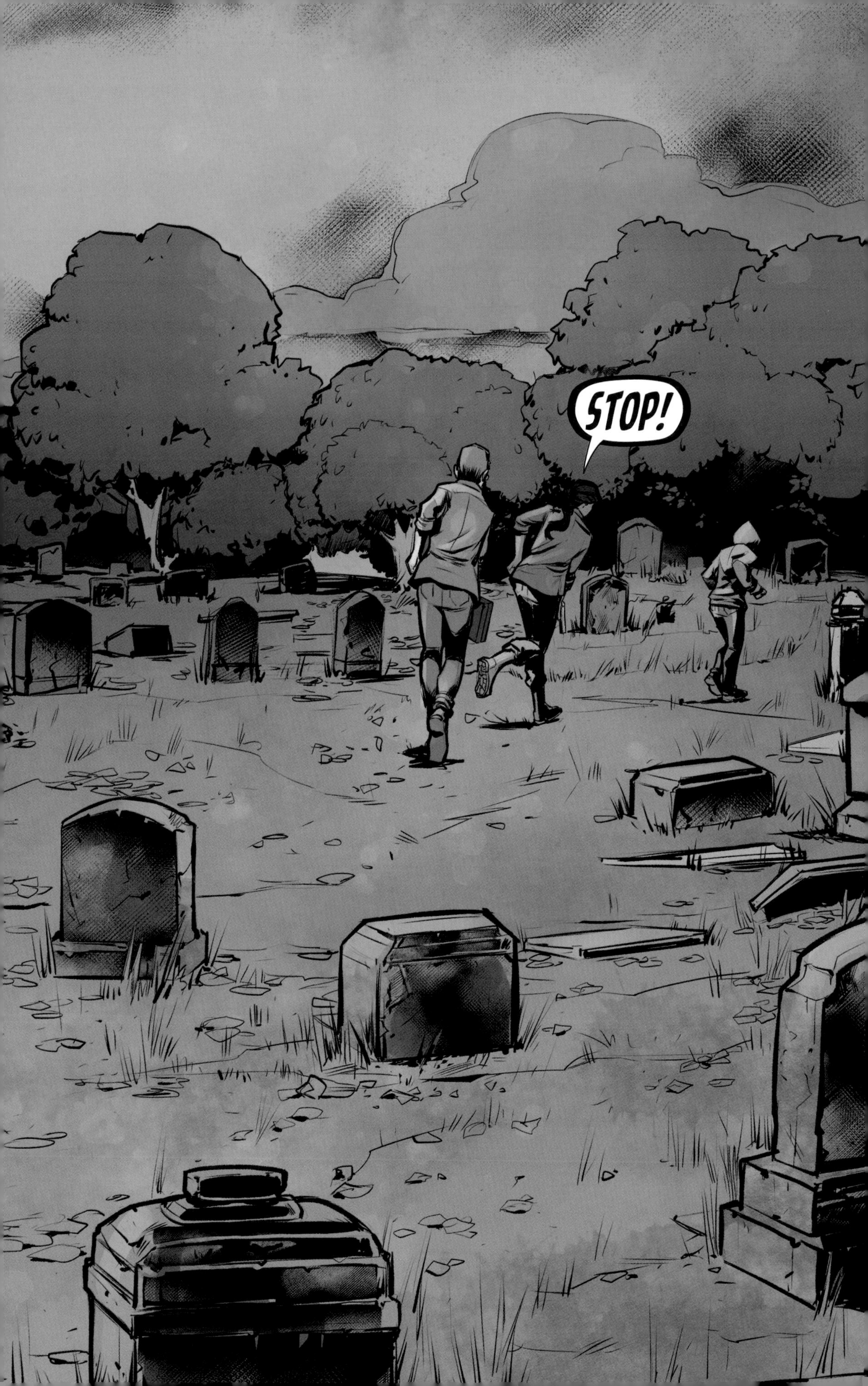
STOP!

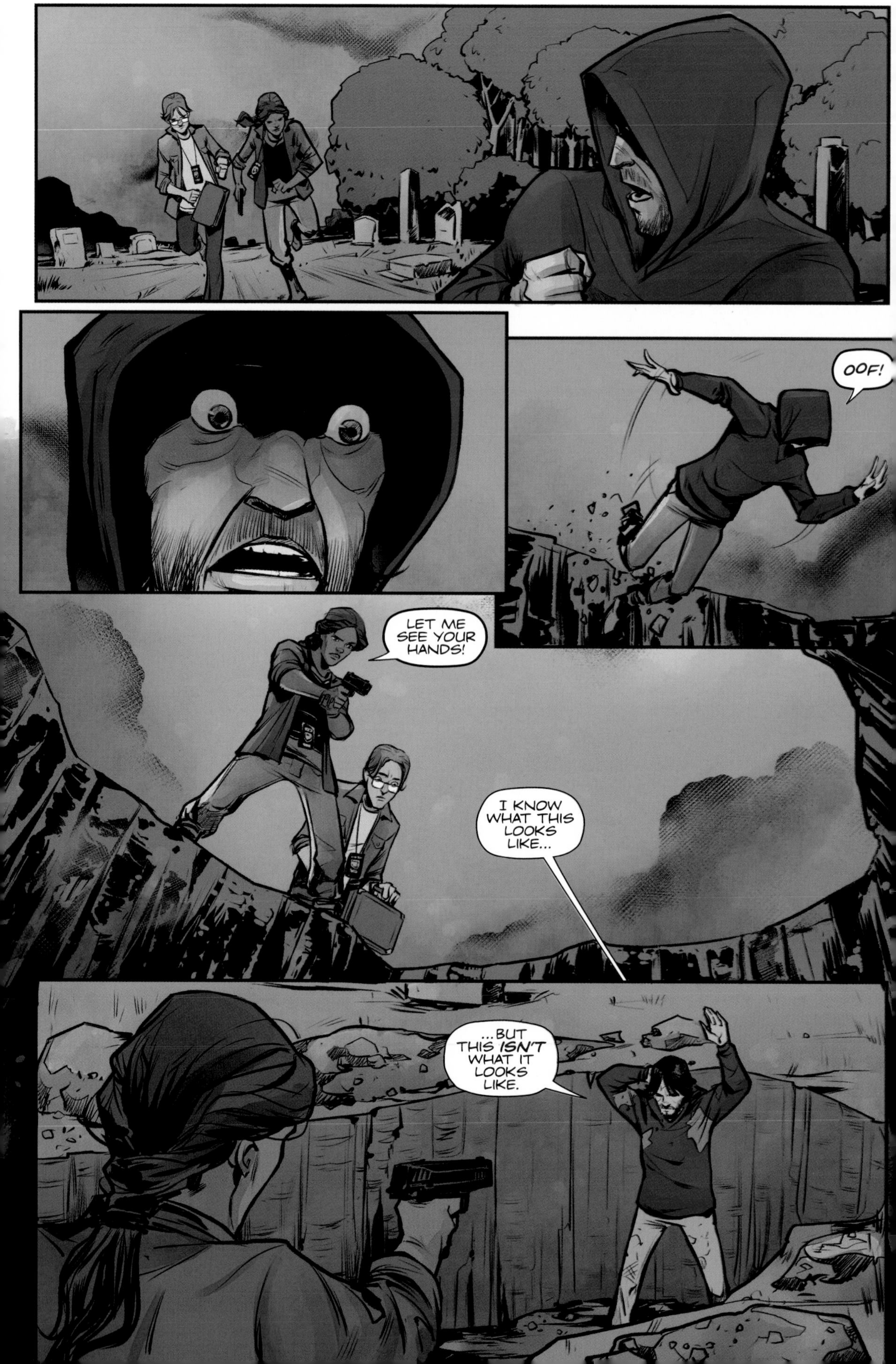
OOF!
LET ME SEE YOUR HANDS!
I KNOW WHAT THIS LOOKS LIKE...
...BUT THIS *ISN'T* WHAT IT LOOKS LIKE.

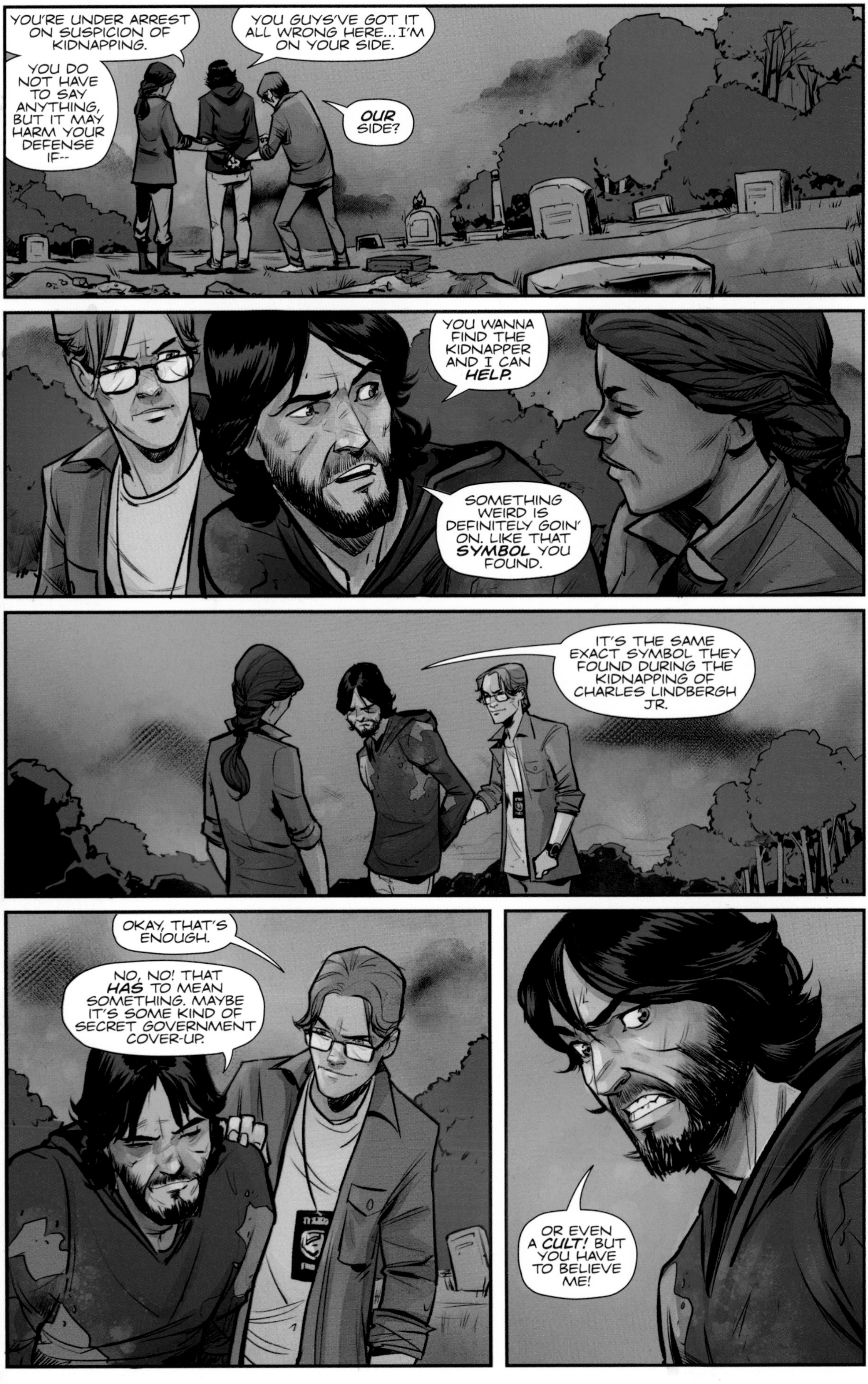
YOU'RE UNDER ARREST ON SUSPICION OF KIDNAPPING.
YOU DO NOT HAVE TO SAY ANYTHING, BUT IT MAY HARM YOUR DEFENSE IF--
YOU GUYS'VE GOT IT ALL WRONG HERE...I'M ON YOUR SIDE.
OUR SIDE?
YOU WANNA FIND THE KIDNAPPER AND I CAN HELP.
SOMETHING WEIRD IS DEFINITELY GOIN' ON. LIKE THAT SYMBOL YOU FOUND.
IT'S THE SAME EXACT SYMBOL THEY FOUND DURING THE KIDNAPPING OF CHARLES LINDBERGH JR.
OKAY, THAT'S ENOUGH.
NO, NO! THAT HAS TO MEAN SOMETHING. MAYBE IT'S SOME KIND OF SECRET GOVERNMENT COVER-UP.
OR EVEN A CULT! BUT YOU HAVE TO BELIEVE ME!

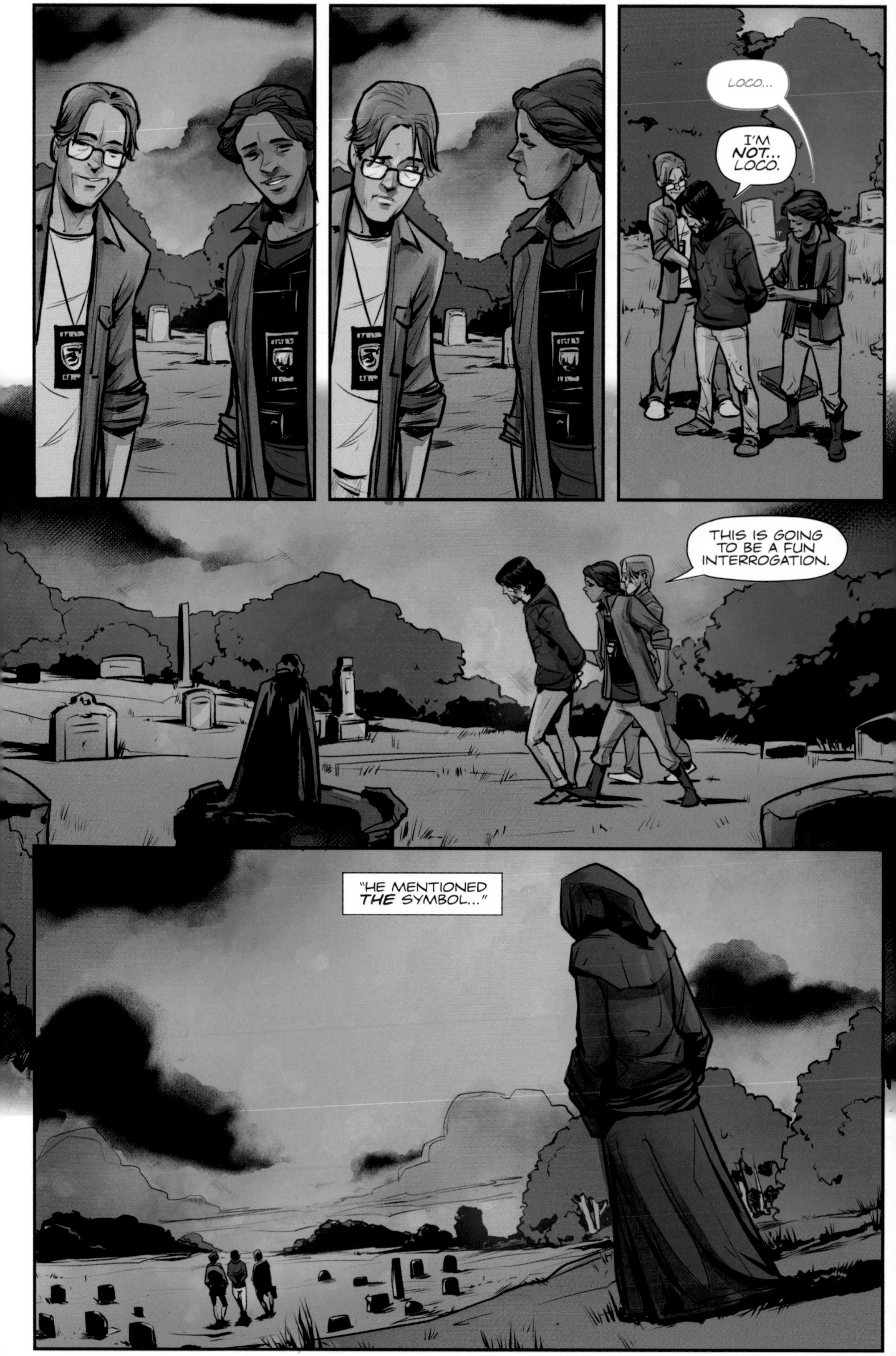
LOCO...
I'M NOT... LOCO.
THIS IS GOING TO BE A FUN INTERROGATION.
"HE MENTIONED THE SYMBOL..."

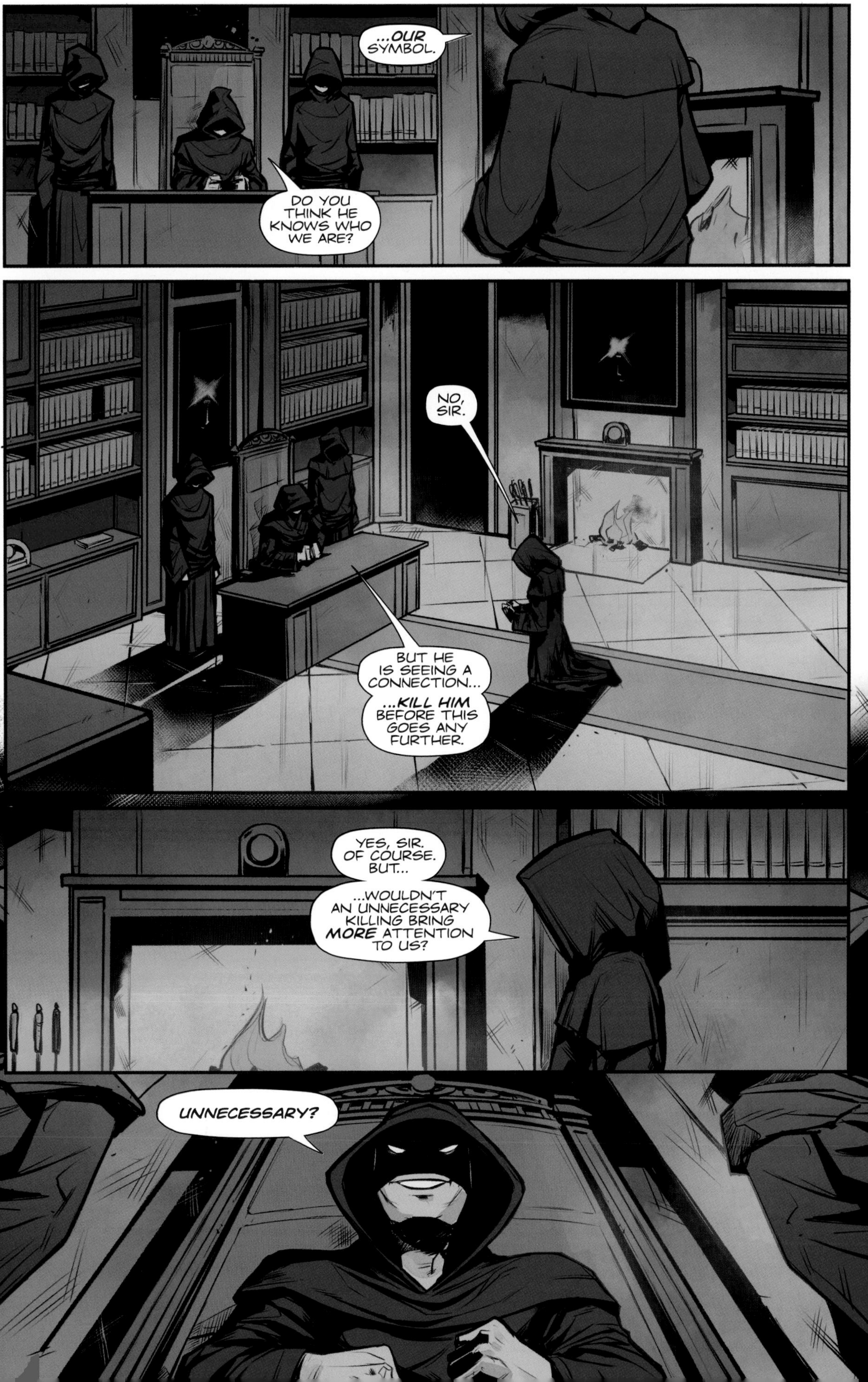
...OUR SYMBOL.
DO YOU THINK HE KNOWS WHO WE ARE?
NO, SIR.
BUT HE IS SEEING A CONNECTION...
...KILL HIM BEFORE THIS GOES ANY FURTHER.
YES, SIR. OF COURSE. BUT...
...WOULDN'T AN UNNECESSARY KILLING BRING MORE ATTENTION TO US?
UNNECESSARY?

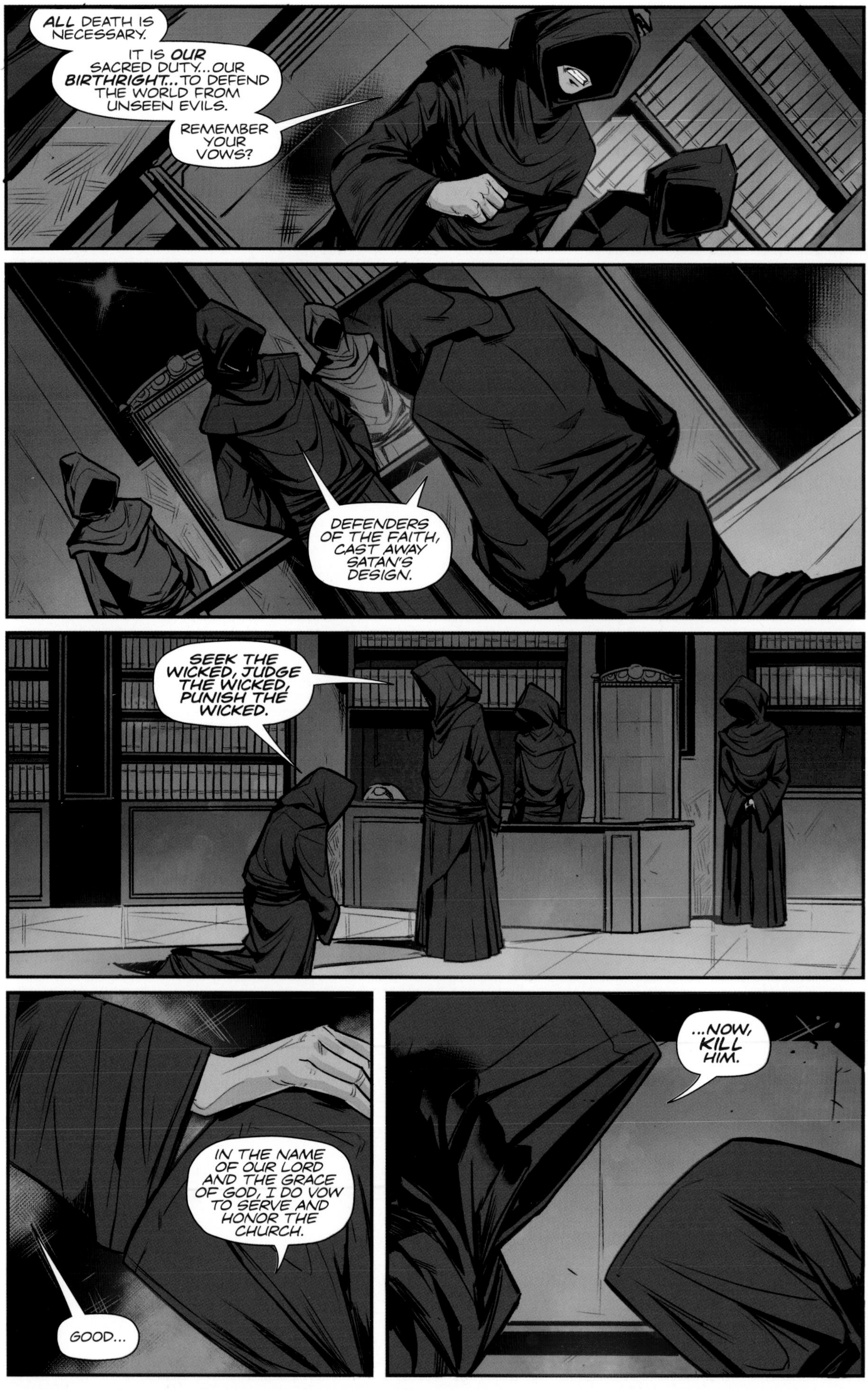
ALL DEATH IS NECESSARY.
IT IS OUR SACRED DUTY...OUR BIRTHRIGHT...TO DEFEND THE WORLD FROM UNSEEN EVILS.
REMEMBER YOUR VOWS?
DEFENDERS OF THE FAITH, CAST AWAY SATAN'S DESIGN.
SEEK THE WICKED, JUDGE THE WICKED, PUNISH THE WICKED.
IN THE NAME OF OUR LORD AND THE GRACE OF GOD, I DO VOW TO SERVE AND HONOR THE CHURCH.
GOOD...
...NOW, KILL HIM.

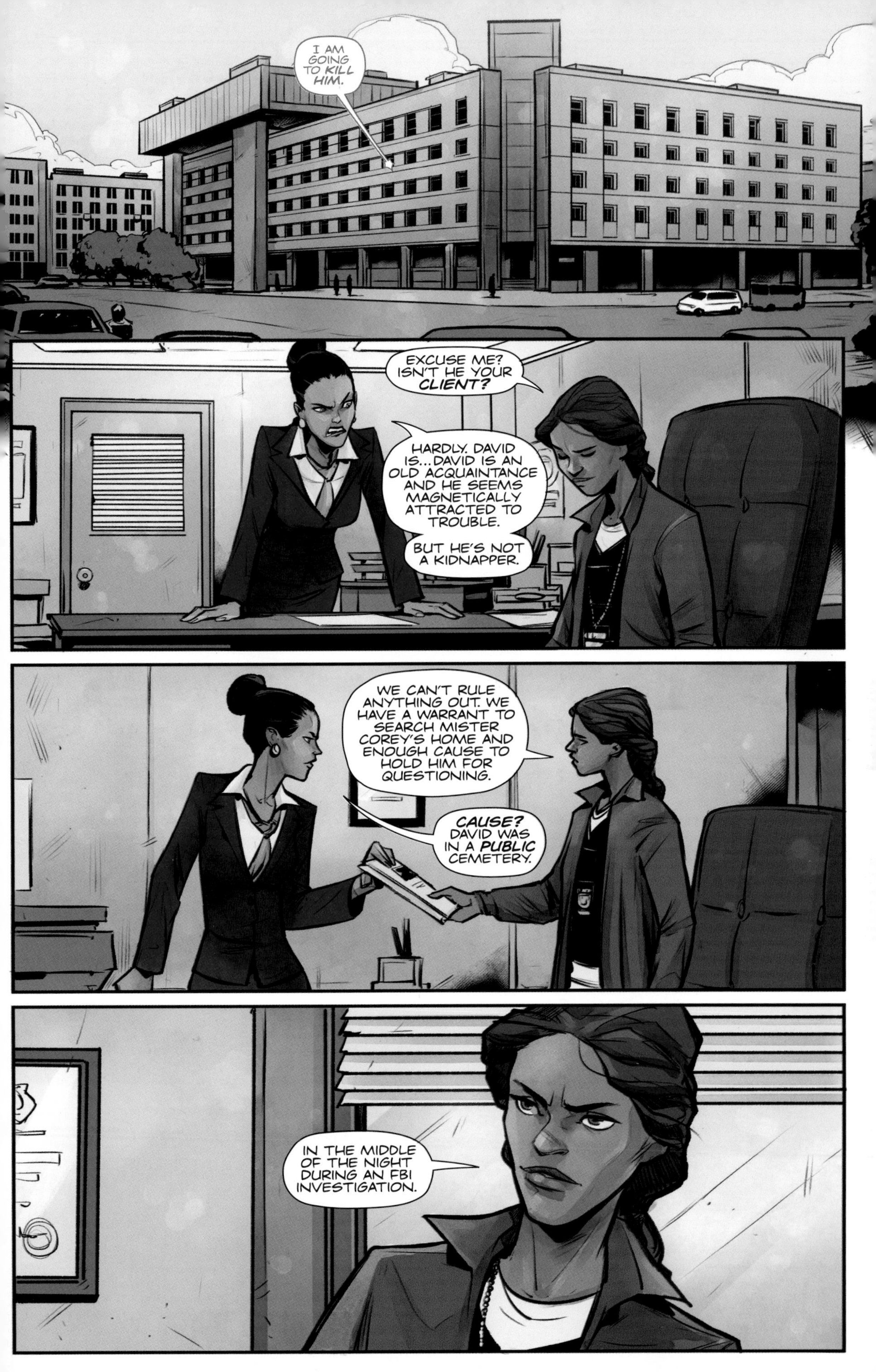
I AM GOING TO KILL HIM.
EXCUSE ME? ISN'T HE YOUR CLIENT?
HARDLY. DAVID IS...DAVID IS AN OLD ACQUAINTANCE AND HE SEEMS MAGNETICALLY ATTRACTED TO TROUBLE.
BUT HE'S NOT A KIDNAPPER.
WE CAN'T RULE ANYTHING OUT. WE HAVE A WARRANT TO SEARCH MISTER COREY'S HOME AND ENOUGH CAUSE TO HOLD HIM FOR QUESTIONING.
CAUSE? DAVID WAS IN A PUBLIC CEMETERY.
IN THE MIDDLE OF THE NIGHT DURING AN FBI INVESTIGATION.

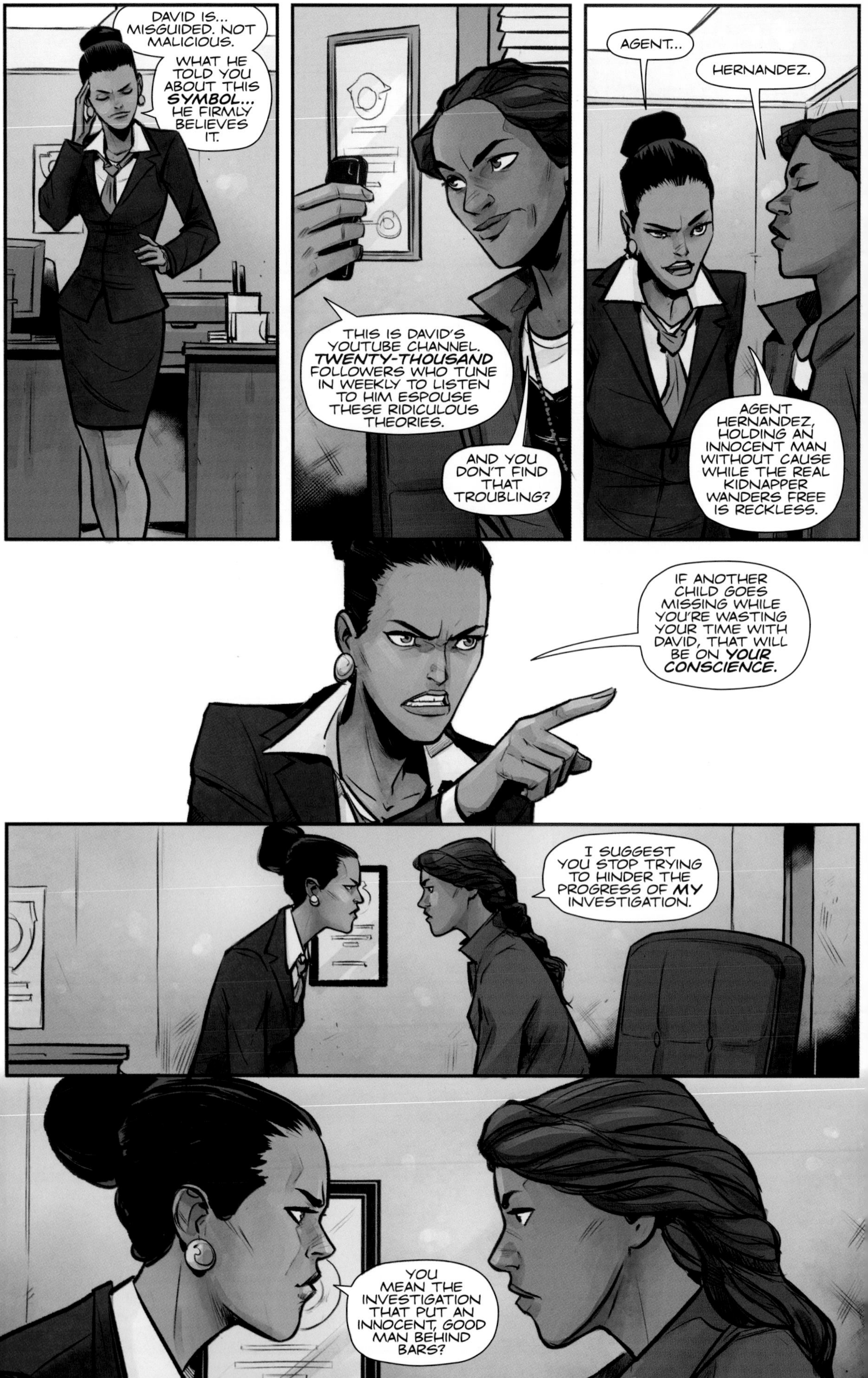

DAVID IS... MISGUIDED. NOT MALICIOUS.
WHAT HE TOLD YOU ABOUT THIS SYMBOL... HE FIRMLY BELIEVES IT.
THIS IS DAVID'S YOUTUBE CHANNEL. TWENTY-THOUSAND FOLLOWERS WHO TUNE IN WEEKLY TO LISTEN TO HIM ESPOUSE THESE RIDICULOUS THEORIES.
AND YOU DON'T FIND THAT TROUBLING?
AGENT...
HERNANDEZ.
AGENT HERNANDEZ, HOLDING AN INNOCENT MAN WITHOUT CAUSE WHILE THE REAL KIDNAPPER WANDERS FREE IS RECKLESS.
IF ANOTHER CHILD GOES MISSING WHILE YOU'RE WASTING YOUR TIME WITH DAVID, THAT WILL BE ON YOUR CONSCIENCE.
I SUGGEST YOU STOP TRYING TO HINDER THE PROGRESS OF MY INVESTIGATION.
YOU MEAN THE INVESTIGATION THAT PUT AN INNOCENT, GOOD MAN BEHIND BARS?

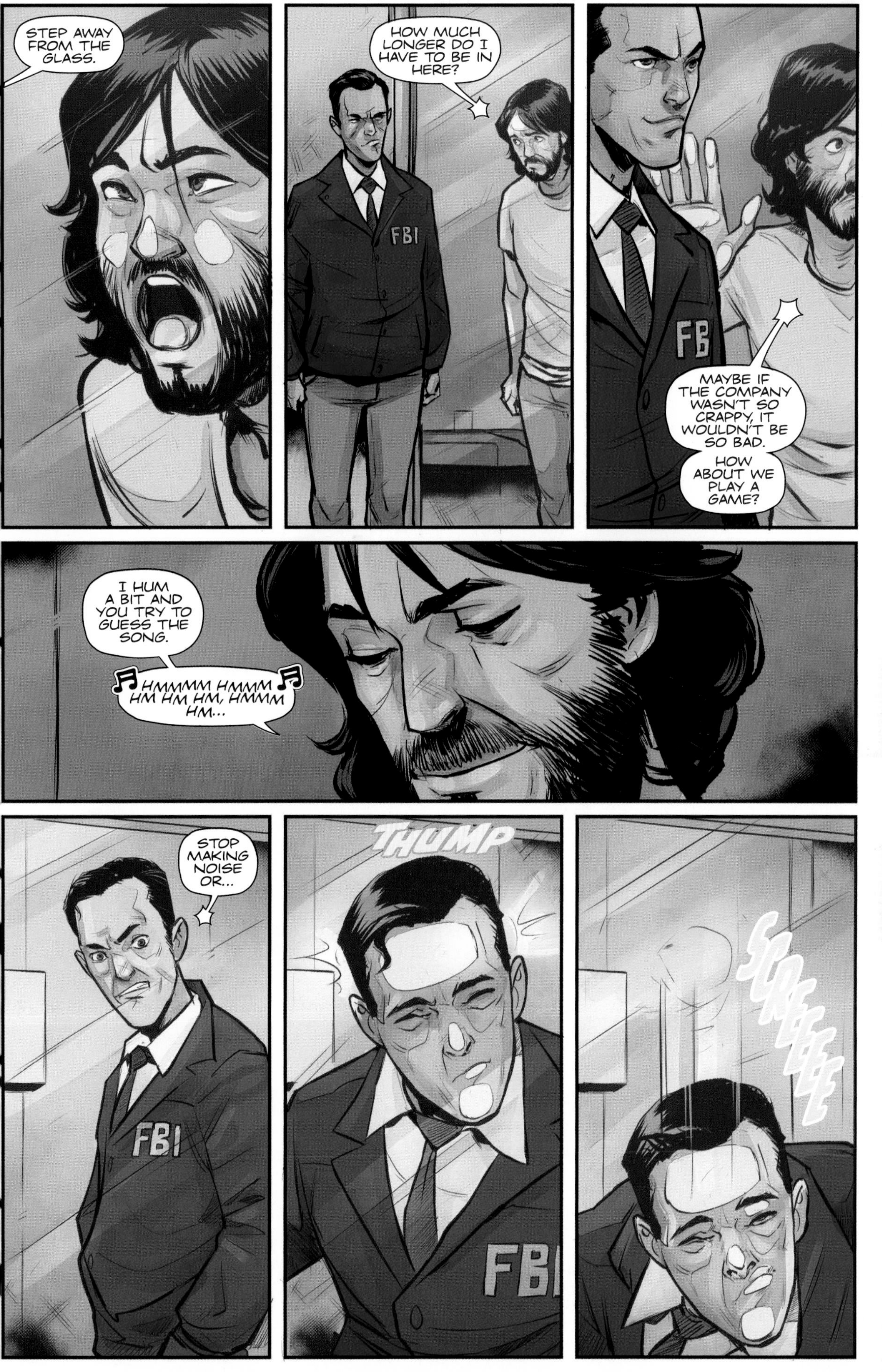
STEP AWAY FROM THE GLASS.
HOW MUCH LONGER DO I HAVE TO BE IN HERE?
FBI
FBI
MAYBE IF THE COMPANY WASN'T SO CRAPPY, IT WOULDN'T BE SO BAD.
HOW ABOUT WE PLAY A GAME?
I HUM A BIT AND YOU TRY TO GUESS THE SONG.
HMMMM HMMM HM HM HM, HMMM HM...
STOP MAKING NOISE OR...
FBI
THUMP
FBI
SCREEEE

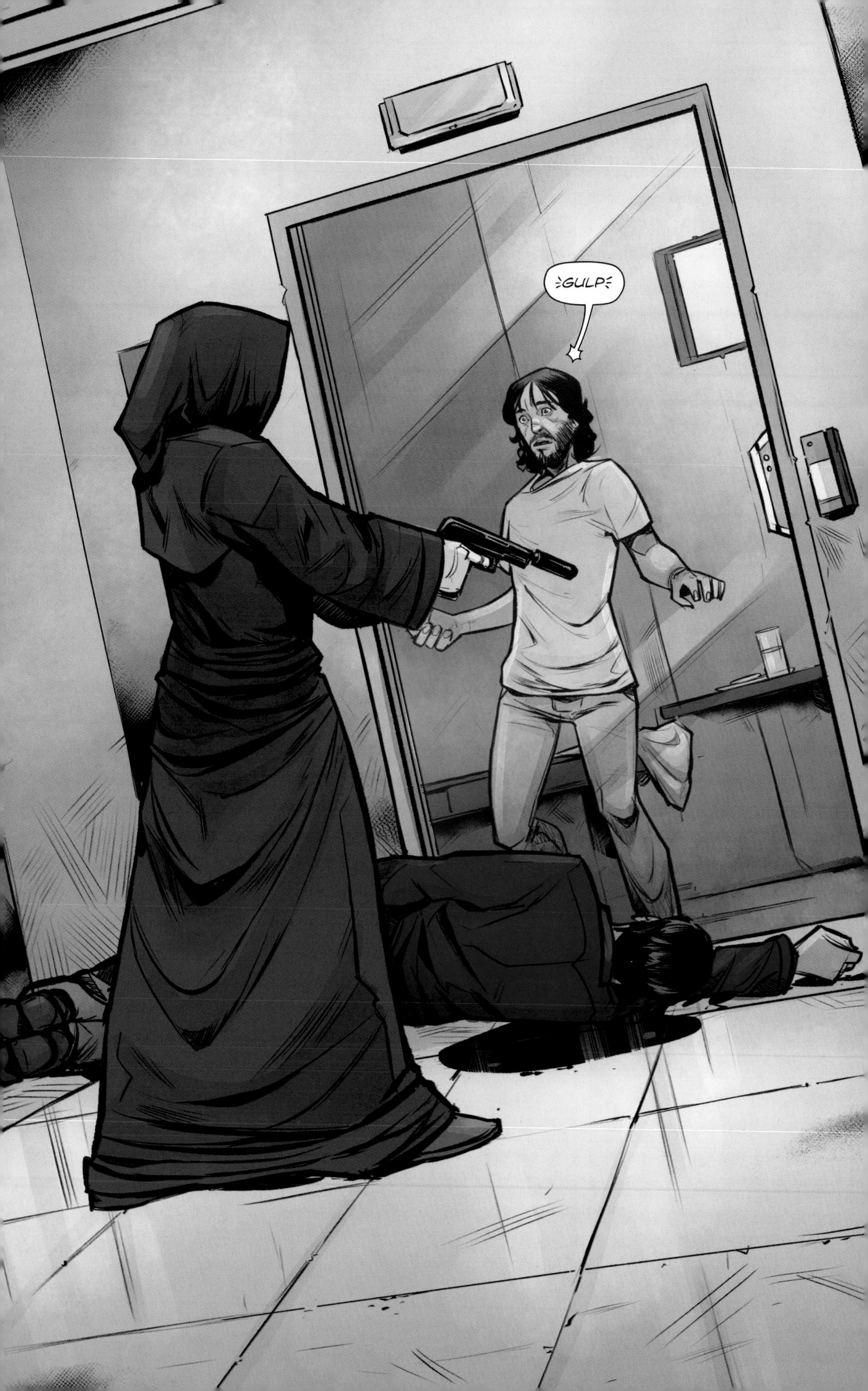
GULP

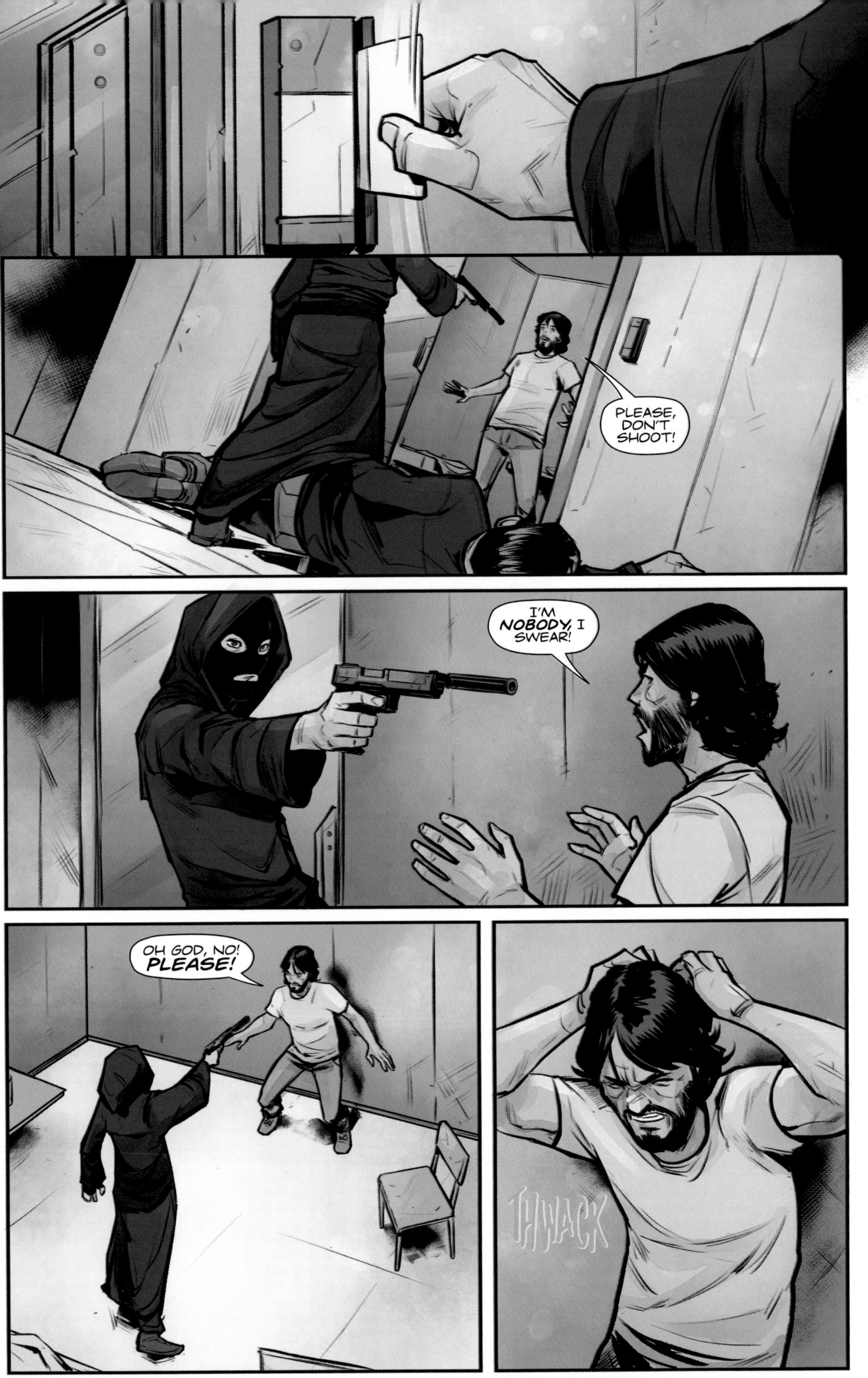
PLEASE, DON'T SHOOT!
I'M NOBODY, I SWEAR!
OH GOD, NO! PLEASE!
THWACK

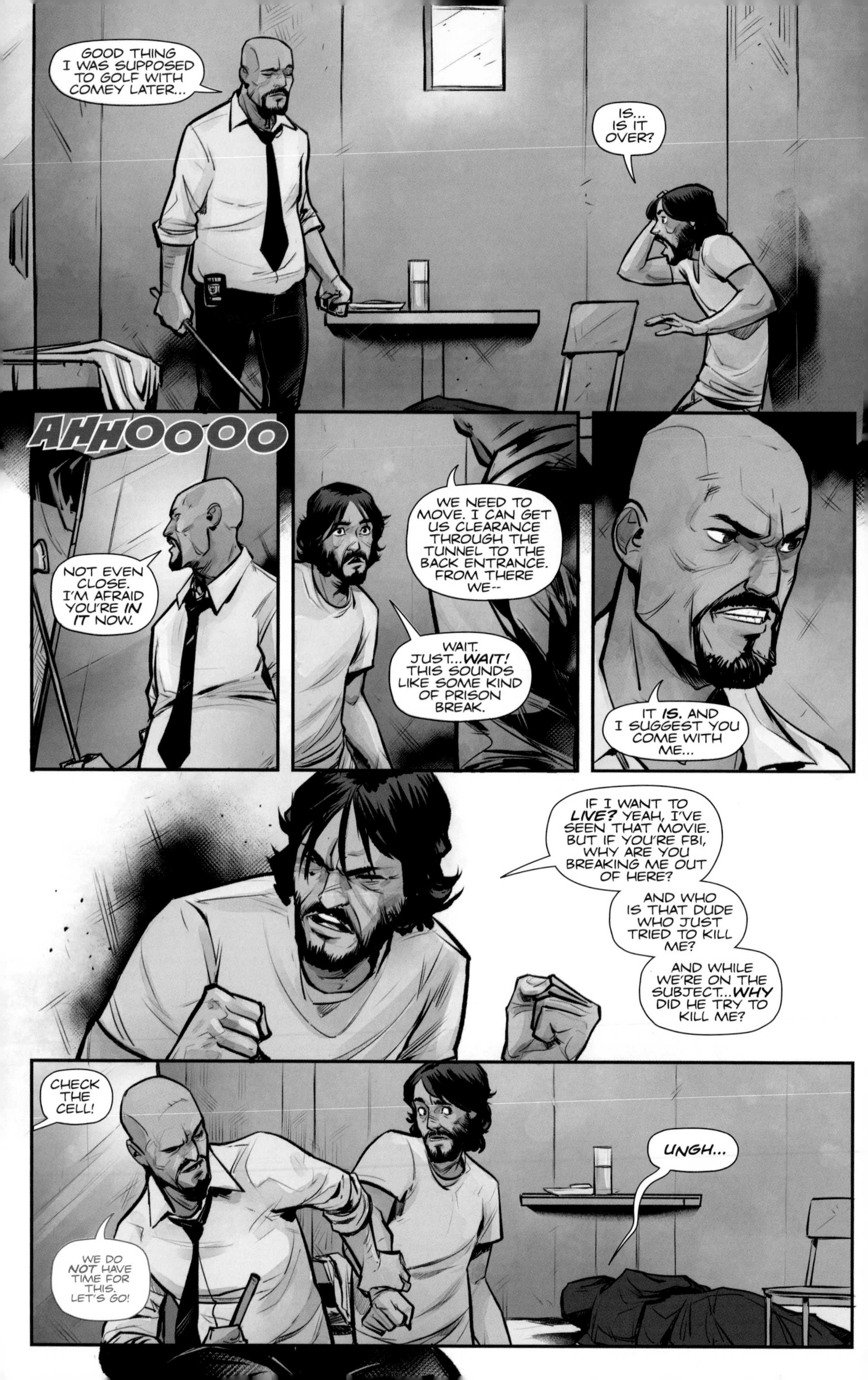
GOOD THING I WAS SUPPOSED TO GOLF WITH COMEY LATER...
IS... IS IT OVER?
AHHOOOO
NOT EVEN CLOSE. I'M AFRAID YOU'RE IN IT NOW.
WE NEED TO MOVE. I CAN GET US CLEARANCE THROUGH THE TUNNEL TO THE BACK ENTRANCE. FROM THERE WE--
WAIT. JUST...WAIT! THIS SOUNDS LIKE SOME KIND OF PRISON BREAK.
IT IS. AND I SUGGEST YOU COME WITH ME...
IF I WANT TO LIVE? YEAH, I'VE SEEN THAT MOVIE. BUT IF YOU'RE FBI, WHY ARE YOU BREAKING ME OUT OF HERE?
AND WHO IS THAT DUDE WHO JUST TRIED TO KILL ME?
AND WHILE WE'RE ON THE SUBJECT...WHY DID HE TRY TO KILL ME?
CHECK THE CELL!
UNGH...
WE DO NOT HAVE TIME FOR THIS. LET'S GO!

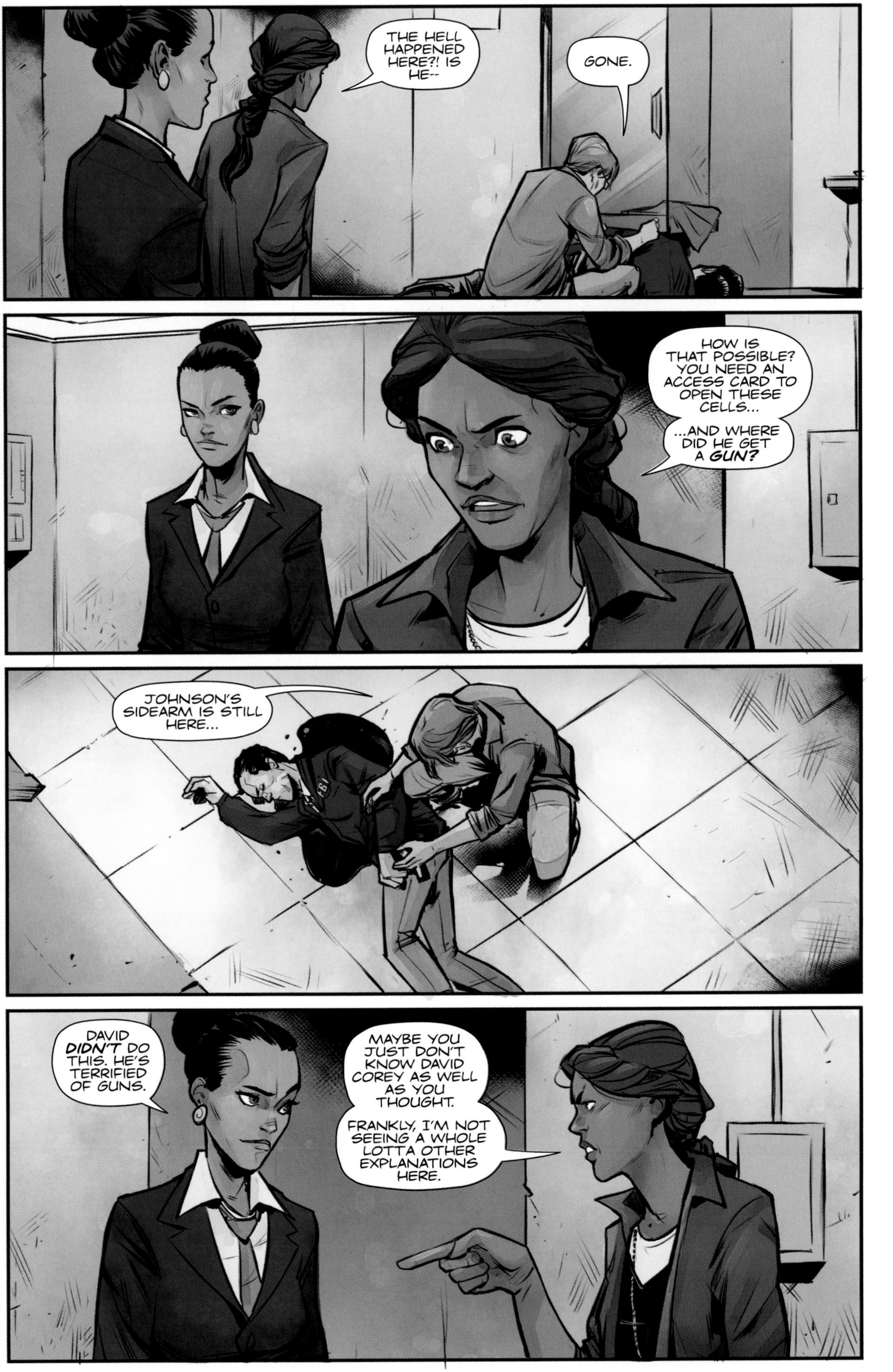

THE HELL HAPPENED HERE?! IS HE--
GONE.
HOW IS THAT POSSIBLE? YOU NEED AN ACCESS CARD TO OPEN THESE CELLS...
...AND WHERE DID HE GET A **GUN?**
JOHNSON'S SIDEARM IS STILL HERE...
FBI
DAVID **DIDN'T** DO THIS. HE'S TERRIFIED OF GUNS.
MAYBE YOU JUST DON'T KNOW DAVID COREY AS WELL AS YOU THOUGHT.
FRANKLY, I'M NOT SEEING A WHOLE LOTTA OTHER EXPLANATIONS HERE.

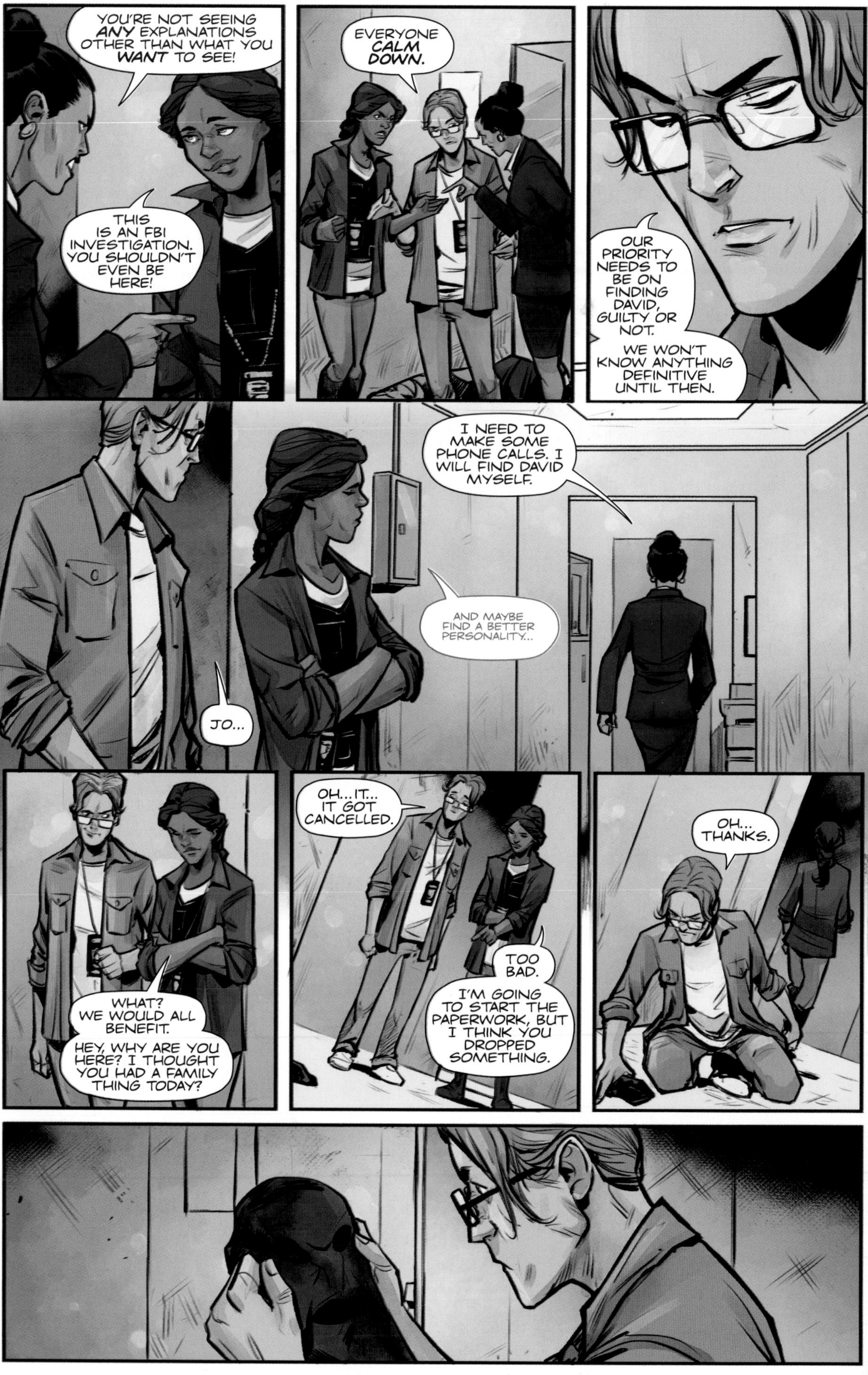
YOU'RE NOT SEEING ANY EXPLANATIONS OTHER THAN WHAT YOU WANT TO SEE!
THIS IS AN FBI INVESTIGATION. YOU SHOULDN'T EVEN BE HERE!
EVERYONE CALM DOWN.
OUR PRIORITY NEEDS TO BE ON FINDING DAVID, GUILTY OR NOT.
WE WON'T KNOW ANYTHING DEFINITIVE UNTIL THEN.
I NEED TO MAKE SOME PHONE CALLS. I WILL FIND DAVID MYSELF.
AND MAYBE FIND A BETTER PERSONALITY...
JO...
WHAT? WE WOULD ALL BENEFIT.
HEY, WHY ARE YOU HERE? I THOUGHT YOU HAD A FAMILY THING TODAY?
OH...IT... IT GOT CANCELLED.
TOO BAD.
I'M GOING TO START THE PAPERWORK, BUT I THINK YOU DROPPED SOMETHING.
OH... THANKS.

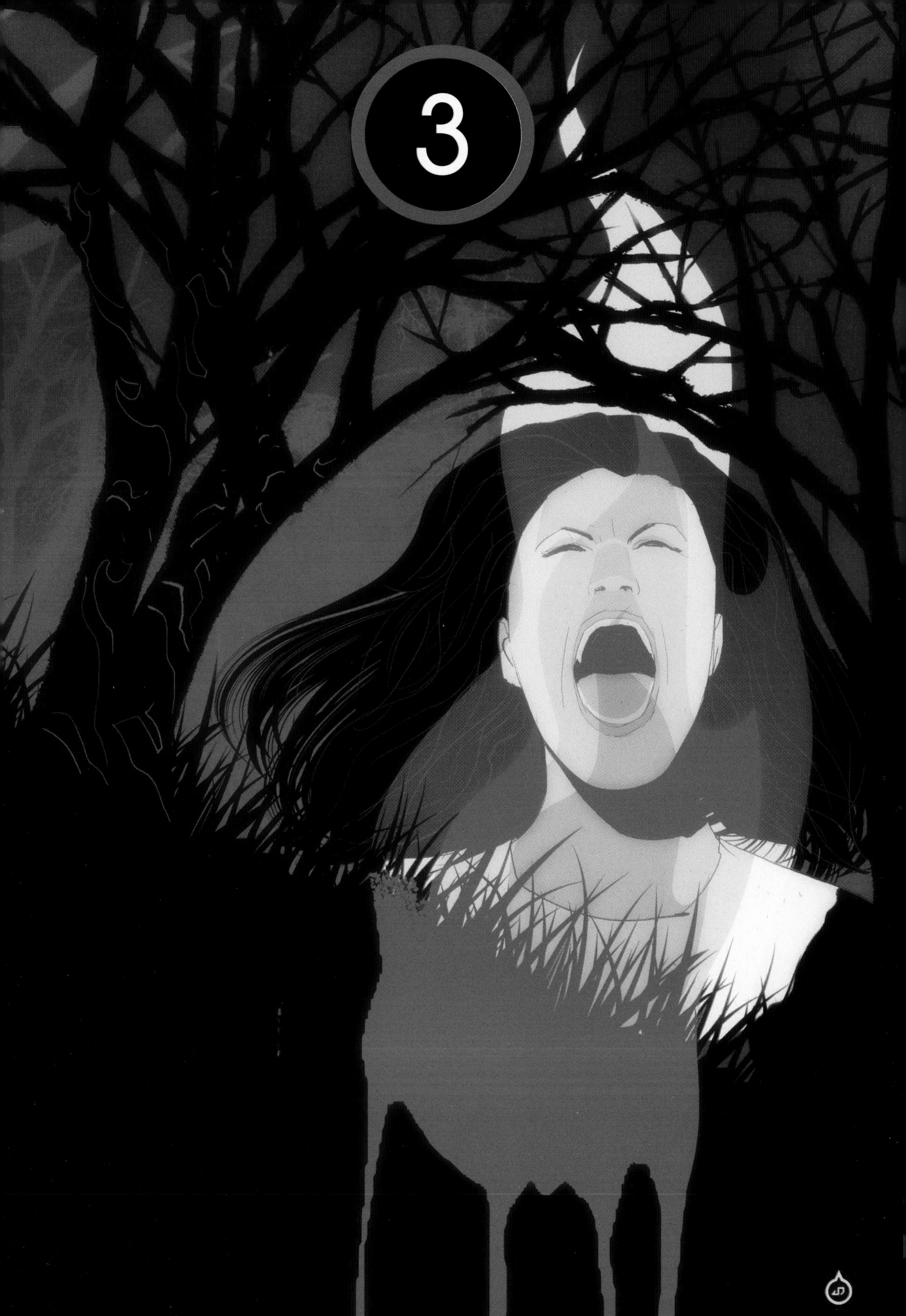

3

KIDNAPPINGS AND MURDER AND JAILBREAKS, OH MY!

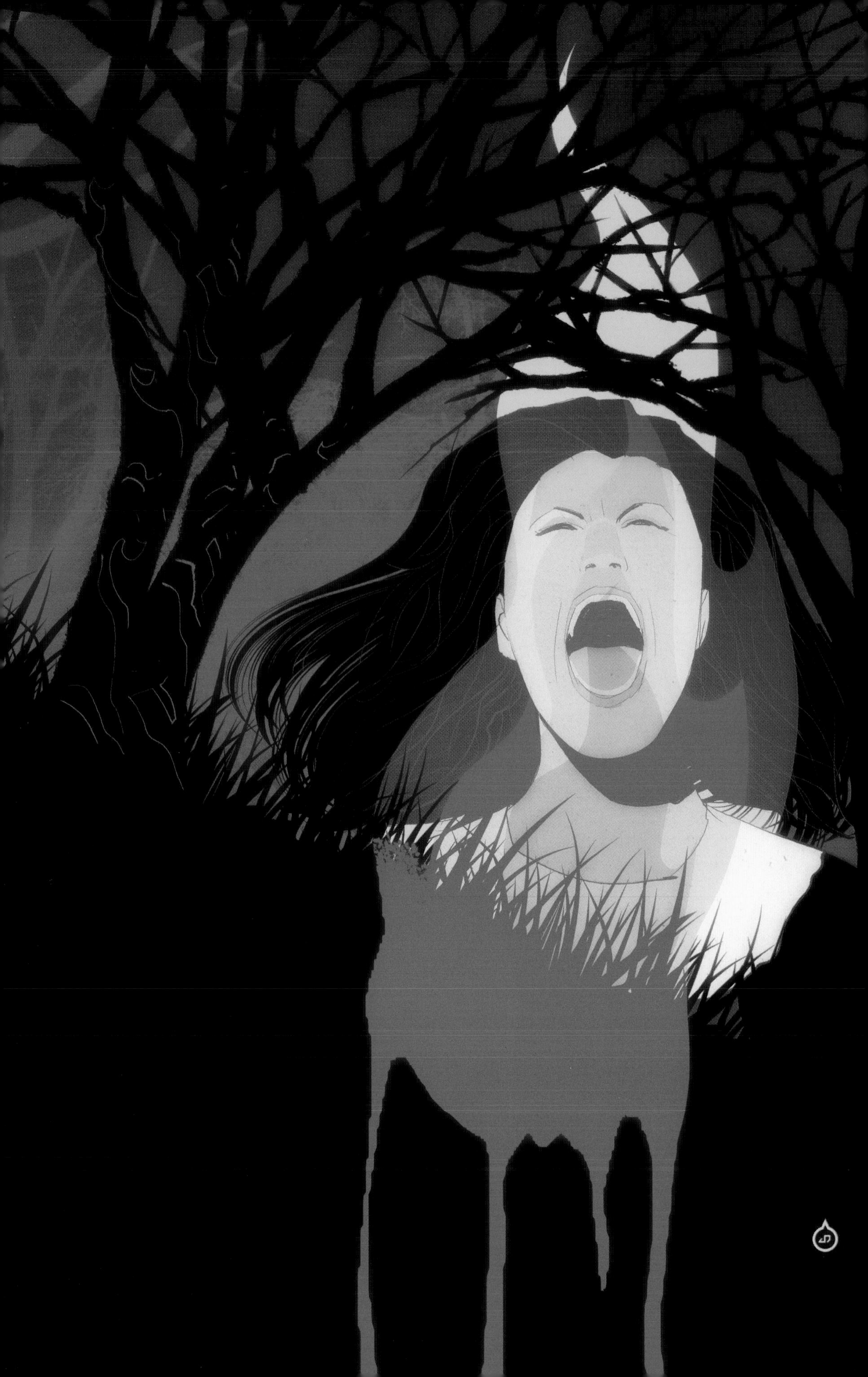

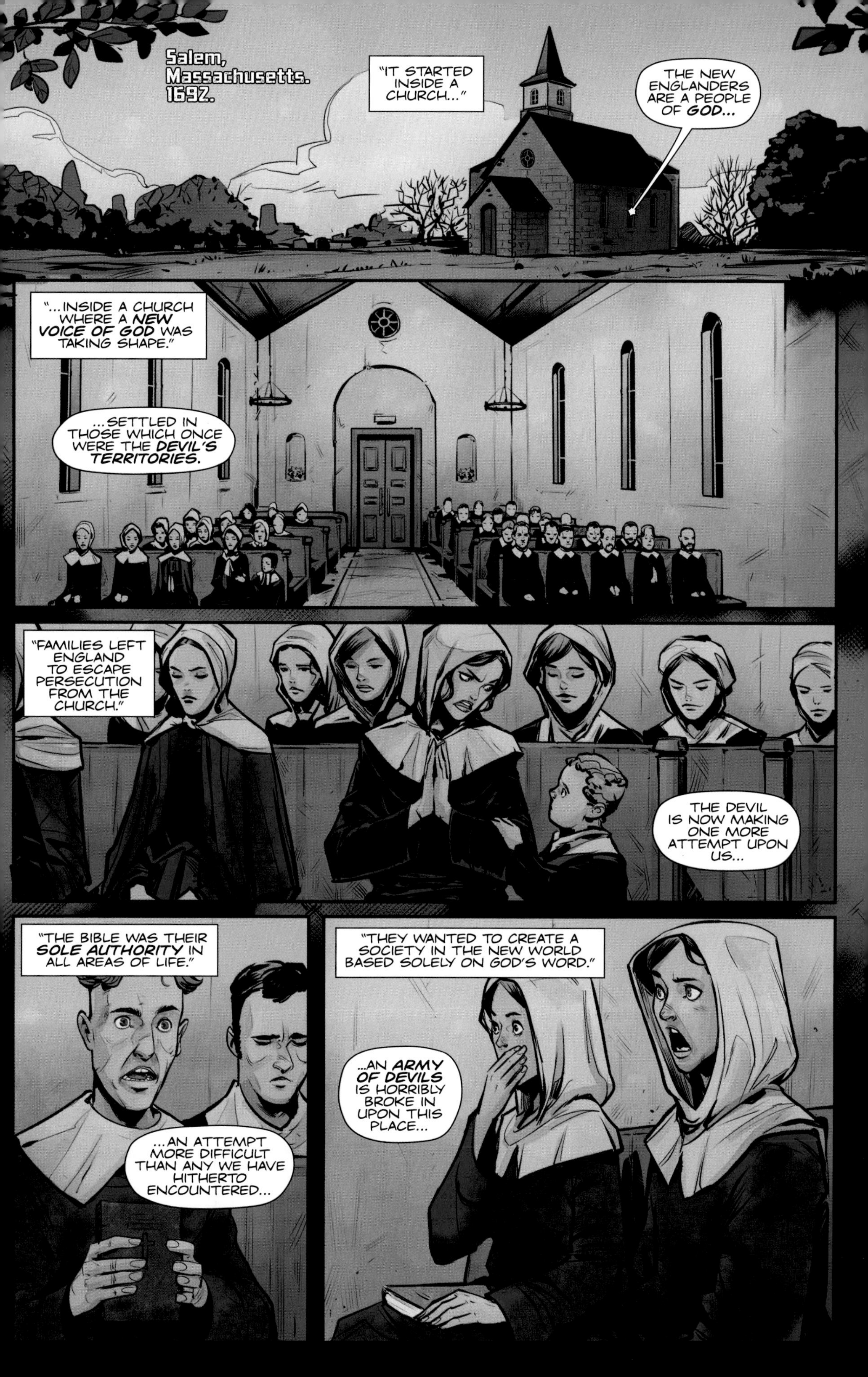
Salem, Massachusetts. 1692.
"IT STARTED INSIDE A CHURCH..."
THE NEW ENGLANDERS ARE A PEOPLE OF GOD...
"...INSIDE A CHURCH WHERE A NEW VOICE OF GOD WAS TAKING SHAPE."
...SETTLED IN THOSE WHICH ONCE WERE THE DEVIL'S TERRITORIES.
"FAMILIES LEFT ENGLAND TO ESCAPE PERSECUTION FROM THE CHURCH."
THE DEVIL IS NOW MAKING ONE MORE ATTEMPT UPON US...
"THE BIBLE WAS THEIR SOLE AUTHORITY IN ALL AREAS OF LIFE."
...AN ATTEMPT MORE DIFFICULT THAN ANY WE HAVE HITHERTO ENCOUNTERED...
"THEY WANTED TO CREATE A SOCIETY IN THE NEW WORLD BASED SOLELY ON GOD'S WORD."
...AN ARMY OF DEVILS IS HORRIBLY BROKE IN UPON THIS PLACE...

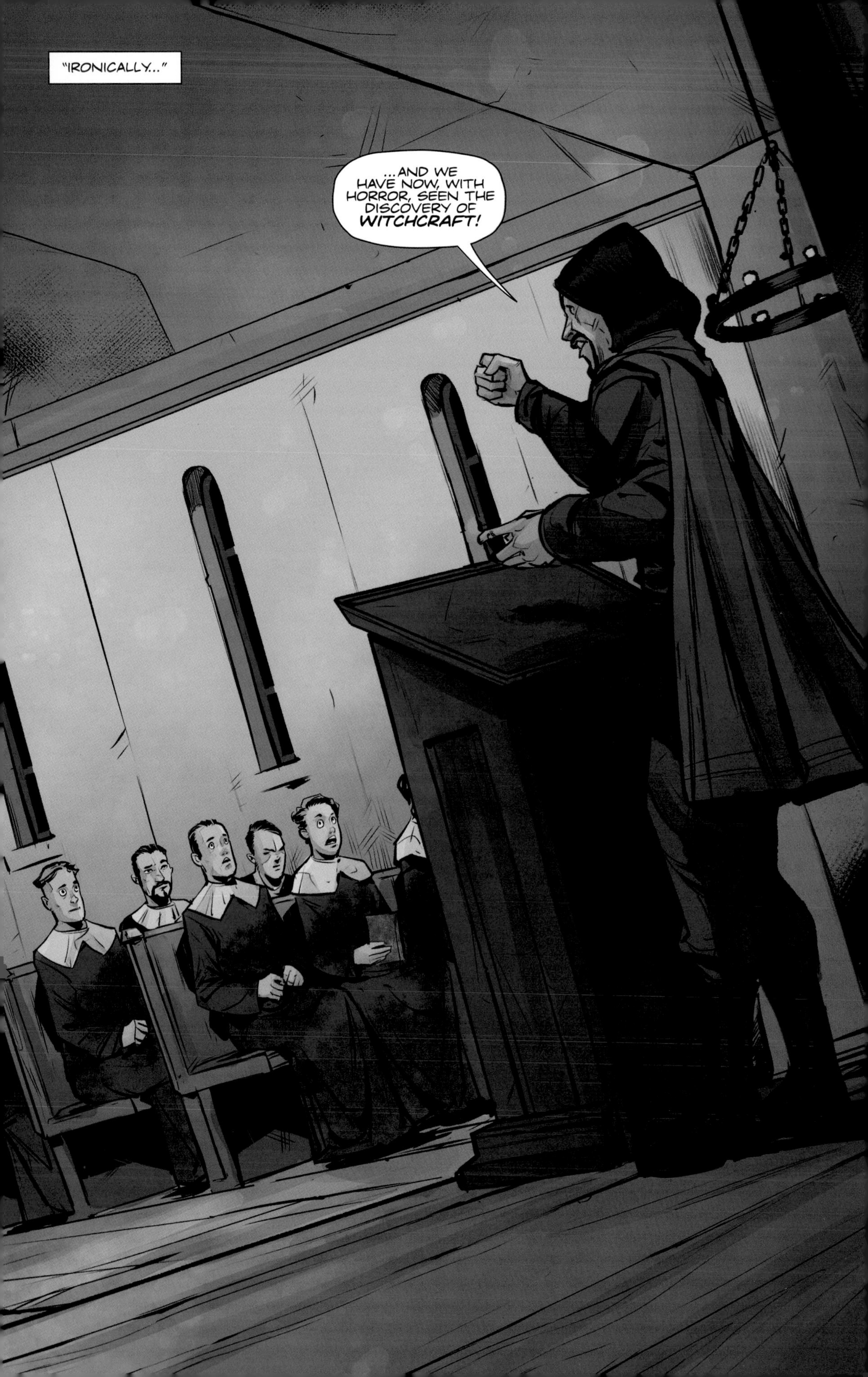
"IRONICALLY..."
...AND WE HAVE NOW, WITH HORROR, SEEN THE DISCOVERY OF WITCHCRAFT!

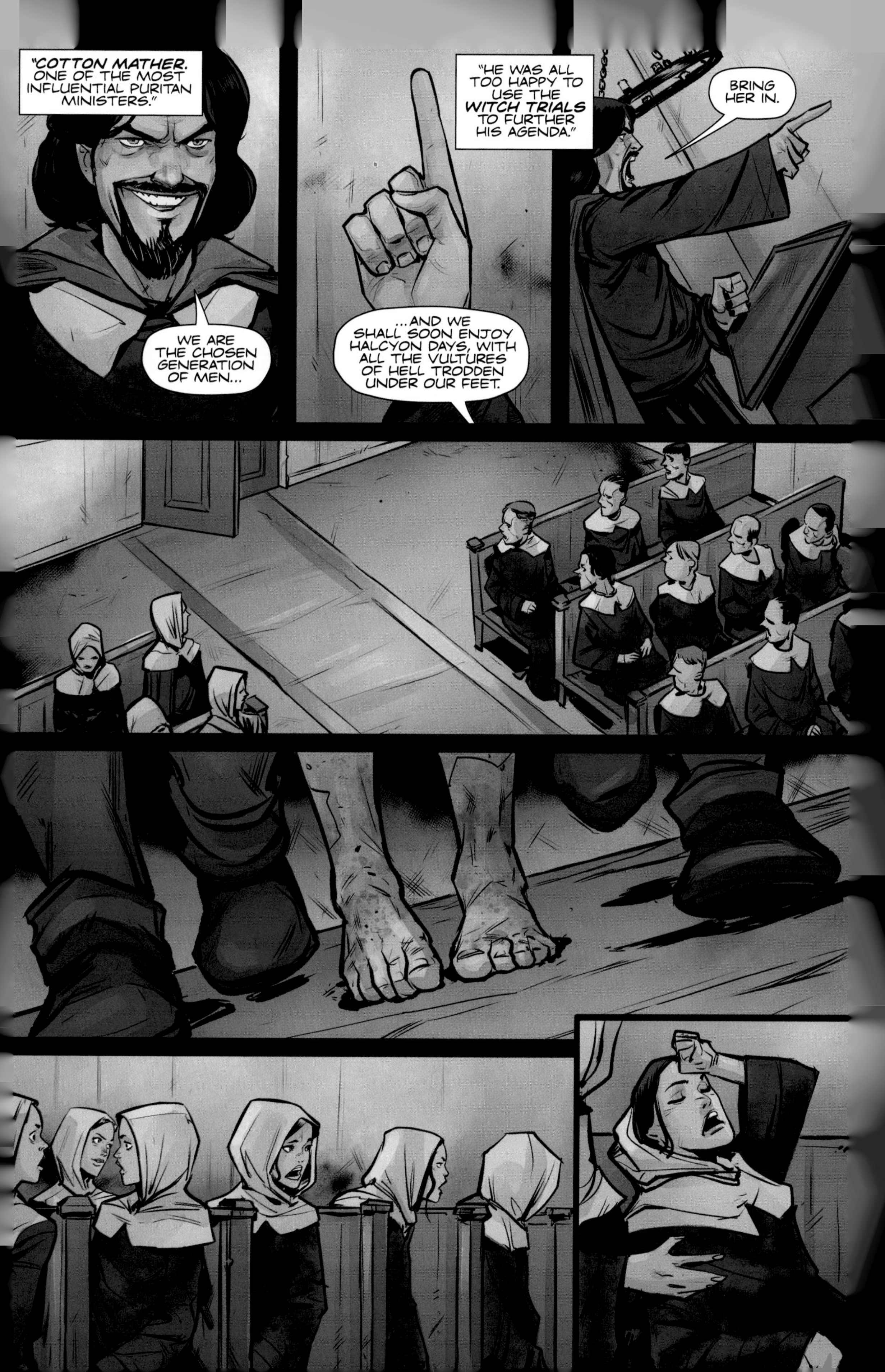
"COTTON MATHER. ONE OF THE MOST INFLUENTIAL PURITAN MINISTERS."
WE ARE THE CHOSEN GENERATION OF MEN...
...AND WE SHALL SOON ENJOY HALCYON DAYS, WITH ALL THE VULTURES OF HELL TRODDEN UNDER OUR FEET.
"HE WAS ALL TOO HAPPY TO USE THE WITCH TRIALS TO FURTHER HIS AGENDA."
BRING HER IN.

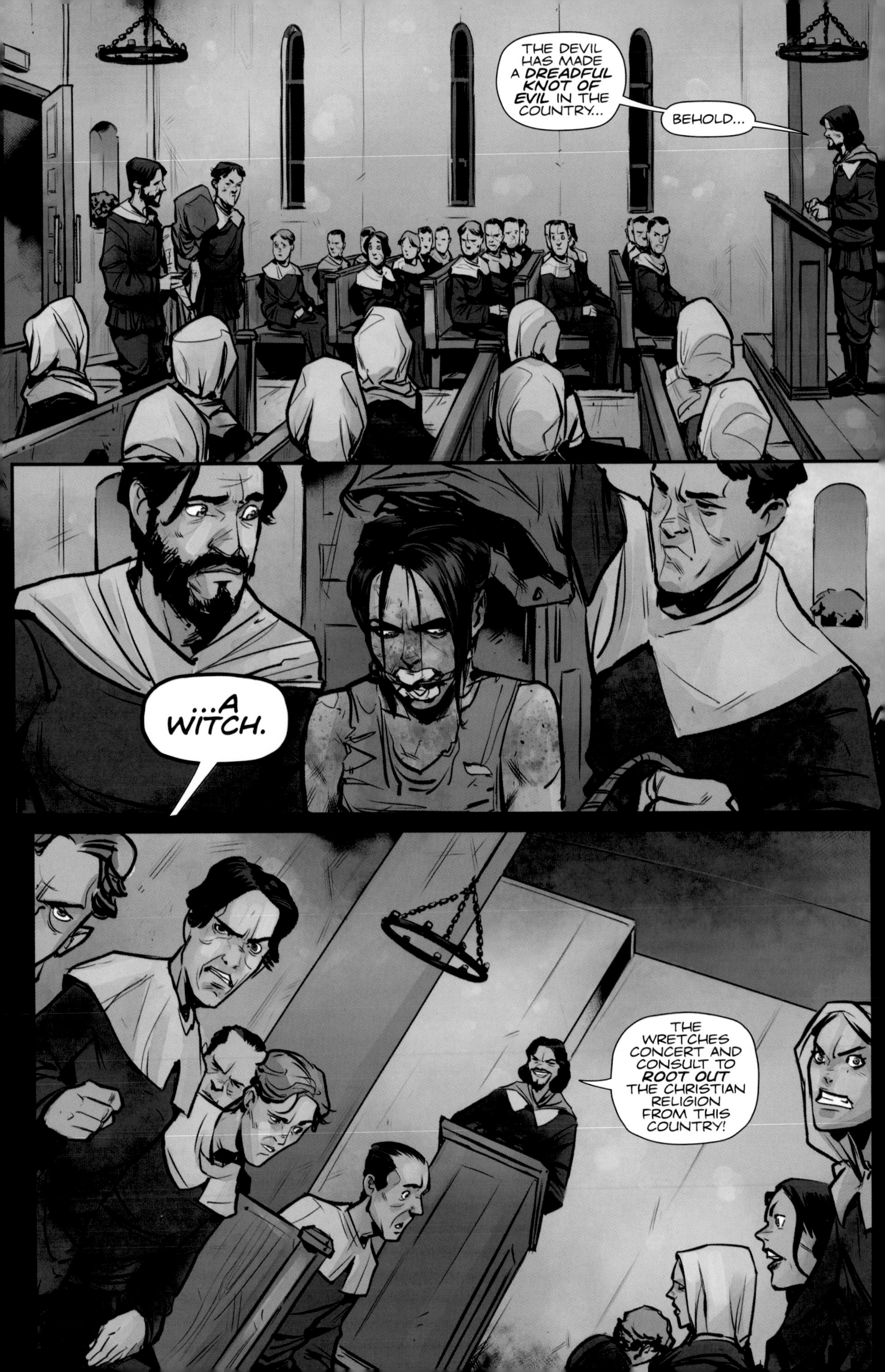
THE DEVIL HAS MADE A **DREADFUL KNOT OF EVIL** IN THE COUNTRY...
BEHOLD...
...A WITCH.
THE WRETCHES CONCERT AND CONSULT TO **ROOT OUT** THE CHRISTIAN RELIGION FROM THIS COUNTRY!

BUT WE SEE THIS TERRIBLE PLAGUE OF EVIL ANGELS...

...WE SEE THEM AND WE WILL *EXTINGUISH* THEM...

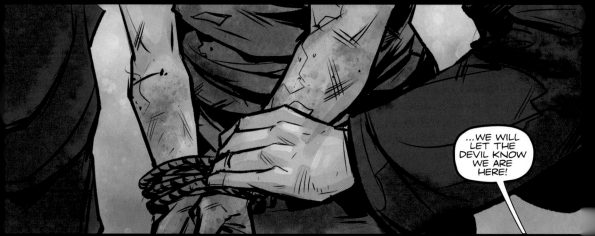

...WE WILL LET THE DEVIL KNOW WE ARE HERE!

SEEK THE WICKED...

...JUDGE THE WICKED...

...PUNISH THE WICKED!

"IT STANDS FOR *CHURCH* AND *STATE*..."

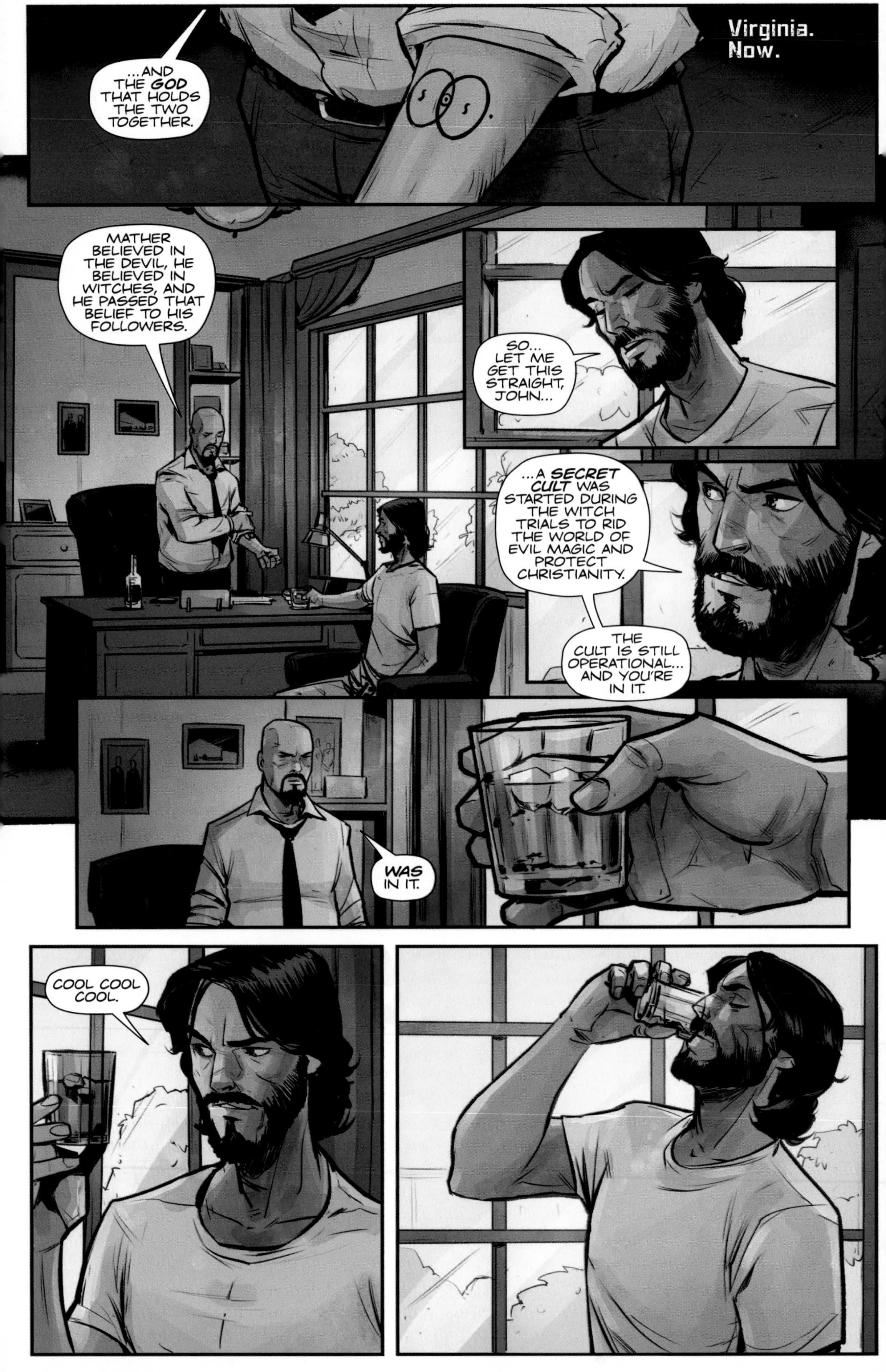

Virginia. Now.
...AND THE GOD THAT HOLDS THE TWO TOGETHER.
MATHER BELIEVED IN THE DEVIL, HE BELIEVED IN WITCHES, AND HE PASSED THAT BELIEF TO HIS FOLLOWERS.
SO... LET ME GET THIS STRAIGHT, JOHN...
...A SECRET CULT WAS STARTED DURING THE WITCH TRIALS TO RID THE WORLD OF EVIL MAGIC AND PROTECT CHRISTIANITY.
THE CULT IS STILL OPERATIONAL... AND YOU'RE IN IT.
WAS IN IT.
COOL COOL COOL.

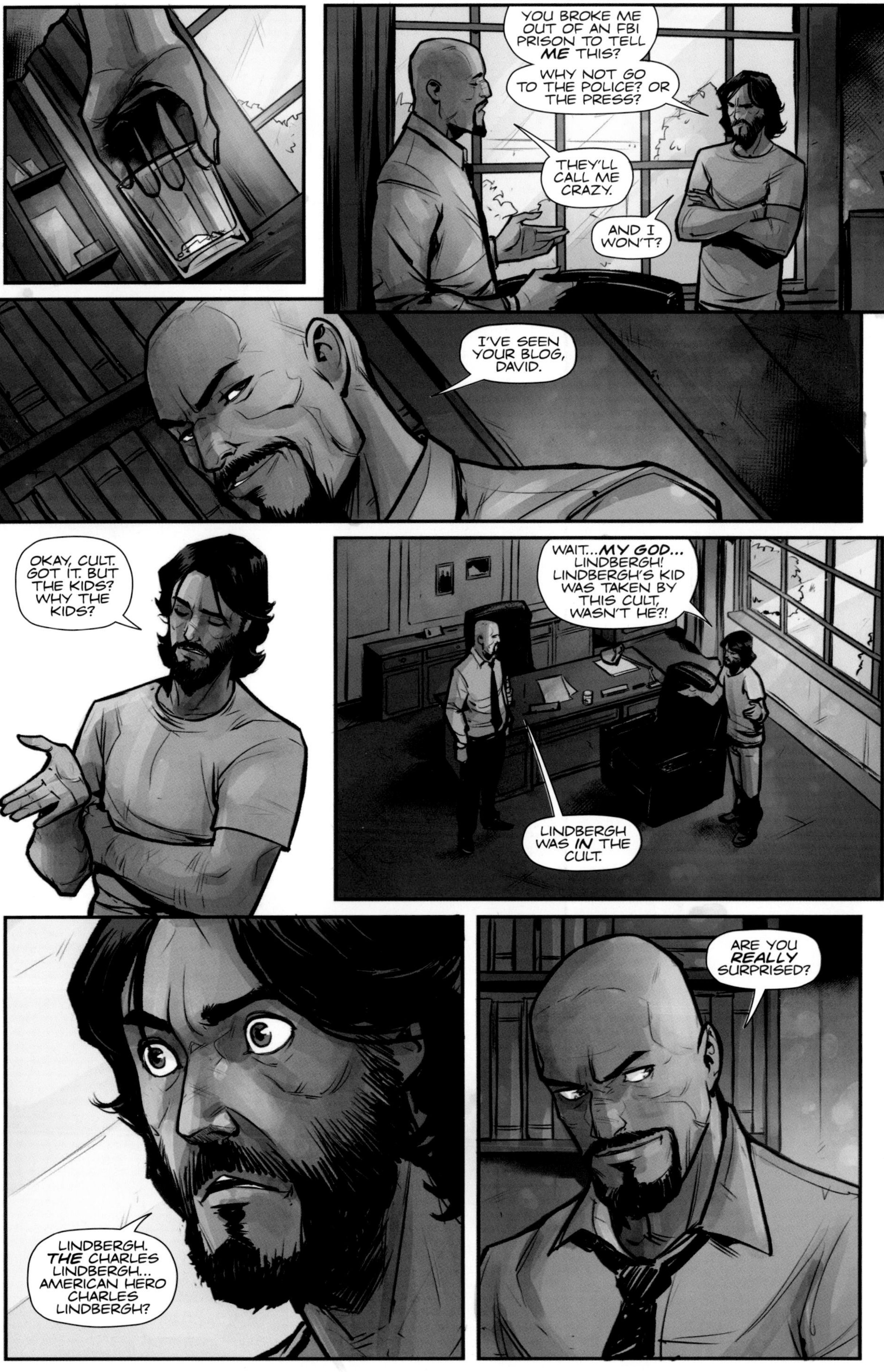
YOU BROKE ME OUT OF AN FBI PRISON TO TELL **ME** THIS?
WHY NOT GO TO THE POLICE? OR THE PRESS?
THEY'LL CALL ME CRAZY.
AND I WON'T?
I'VE SEEN YOUR BLOG, DAVID.
OKAY, CULT. GOT IT. BUT THE KIDS? WHY THE KIDS?
WAIT... **MY GOD...** LINDBERGH! LINDBERGH'S KID WAS TAKEN BY THIS CULT, WASN'T HE?!
LINDBERGH WAS **IN** THE CULT.
LINDBERGH. **THE** CHARLES LINDBERGH... AMERICAN HERO CHARLES LINDBERGH?
ARE YOU **REALLY** SURPRISED?

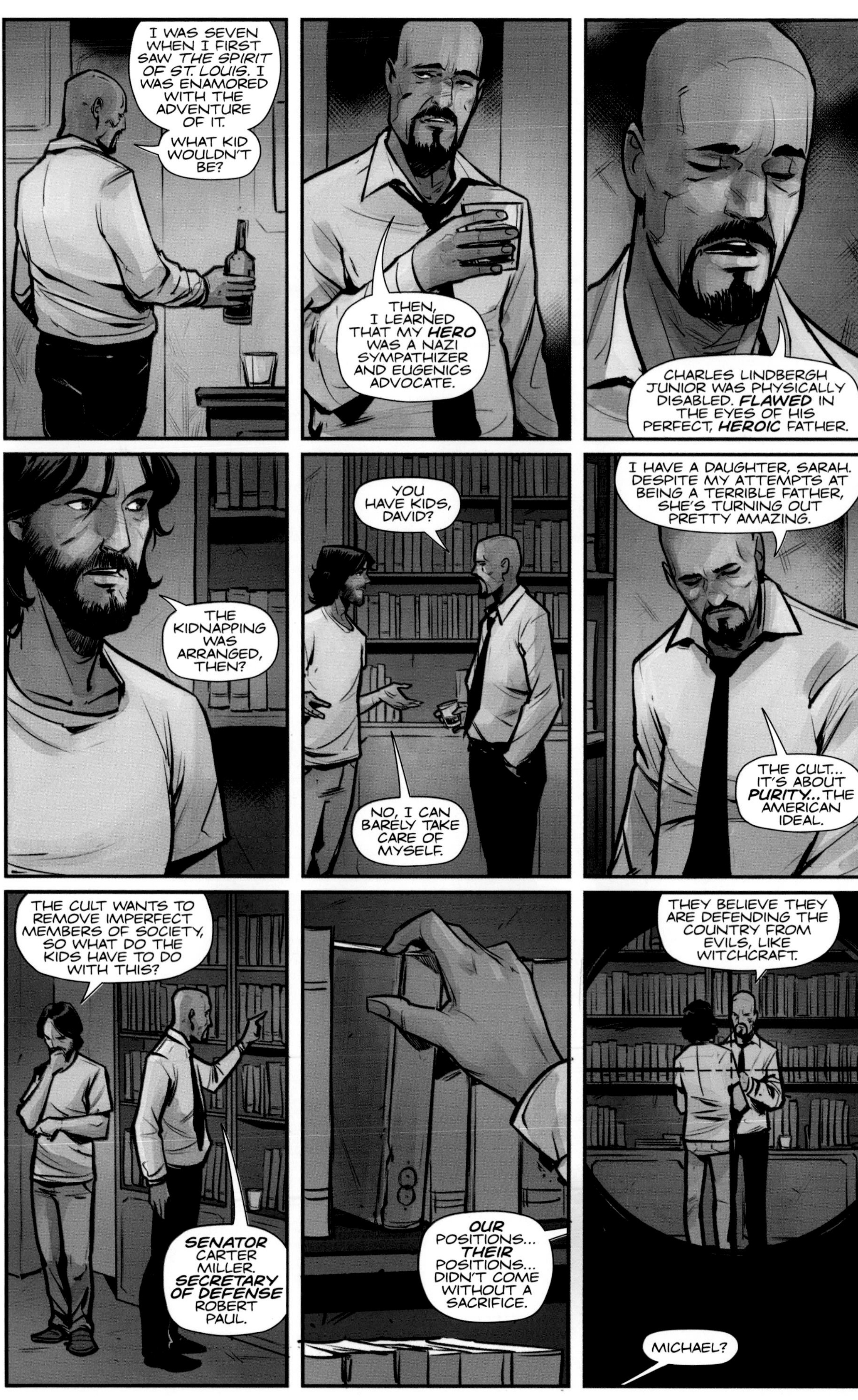
I WAS SEVEN WHEN I FIRST SAW *THE SPIRIT OF ST. LOUIS*. I WAS ENAMORED WITH THE ADVENTURE OF IT.
WHAT KID WOULDN'T BE?
THEN, I LEARNED THAT MY **HERO** WAS A NAZI SYMPATHIZER AND EUGENICS ADVOCATE.
CHARLES LINDBERGH JUNIOR WAS PHYSICALLY DISABLED. **FLAWED** IN THE EYES OF HIS PERFECT, **HEROIC** FATHER.
THE KIDNAPPING WAS ARRANGED, THEN?
YOU HAVE KIDS, DAVID?
NO, I CAN BARELY TAKE CARE OF MYSELF.
I HAVE A DAUGHTER, SARAH. DESPITE MY ATTEMPTS AT BEING A TERRIBLE FATHER, SHE'S TURNING OUT PRETTY AMAZING.
THE CULT... IT'S ABOUT **PURITY**... THE AMERICAN IDEAL.
THE CULT WANTS TO REMOVE IMPERFECT MEMBERS OF SOCIETY, SO WHAT DO THE KIDS HAVE TO DO WITH THIS?
SENATOR CARTER MILLER. **SECRETARY OF DEFENSE** ROBERT PAUL.
OUR POSITIONS... **THEIR** POSITIONS... DIDN'T COME WITHOUT A SACRIFICE.
THEY BELIEVE THEY ARE DEFENDING THE COUNTRY FROM EVILS, LIKE WITCHCRAFT.
MICHAEL?

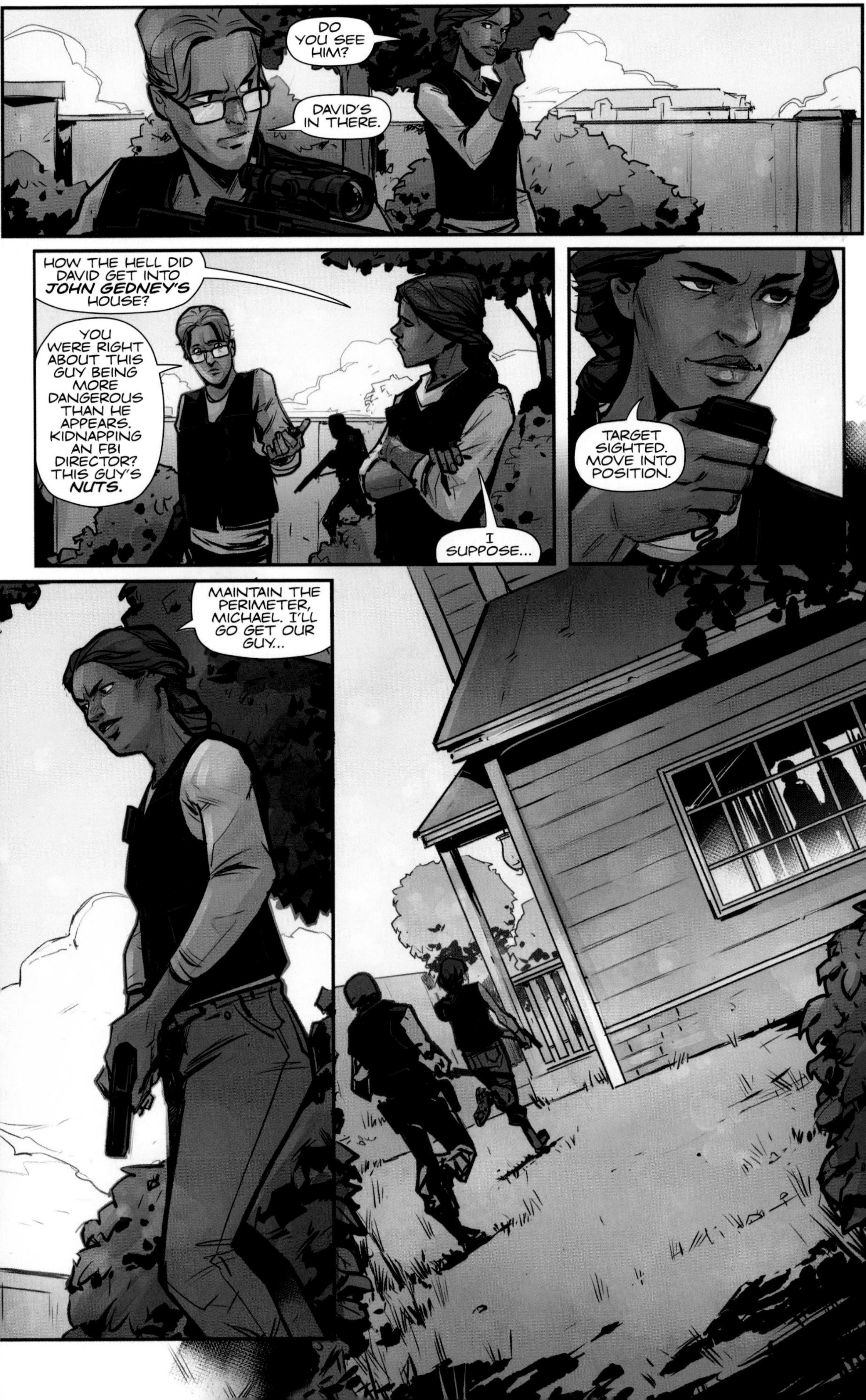
DO YOU SEE HIM?
DAVID'S IN THERE.
HOW THE HELL DID DAVID GET INTO **JOHN GEDNEY'S** HOUSE?
YOU WERE RIGHT ABOUT THIS GUY BEING MORE DANGEROUS THAN HE APPEARS. KIDNAPPING AN FBI DIRECTOR? THIS GUY'S **NUTS.**
I SUPPOSE...
TARGET SIGHTED. MOVE INTO POSITION.
MAINTAIN THE PERIMETER, MICHAEL. I'LL GO GET OUR GUY...

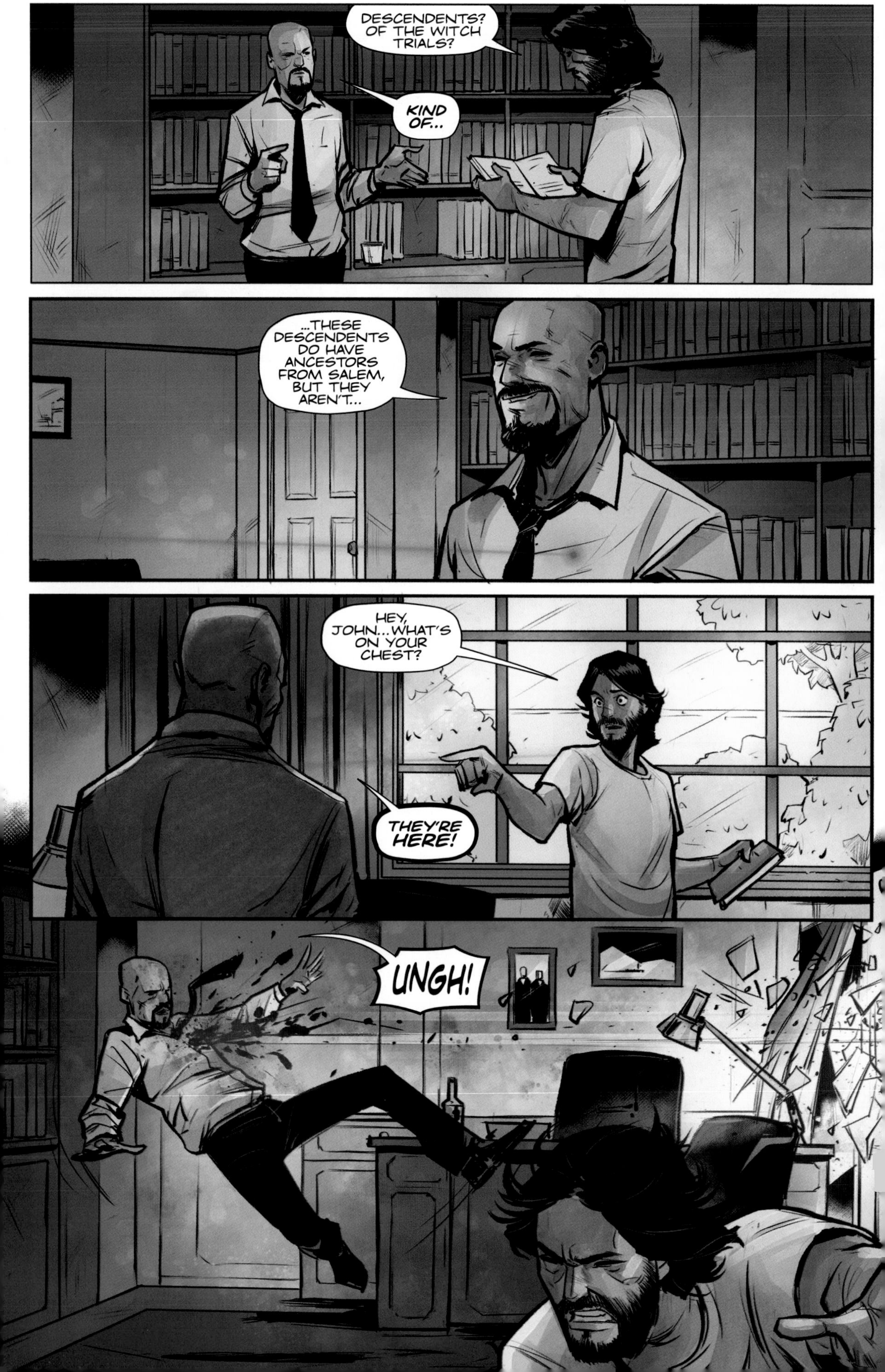
DESCENDENTS? OF THE WITCH TRIALS?
KIND OF...
...THESE DESCENDENTS DO HAVE ANCESTORS FROM SALEM, BUT THEY AREN'T...
HEY, JOHN...WHAT'S ON YOUR CHEST?
THEY'RE HERE!
UNGH!

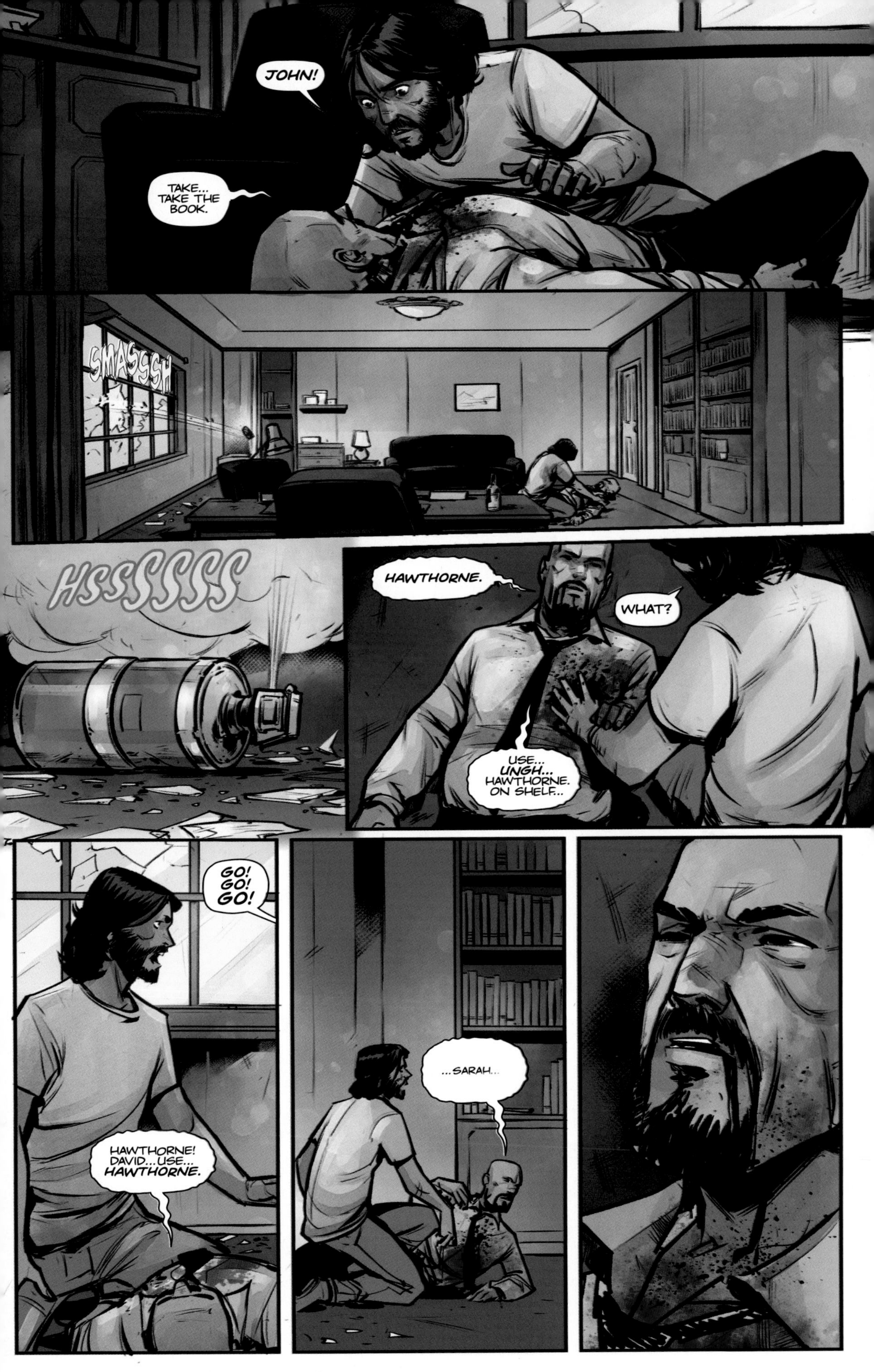
JOHN!
TAKE... TAKE THE BOOK.
SMASSSH
HSSSSSS
HAWTHORNE.
WHAT?
USE... UNGH... HAWTHORNE. ON SHELF...
GO! GO! GO!
HAWTHORNE! DAVID...USE... HAWTHORNE.
...SARAH...

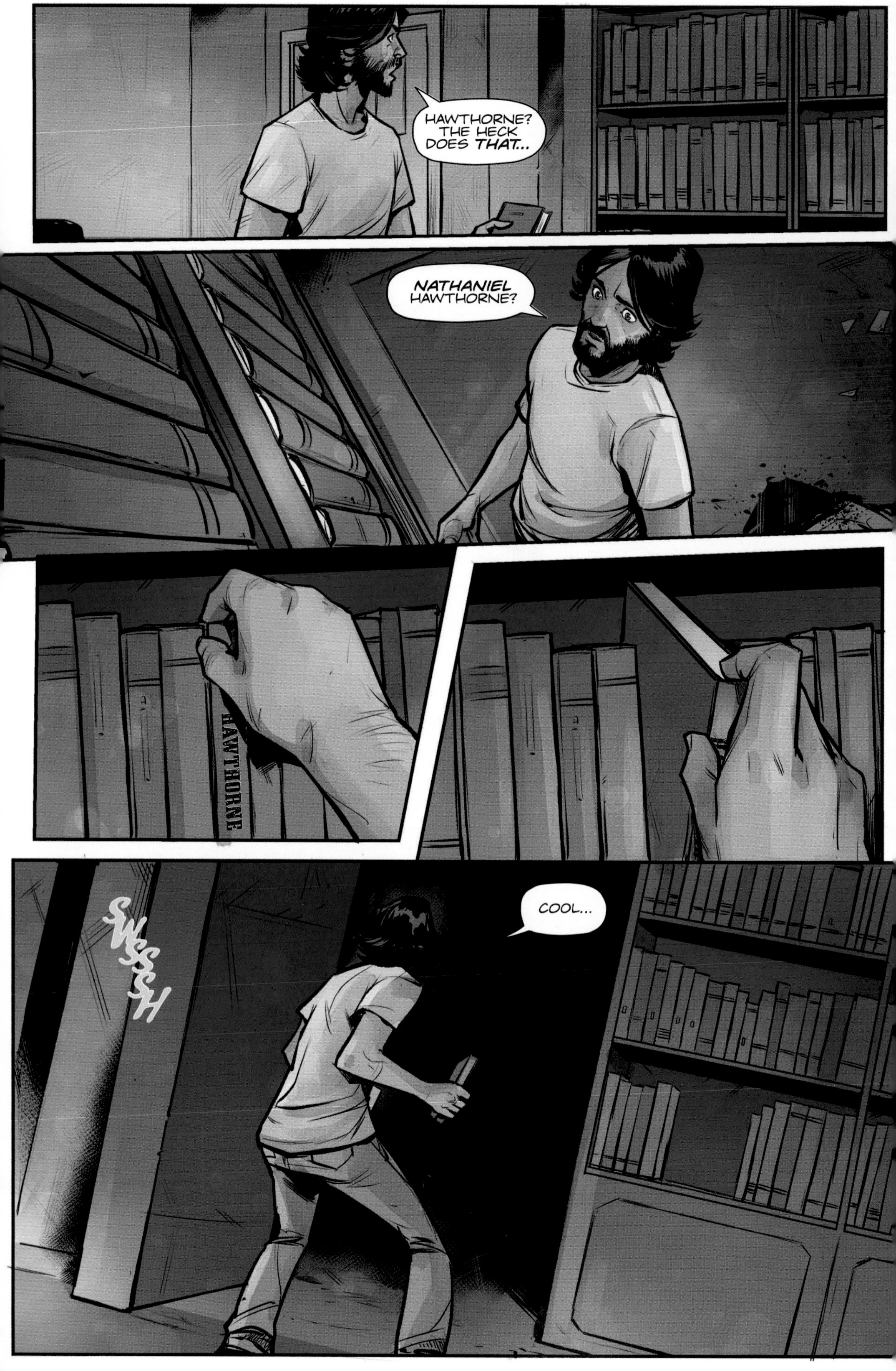
HAWTHORNE? THE HECK DOES *THAT*...
NATHANIEL HAWTHORNE?
HAWTHORNE
SWSSSH
COOL...

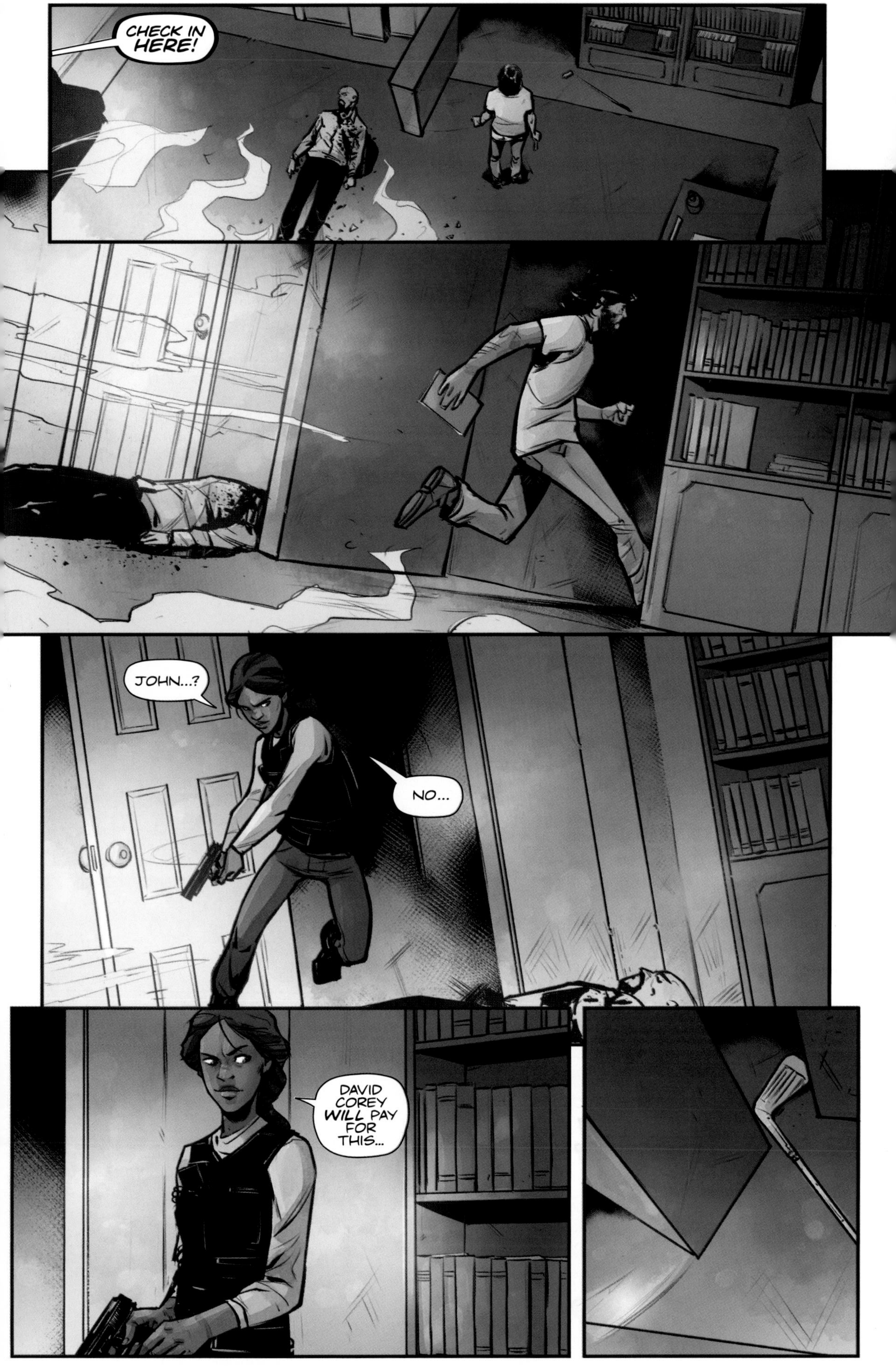
CHECK IN HERE!
JOHN...?
NO...
DAVID COREY WILL PAY FOR THIS...

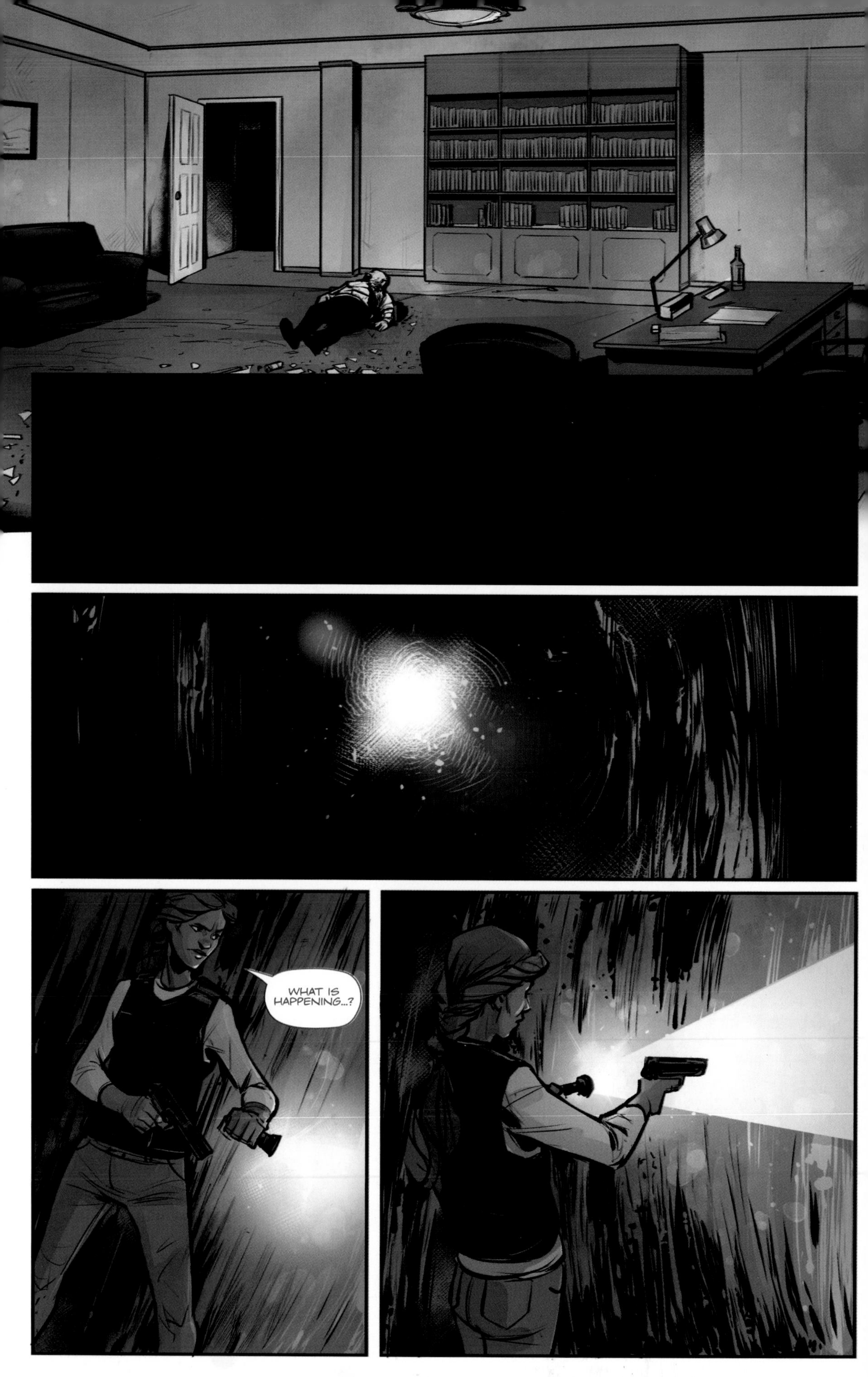
WHAT IS HAPPENING...?

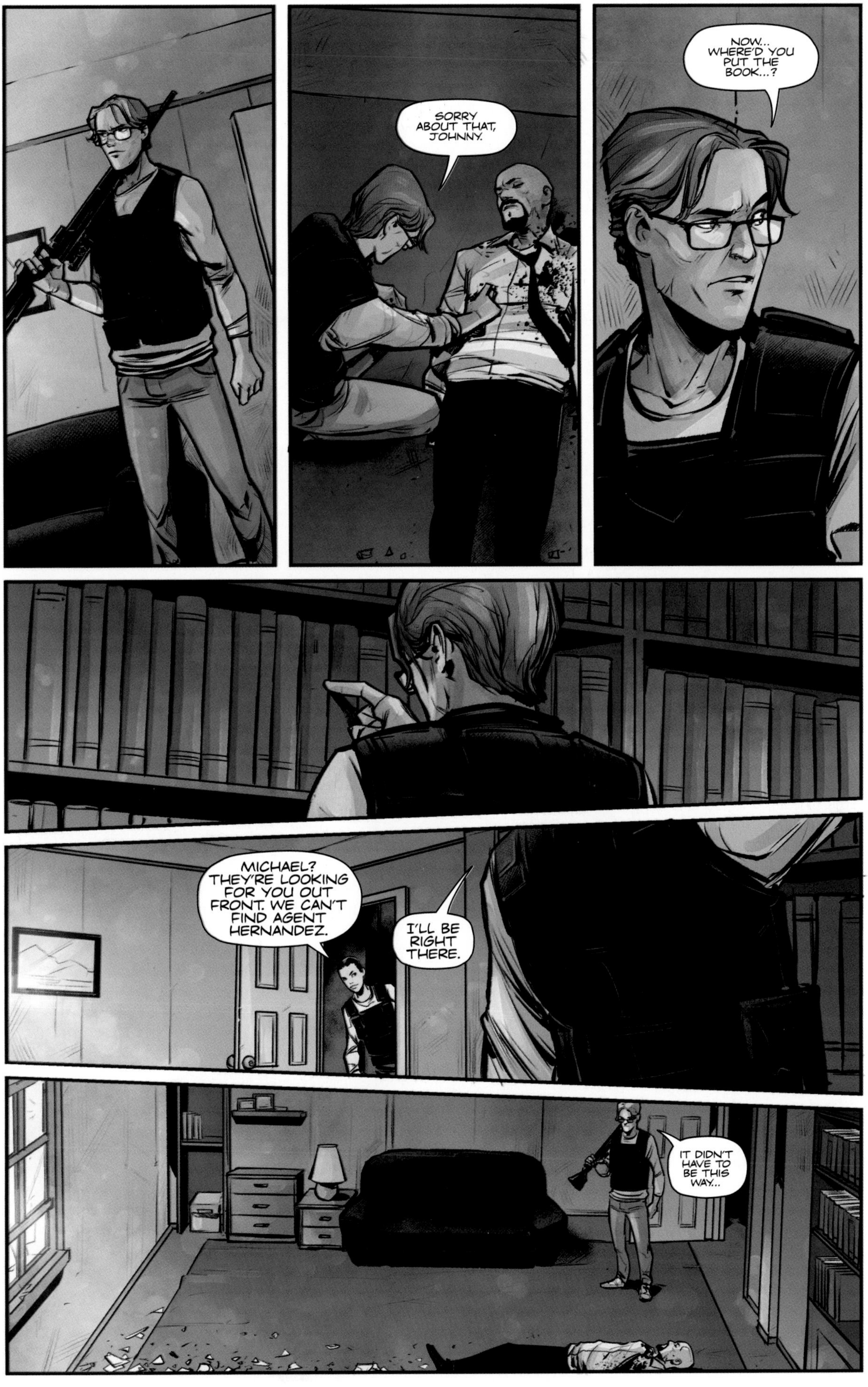
SORRY ABOUT THAT, JOHNNY.
NOW... WHERE'D YOU PUT THE BOOK...?
MICHAEL? THEY'RE LOOKING FOR YOU OUT FRONT. WE CAN'T FIND AGENT HERNANDEZ.
I'LL BE RIGHT THERE.
IT DIDN'T HAVE TO BE THIS WAY...

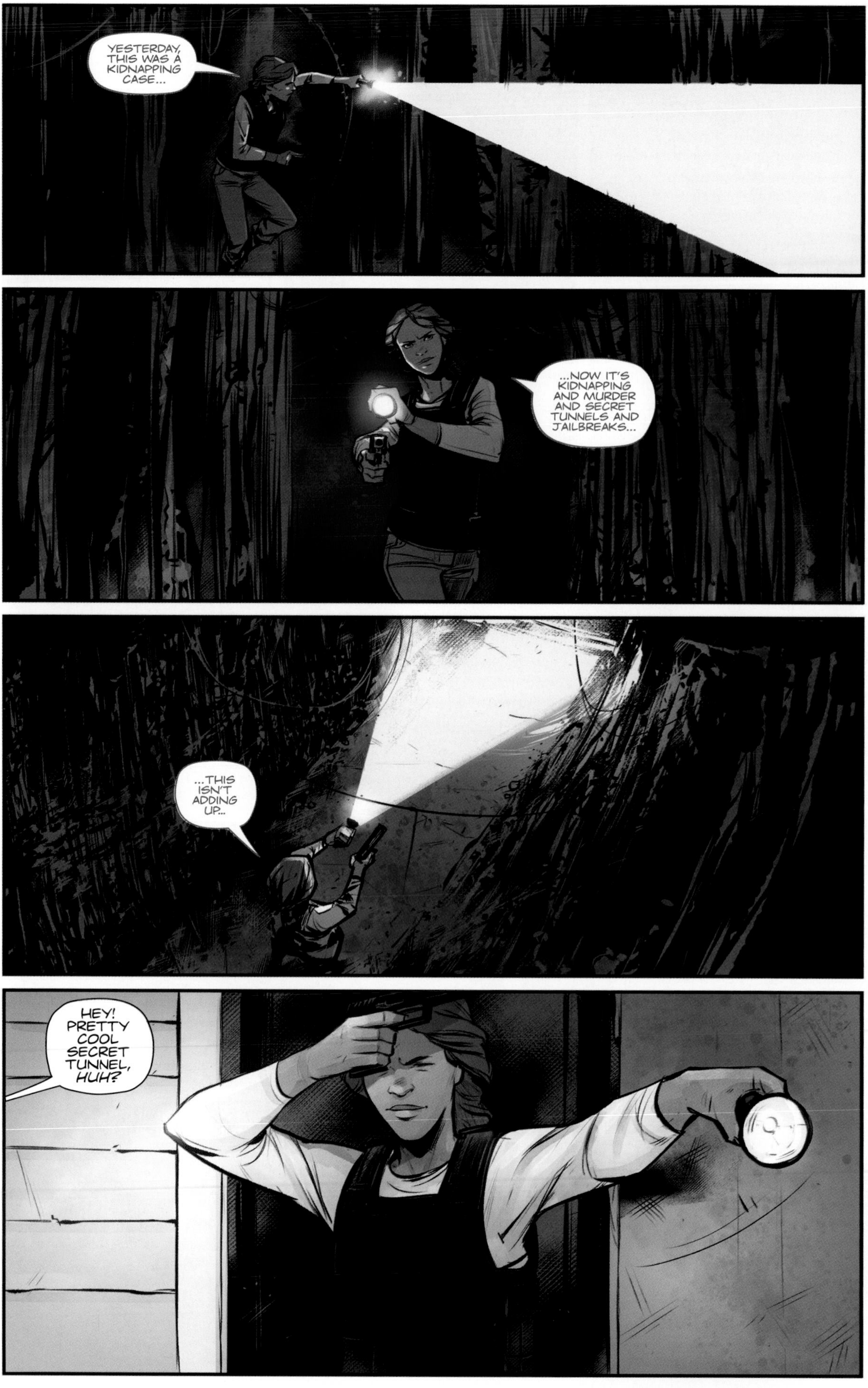
YESTERDAY, THIS WAS A KIDNAPPING CASE...
...NOW IT'S KIDNAPPING AND MURDER AND SECRET TUNNELS AND JAILBREAKS...
...THIS ISN'T ADDING UP...
HEY! PRETTY COOL SECRET TUNNEL, HUH?

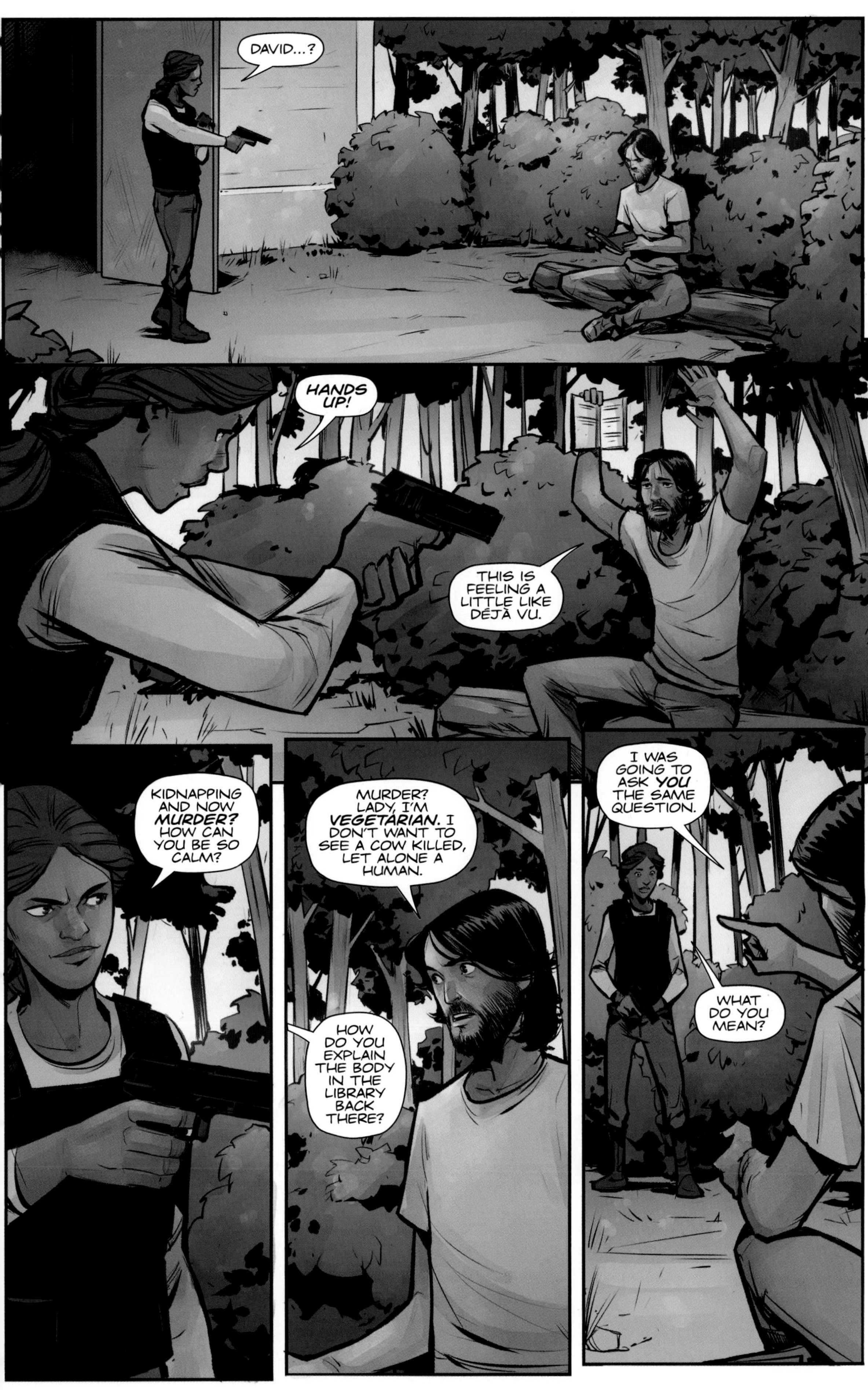
DAVID...?
HANDS UP!
THIS IS FEELING A LITTLE LIKE DÉJÀ VU.
KIDNAPPING AND NOW MURDER? HOW CAN YOU BE SO CALM?
MURDER? LADY, I'M VEGETARIAN. I DON'T WANT TO SEE A COW KILLED, LET ALONE A HUMAN.
HOW DO YOU EXPLAIN THE BODY IN THE LIBRARY BACK THERE?
I WAS GOING TO ASK YOU THE SAME QUESTION.
WHAT DO YOU MEAN?

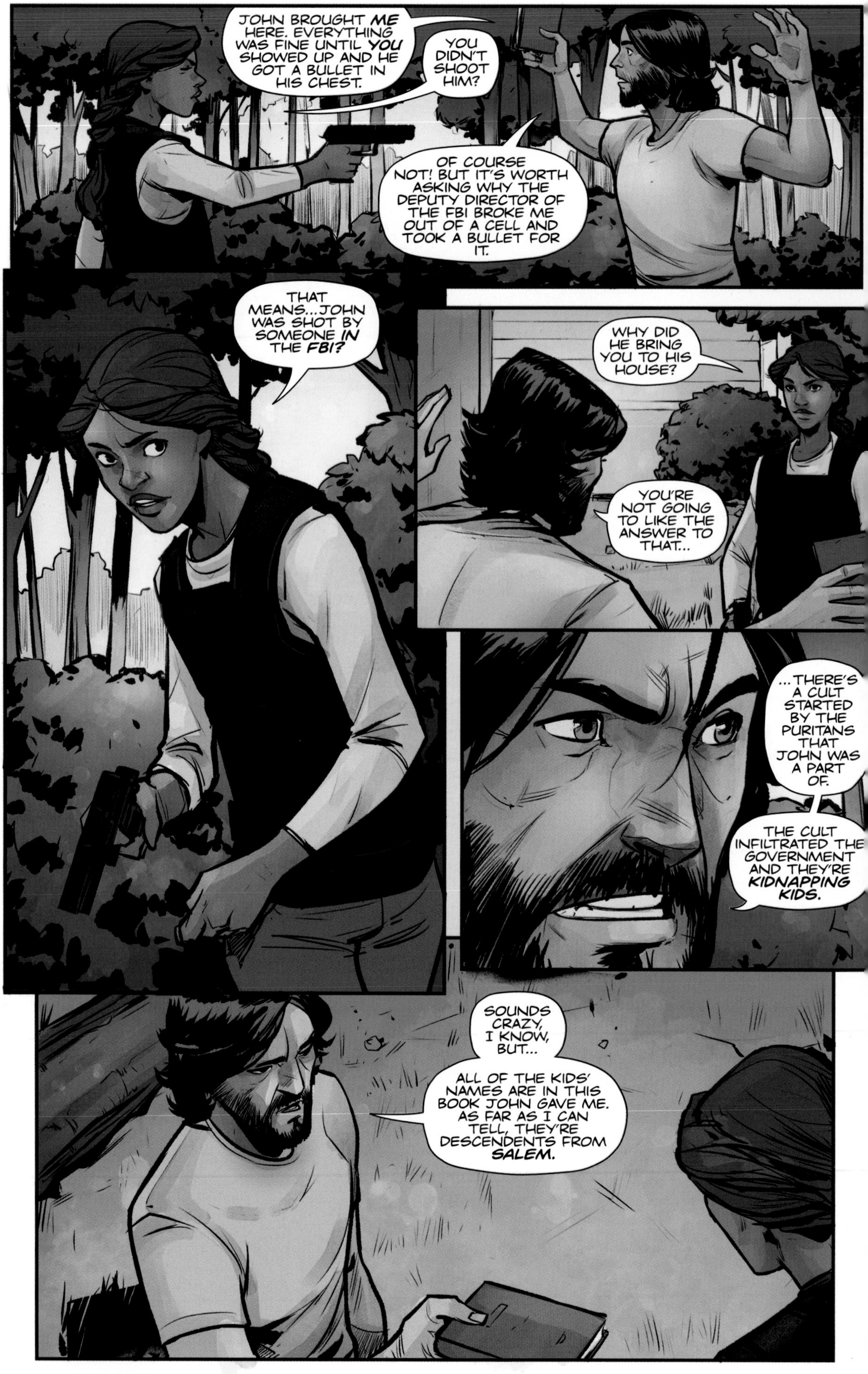
JOHN BROUGHT ME HERE. EVERYTHING WAS FINE UNTIL YOU SHOWED UP AND HE GOT A BULLET IN HIS CHEST.
YOU DIDN'T SHOOT HIM?
OF COURSE NOT! BUT IT'S WORTH ASKING WHY THE DEPUTY DIRECTOR OF THE FBI BROKE ME OUT OF A CELL AND TOOK A BULLET FOR IT.
THAT MEANS...JOHN WAS SHOT BY SOMEONE IN THE FBI?
WHY DID HE BRING YOU TO HIS HOUSE?
YOU'RE NOT GOING TO LIKE THE ANSWER TO THAT...
...THERE'S A CULT STARTED BY THE PURITANS THAT JOHN WAS A PART OF.
THE CULT INFILTRATED THE GOVERNMENT AND THEY'RE KIDNAPPING KIDS.
SOUNDS CRAZY, I KNOW, BUT...
ALL OF THE KIDS' NAMES ARE IN THIS BOOK JOHN GAVE ME. AS FAR AS I CAN TELL, THEY'RE DESCENDENTS FROM SALEM.

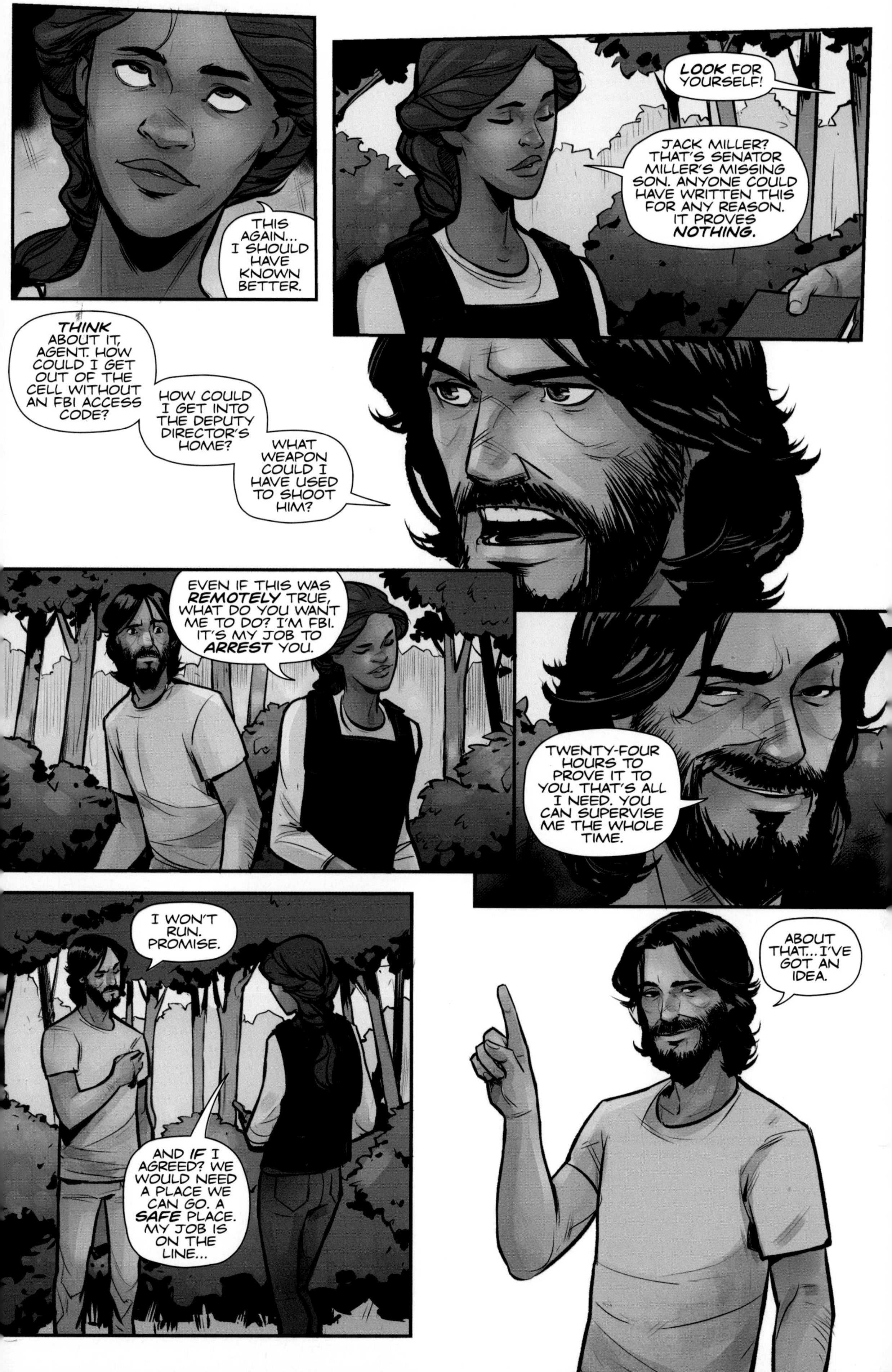
THIS AGAIN... I SHOULD HAVE KNOWN BETTER.
LOOK FOR YOURSELF!
JACK MILLER? THAT'S SENATOR MILLER'S MISSING SON. ANYONE COULD HAVE WRITTEN THIS FOR ANY REASON. IT PROVES NOTHING.
THINK ABOUT IT, AGENT. HOW COULD I GET OUT OF THE CELL WITHOUT AN FBI ACCESS CODE?
HOW COULD I GET INTO THE DEPUTY DIRECTOR'S HOME?
WHAT WEAPON COULD I HAVE USED TO SHOOT HIM?
EVEN IF THIS WAS REMOTELY TRUE, WHAT DO YOU WANT ME TO DO? I'M FBI. IT'S MY JOB TO ARREST YOU.
TWENTY-FOUR HOURS TO PROVE IT TO YOU. THAT'S ALL I NEED. YOU CAN SUPERVISE ME THE WHOLE TIME.
I WON'T RUN. PROMISE.
AND IF I AGREED? WE WOULD NEED A PLACE WE CAN GO. A SAFE PLACE. MY JOB IS ON THE LINE...
ABOUT THAT... I'VE GOT AN IDEA.

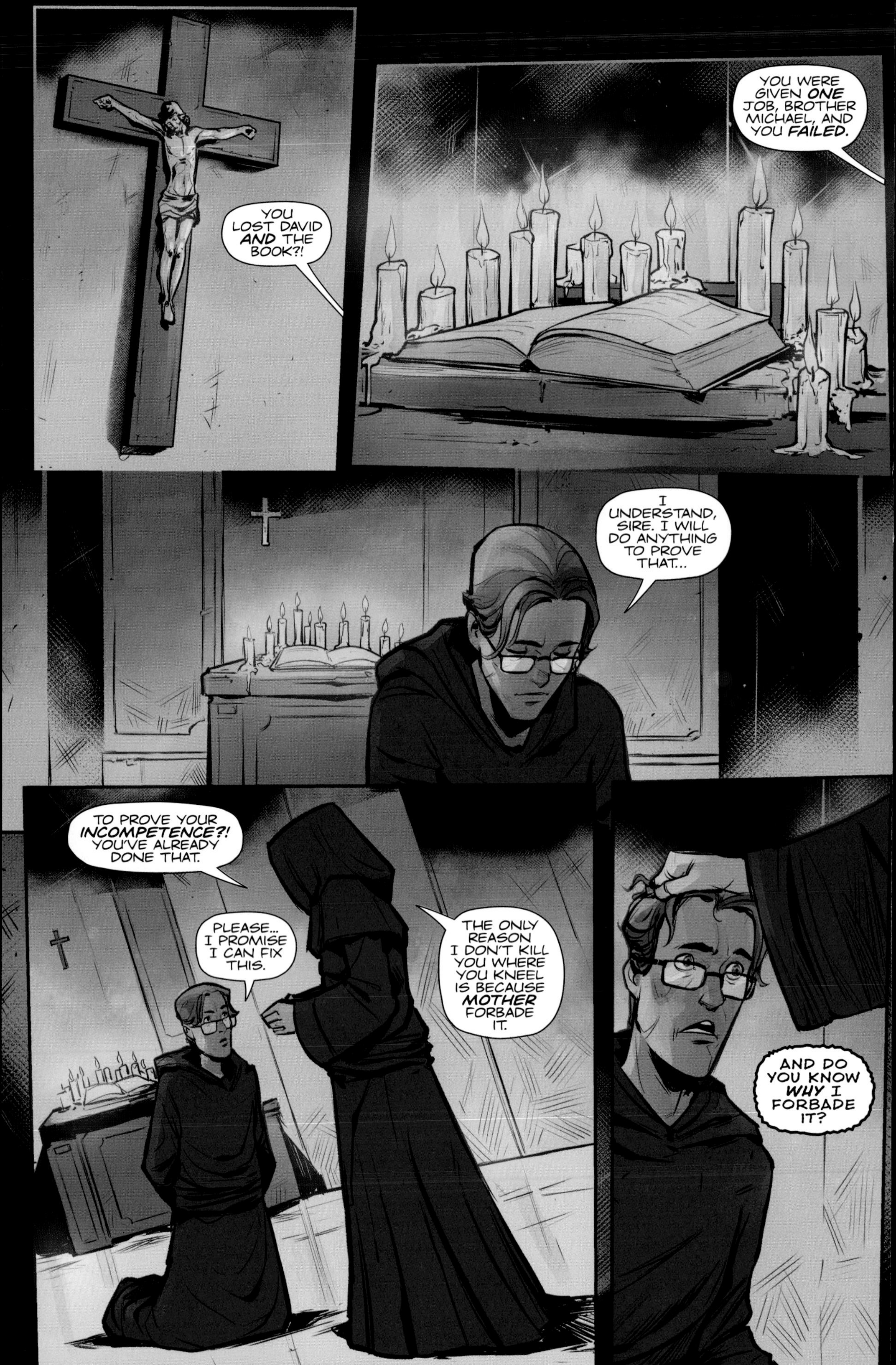
YOU LOST DAVID AND THE BOOK?!
YOU WERE GIVEN ONE JOB, BROTHER MICHAEL, AND YOU FAILED.
I UNDERSTAND, SIRE. I WILL DO ANYTHING TO PROVE THAT...
TO PROVE YOUR INCOMPETENCE?! YOU'VE ALREADY DONE THAT.
PLEASE... I PROMISE I CAN FIX THIS.
THE ONLY REASON I DON'T KILL YOU WHERE YOU KNEEL IS BECAUSE MOTHER FORBADE IT.
AND DO YOU KNOW WHY I FORBADE IT?

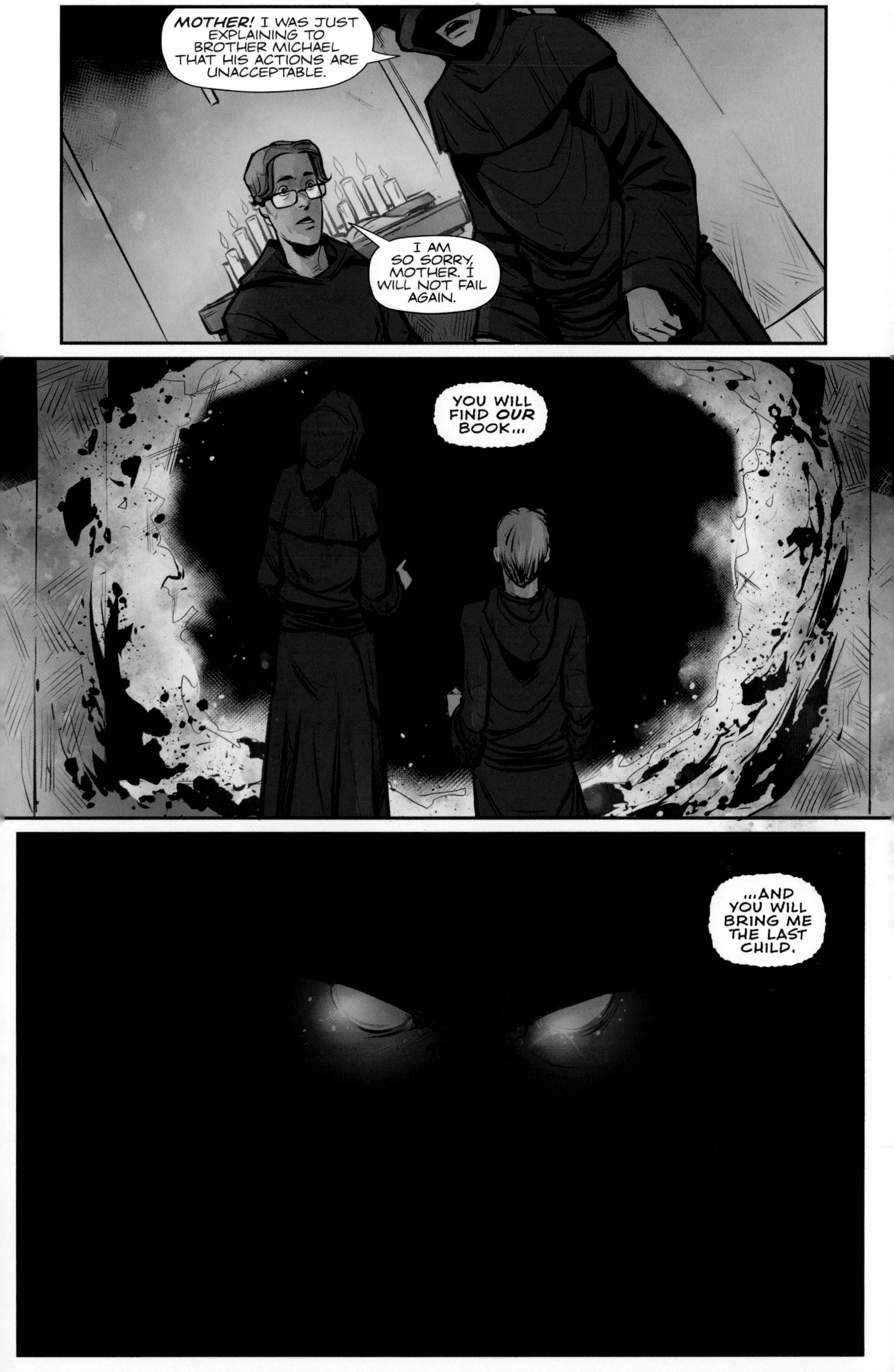
MOTHER! I WAS JUST EXPLAINING TO BROTHER MICHAEL THAT HIS ACTIONS ARE UNACCEPTABLE.
I AM SO SORRY, MOTHER. I WILL NOT FAIL AGAIN.
YOU WILL FIND OUR BOOK...
...AND YOU WILL BRING ME THE LAST CHILD.

4

WORST. STAKEOUT. EVER.

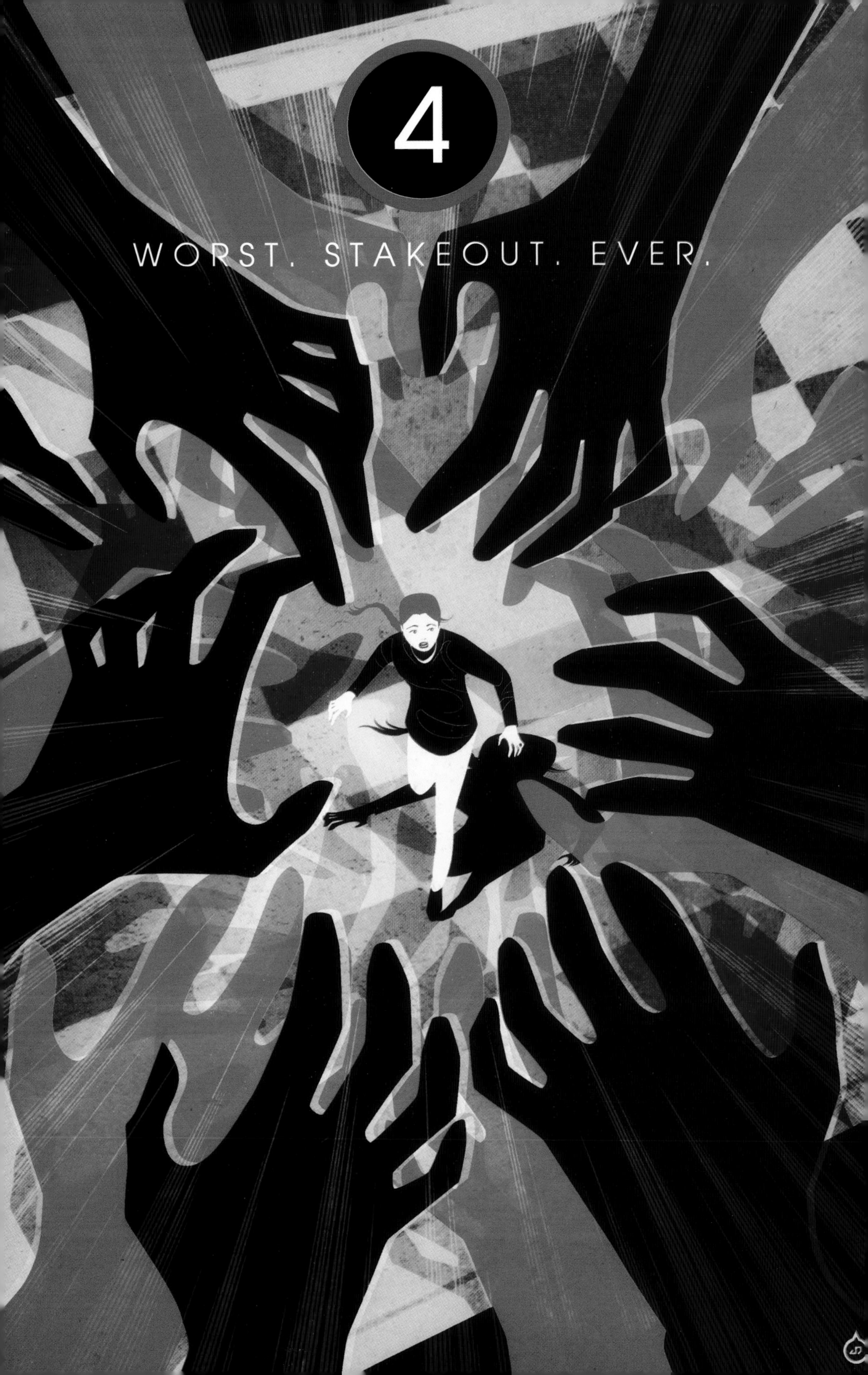

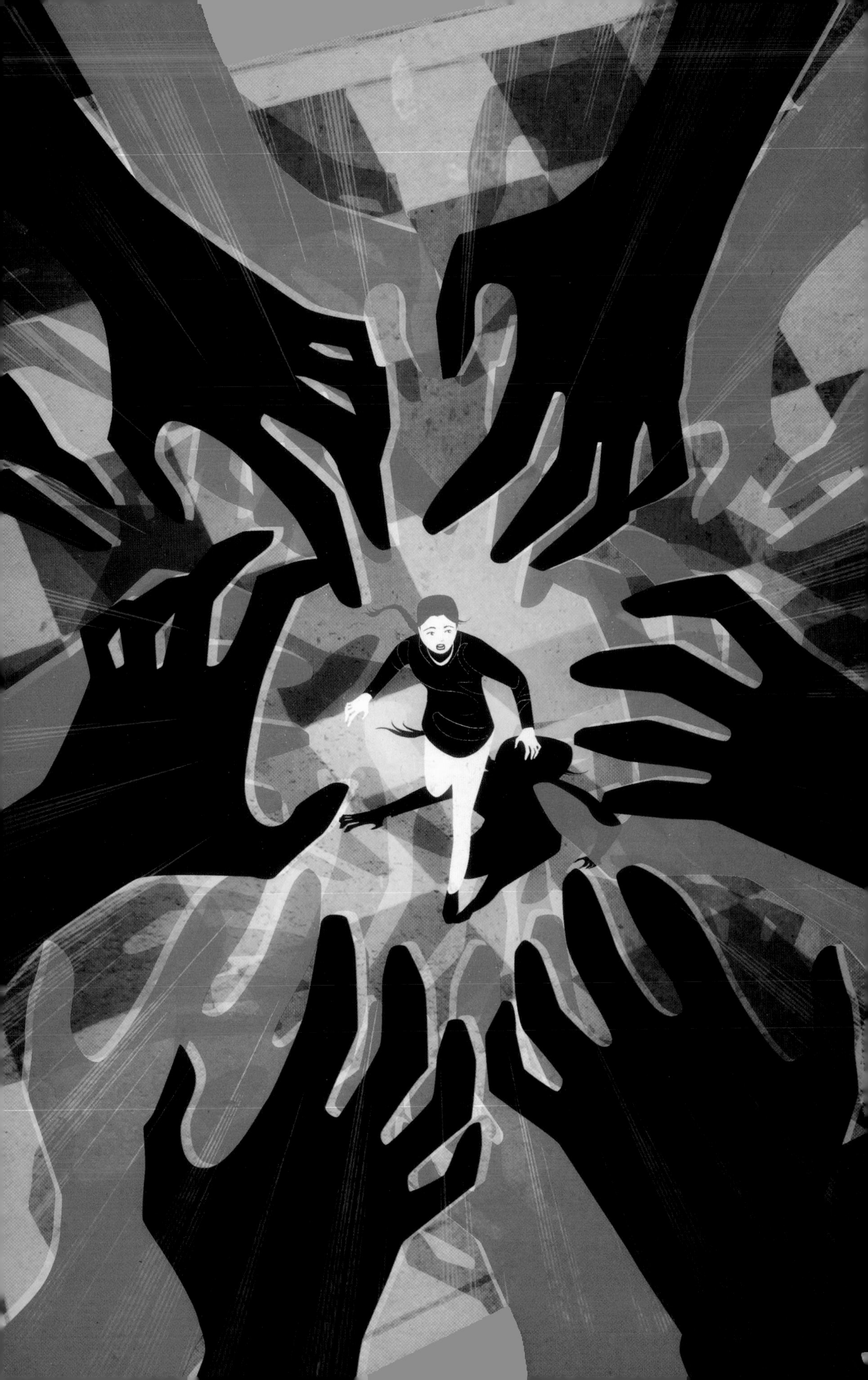

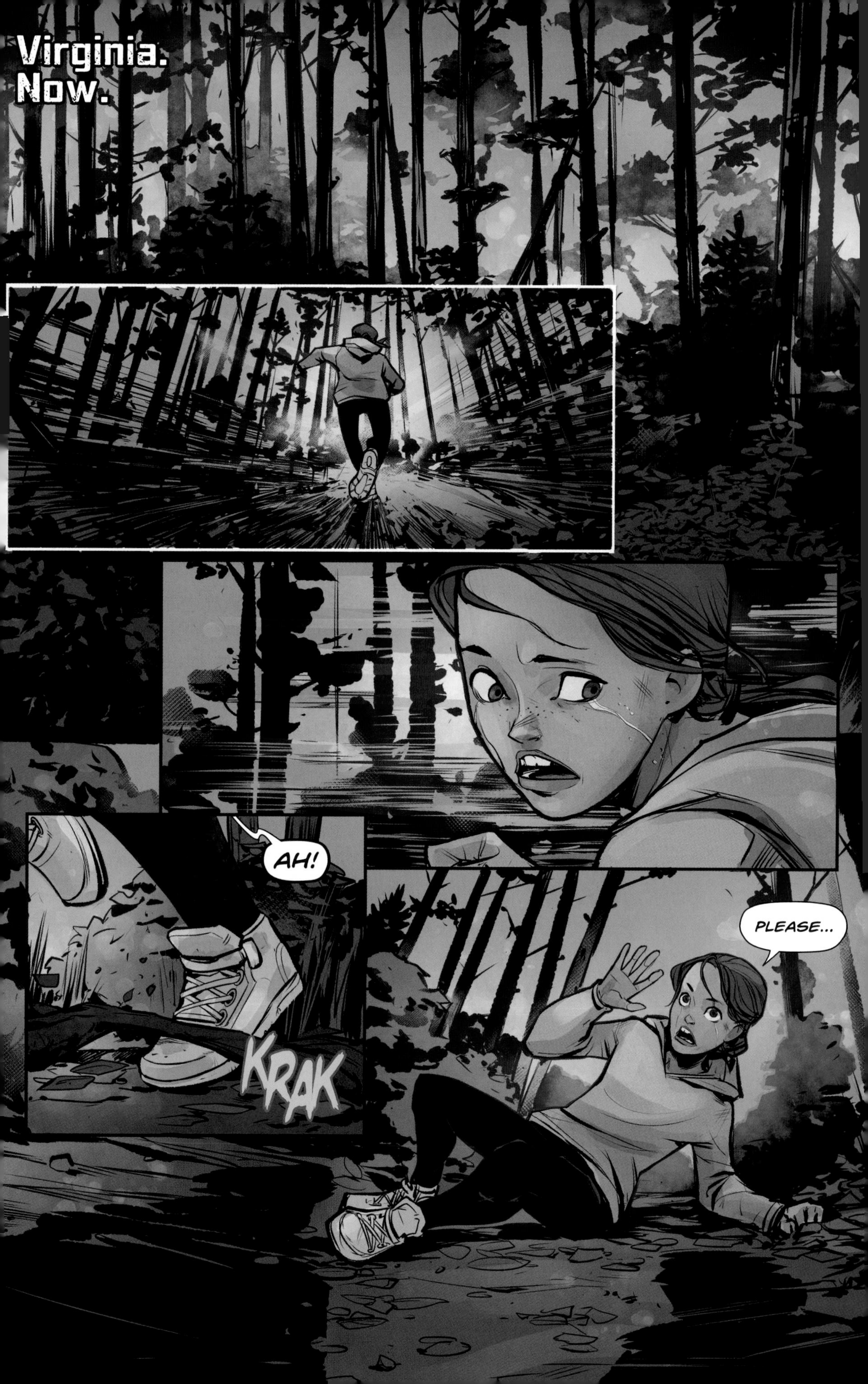
Virginia.
Now.
AH!
KRAK
PLEASE...

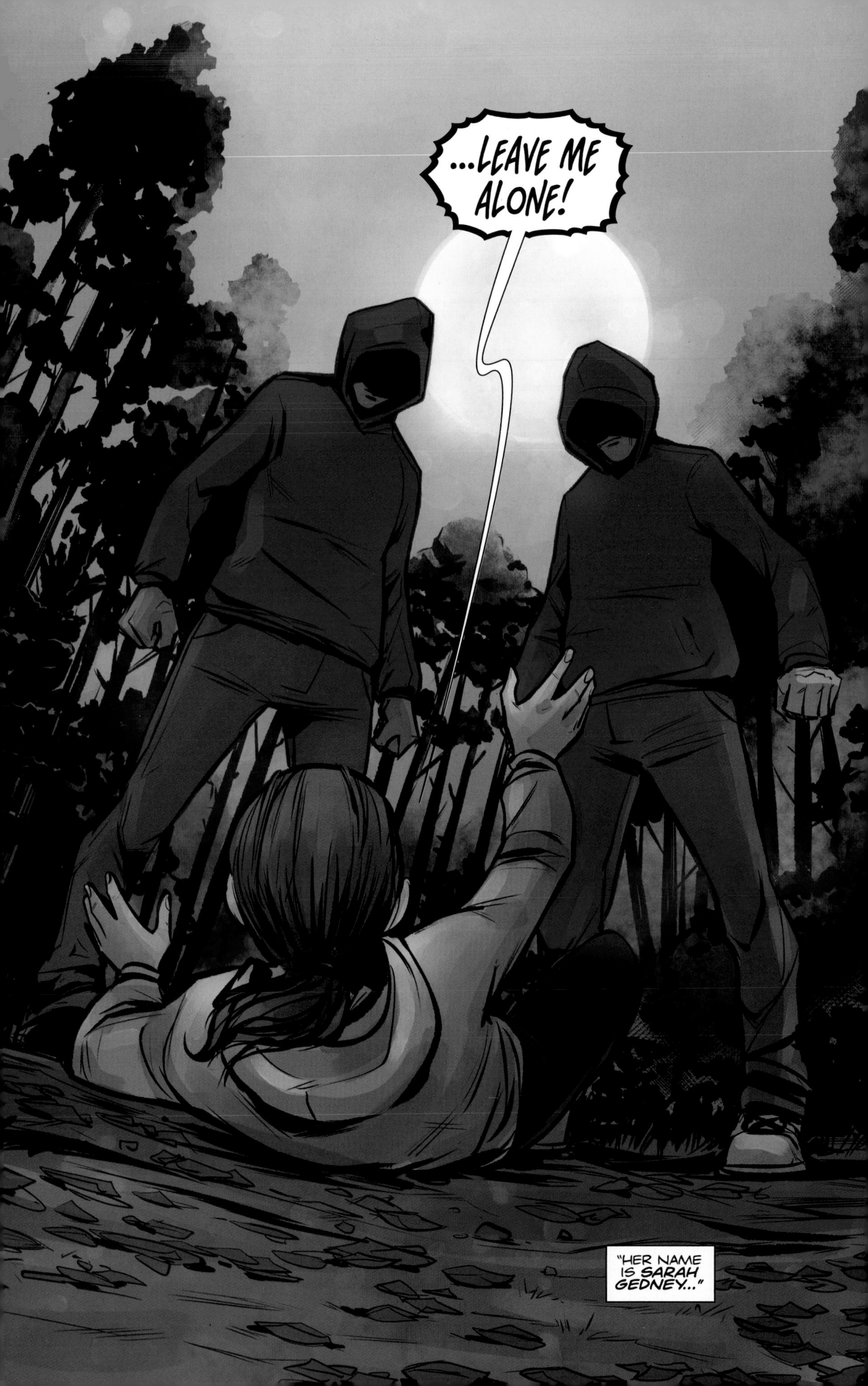
...LEAVE ME ALONE!
"HER NAME IS SARAH GEDNEY..."

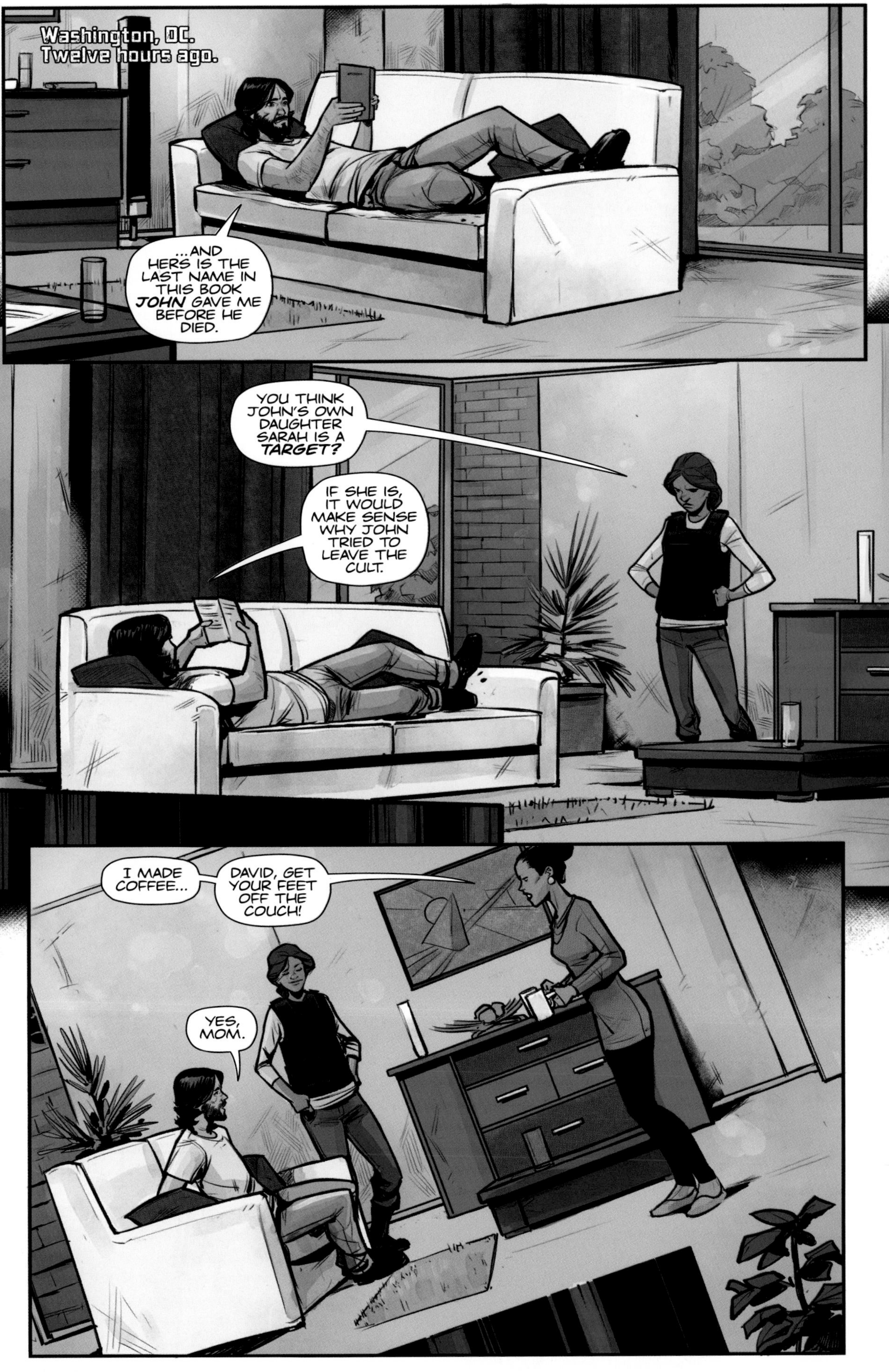
Washington, DC.
Twelve hours ago.
...AND HERS IS THE LAST NAME IN THIS BOOK JOHN GAVE ME BEFORE HE DIED.
YOU THINK JOHN'S OWN DAUGHTER SARAH IS A TARGET?
IF SHE IS, IT WOULD MAKE SENSE WHY JOHN TRIED TO LEAVE THE CULT.
I MADE COFFEE...
DAVID, GET YOUR FEET OFF THE COUCH!
YES, MOM.

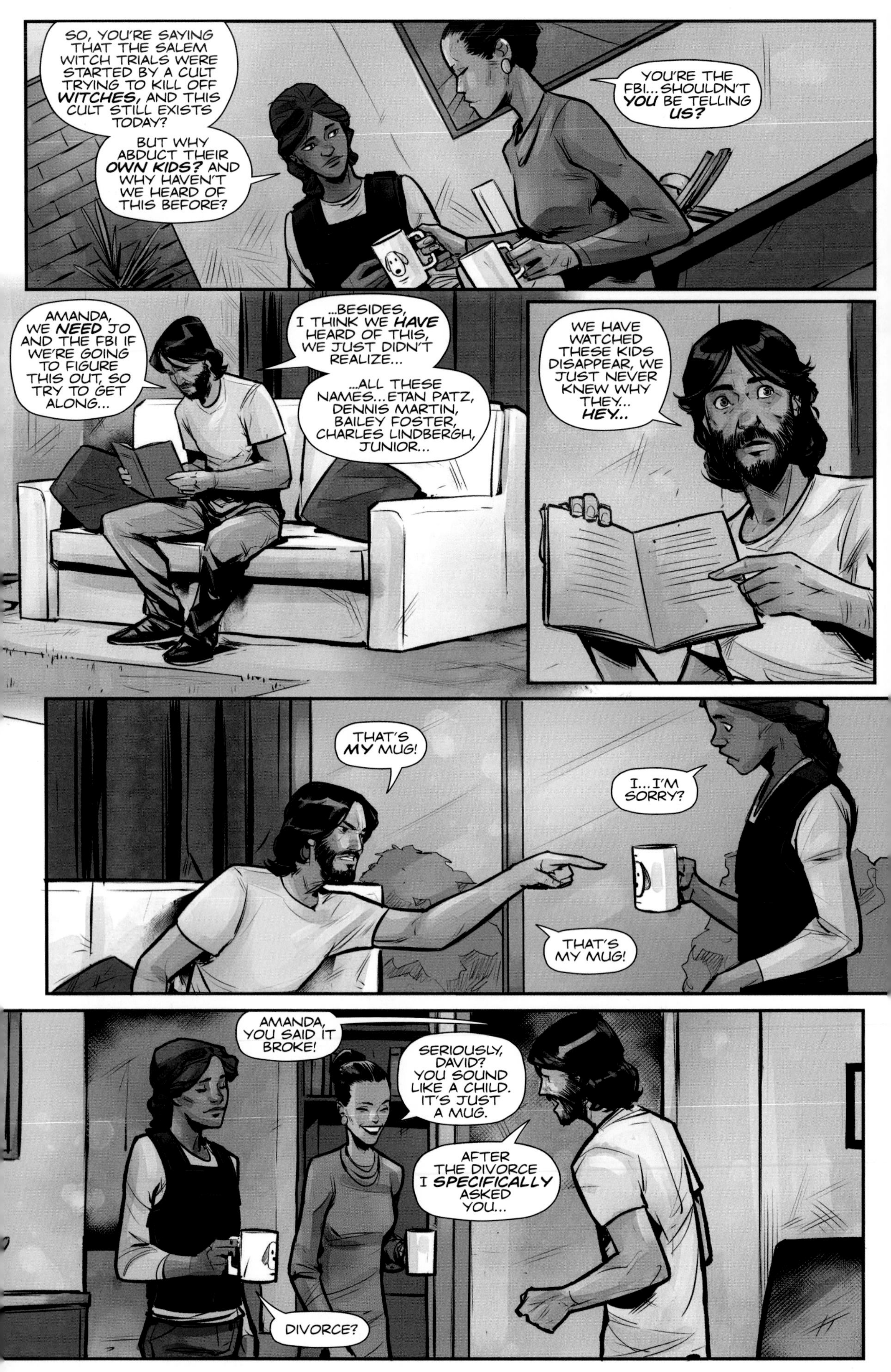
SO, YOU'RE SAYING THAT THE SALEM WITCH TRIALS WERE STARTED BY A CULT TRYING TO KILL OFF WITCHES, AND THIS CULT STILL EXISTS TODAY?
BUT WHY ABDUCT THEIR OWN KIDS? AND WHY HAVEN'T WE HEARD OF THIS BEFORE?
YOU'RE THE FBI...SHOULDN'T YOU BE TELLING US?
AMANDA, WE NEED JO AND THE FBI IF WE'RE GOING TO FIGURE THIS OUT, SO TRY TO GET ALONG...
...BESIDES, I THINK WE HAVE HEARD OF THIS, WE JUST DIDN'T REALIZE...
...ALL THESE NAMES...ETAN PATZ, DENNIS MARTIN, BAILEY FOSTER, CHARLES LINDBERGH, JUNIOR...
WE HAVE WATCHED THESE KIDS DISAPPEAR, WE JUST NEVER KNEW WHY THEY... HEY...
THAT'S MY MUG!
I...I'M SORRY?
THAT'S MY MUG!
AMANDA, YOU SAID IT BROKE!
SERIOUSLY, DAVID? YOU SOUND LIKE A CHILD. IT'S JUST A MUG.
AFTER THE DIVORCE I SPECIFICALLY ASKED YOU...
DIVORCE?

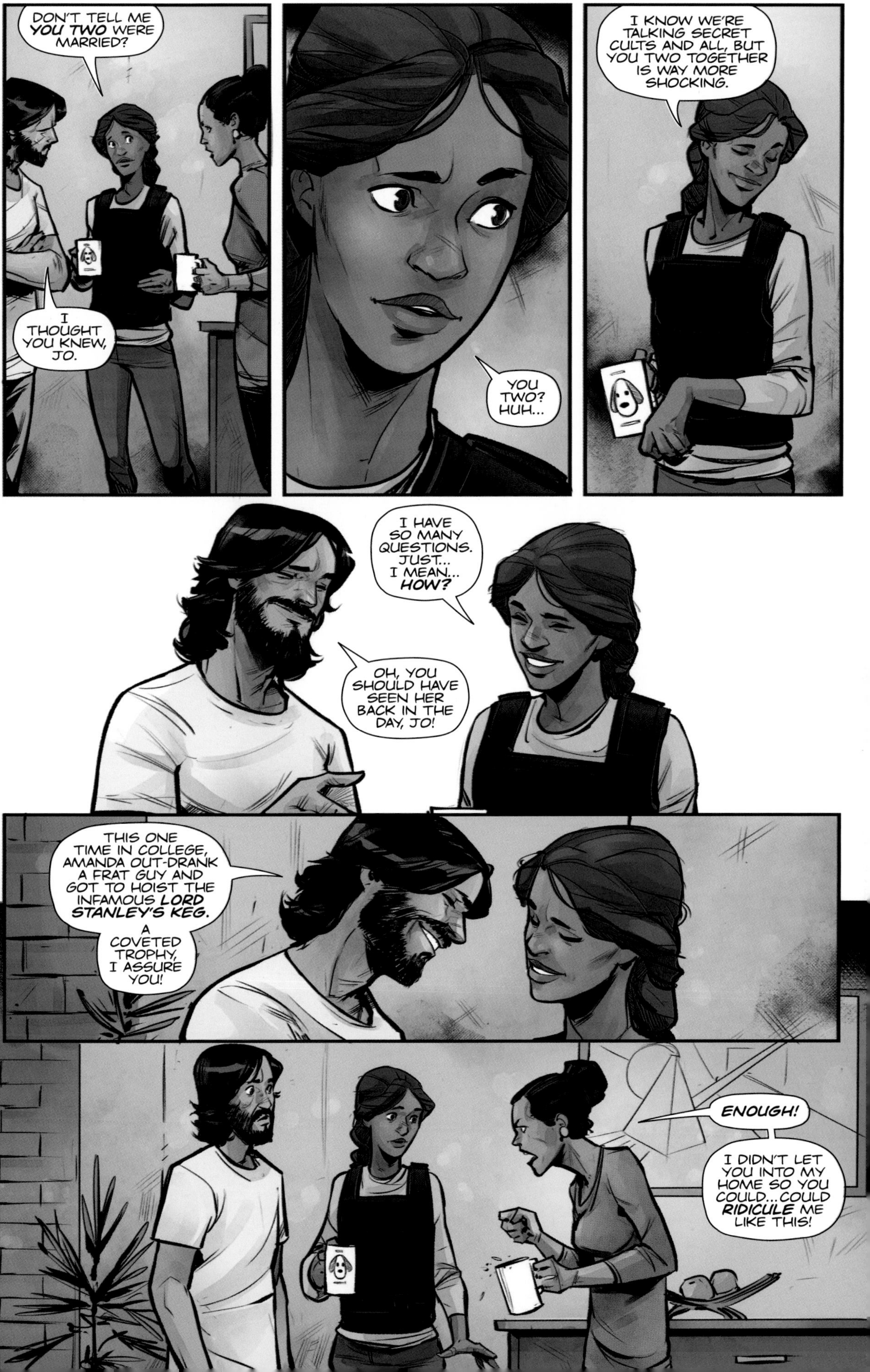
DON'T TELL ME YOU TWO WERE MARRIED?
I THOUGHT YOU KNEW, JO.
YOU TWO? HUH...
I KNOW WE'RE TALKING SECRET CULTS AND ALL, BUT YOU TWO TOGETHER IS WAY MORE SHOCKING.
I HAVE SO MANY QUESTIONS. JUST... I MEAN... HOW?
OH, YOU SHOULD HAVE SEEN HER BACK IN THE DAY, JO!
THIS ONE TIME IN COLLEGE, AMANDA OUT-DRANK A FRAT GUY AND GOT TO HOIST THE INFAMOUS LORD STANLEY'S KEG.
A COVETED TROPHY, I ASSURE YOU!
ENOUGH!
I DIDN'T LET YOU INTO MY HOME SO YOU COULD...COULD RIDICULE ME LIKE THIS!

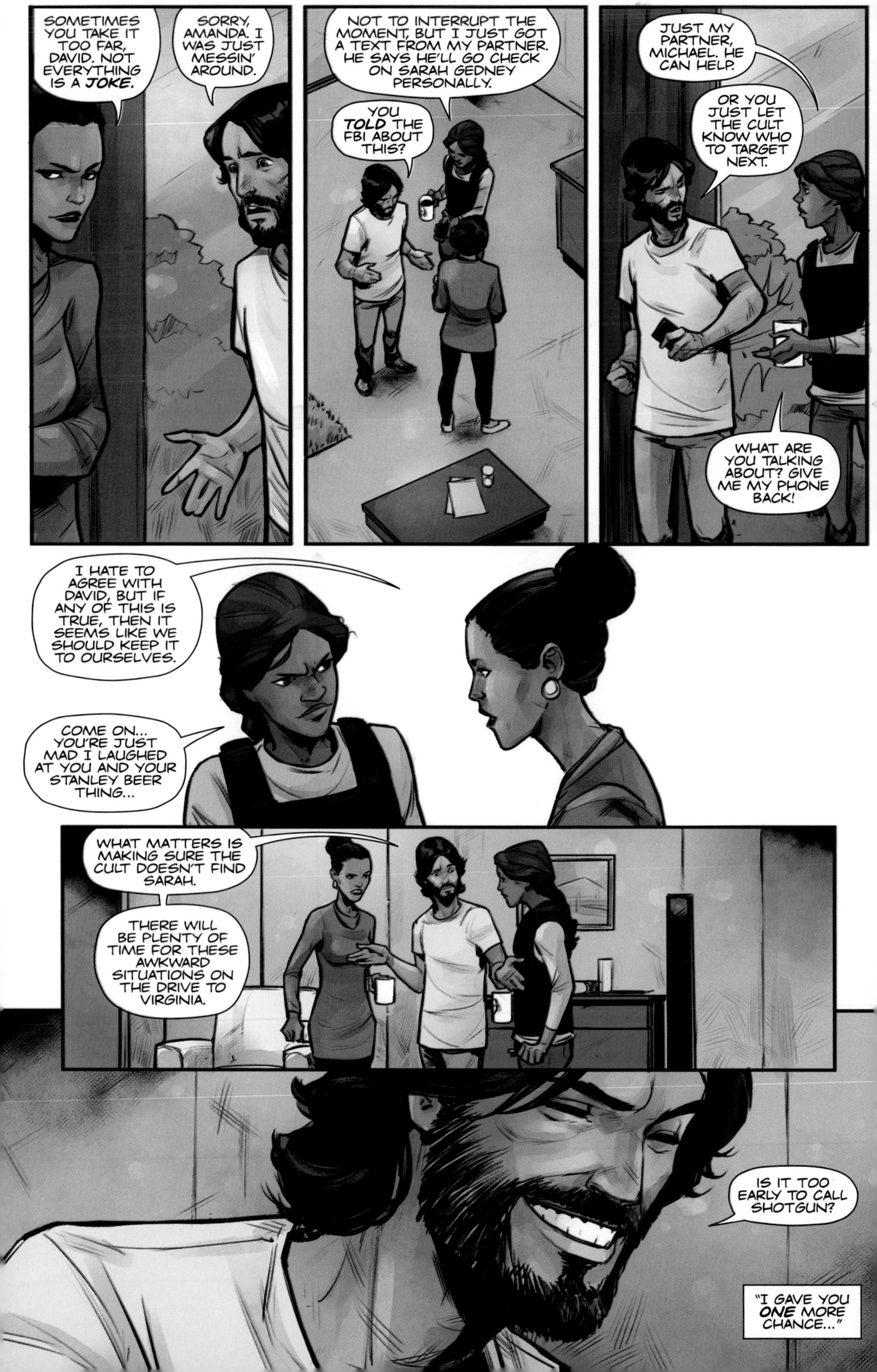
SOMETIMES YOU TAKE IT TOO FAR, DAVID. NOT EVERYTHING IS A ***JOKE.***
SORRY, AMANDA. I WAS JUST MESSIN' AROUND.
NOT TO INTERRUPT THE MOMENT, BUT I JUST GOT A TEXT FROM MY PARTNER. HE SAYS HE'LL GO CHECK ON SARAH GEDNEY PERSONALLY.
YOU ***TOLD*** THE FBI ABOUT THIS?
JUST MY PARTNER, MICHAEL. HE CAN HELP.
OR YOU JUST LET THE CULT KNOW WHO TO TARGET NEXT.
WHAT ARE YOU TALKING ABOUT? GIVE ME MY PHONE BACK!
I HATE TO AGREE WITH DAVID, BUT IF ANY OF THIS IS TRUE, THEN IT SEEMS LIKE WE SHOULD KEEP IT TO OURSELVES.
COME ON... YOU'RE JUST MAD I LAUGHED AT YOU AND YOUR STANLEY BEER THING...
WHAT MATTERS IS MAKING SURE THE CULT DOESN'T FIND SARAH.
THERE WILL BE PLENTY OF TIME FOR THESE AWKWARD SITUATIONS ON THE DRIVE TO VIRGINIA.
IS IT TOO EARLY TO CALL SHOTGUN?
"I GAVE YOU ***ONE*** MORE CHANCE..."

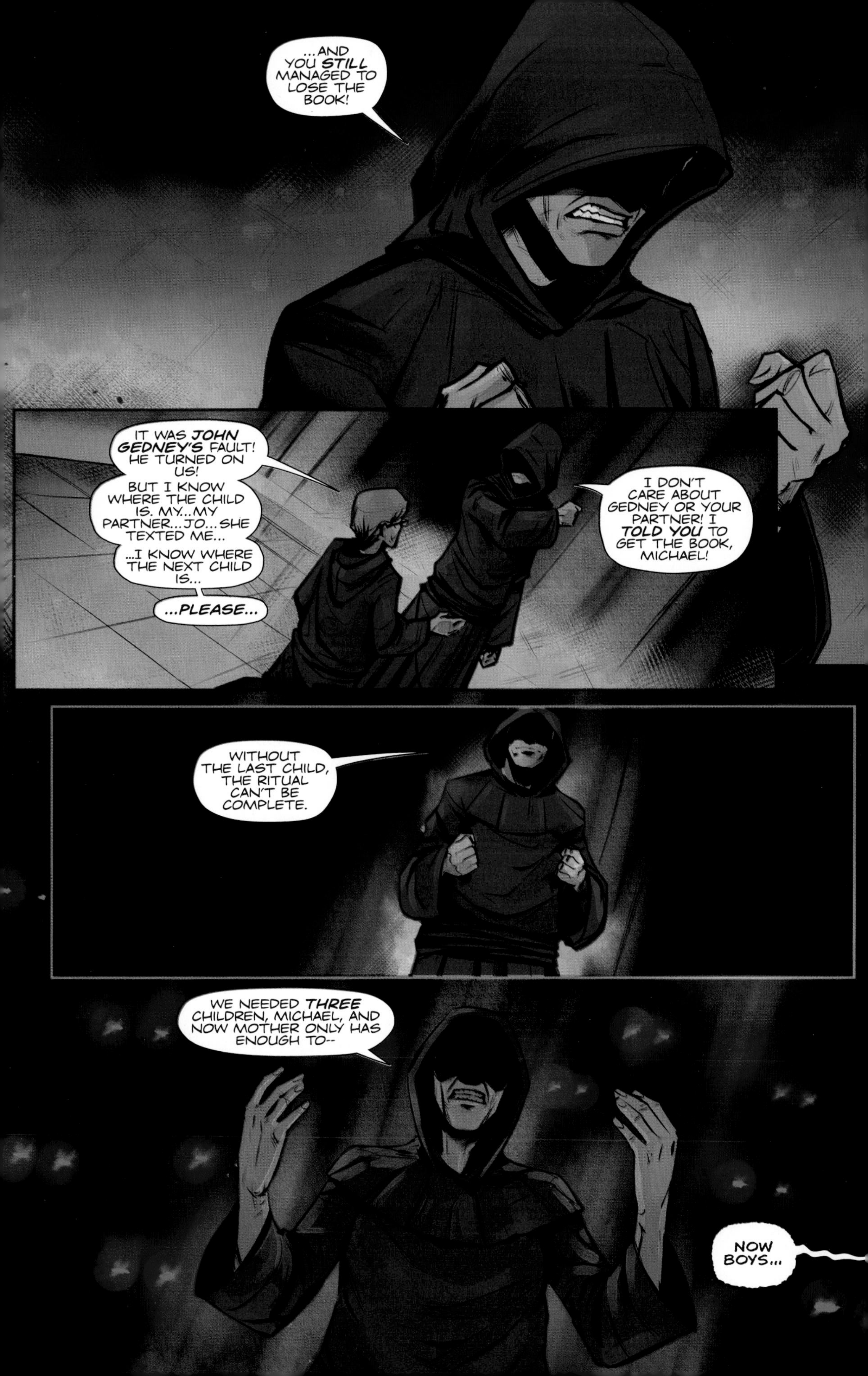
...AND YOU STILL MANAGED TO LOSE THE BOOK!
IT WAS JOHN GEDNEY'S FAULT! HE TURNED ON US!
BUT I KNOW WHERE THE CHILD IS. MY...MY PARTNER...JO...SHE TEXTED ME...
...I KNOW WHERE THE NEXT CHILD IS...
...PLEASE...
I DON'T CARE ABOUT GEDNEY OR YOUR PARTNER! I TOLD YOU TO GET THE BOOK, MICHAEL!
WITHOUT THE LAST CHILD, THE RITUAL CAN'T BE COMPLETE.
WE NEEDED THREE CHILDREN, MICHAEL, AND NOW MOTHER ONLY HAS ENOUGH TO--
NOW BOYS...

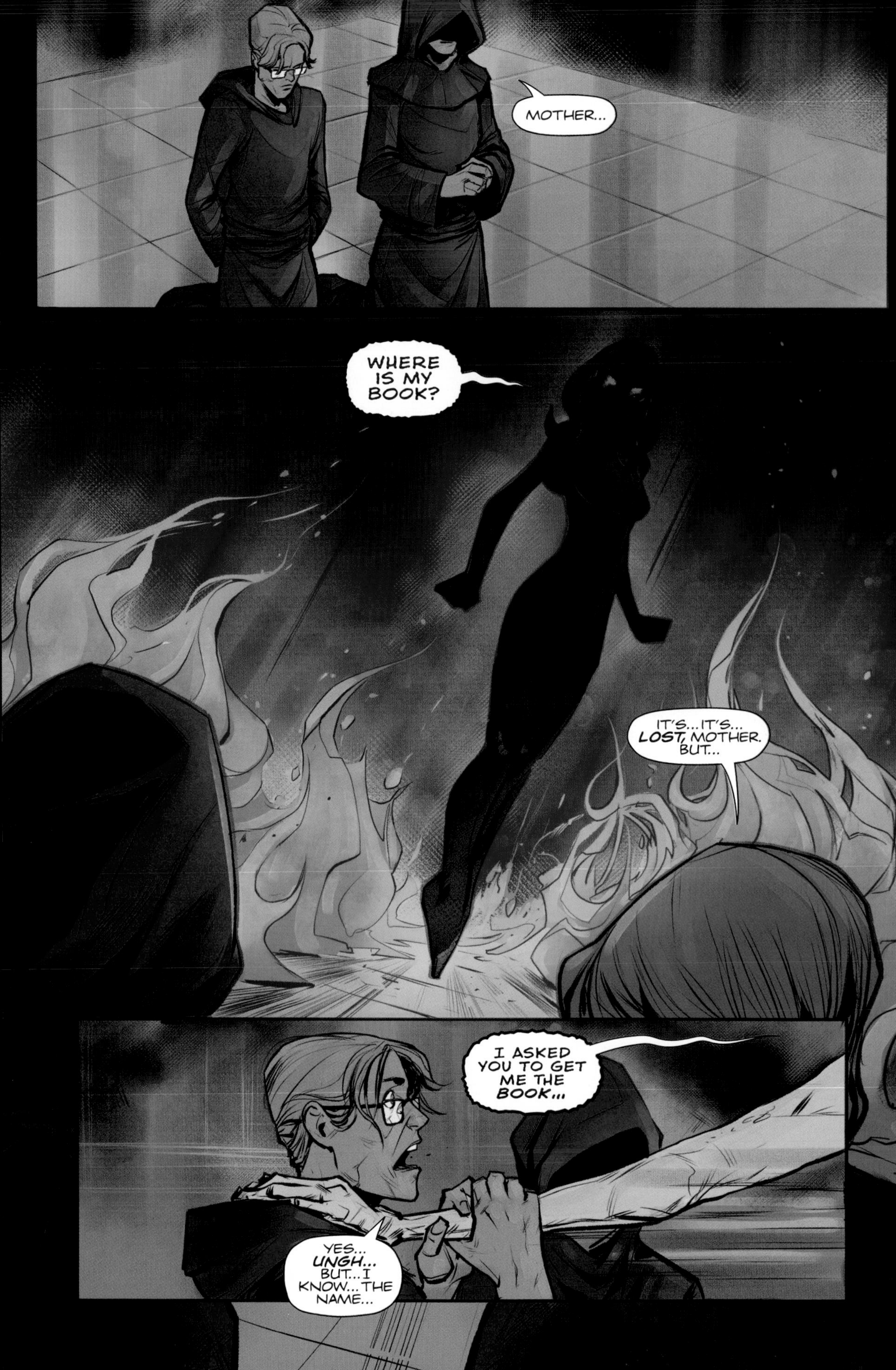
MOTHER...
WHERE IS MY BOOK?
IT'S...IT'S... LOST, MOTHER. BUT...
I ASKED YOU TO GET ME THE BOOK...
YES... UNGH... BUT...I KNOW...THE NAME...

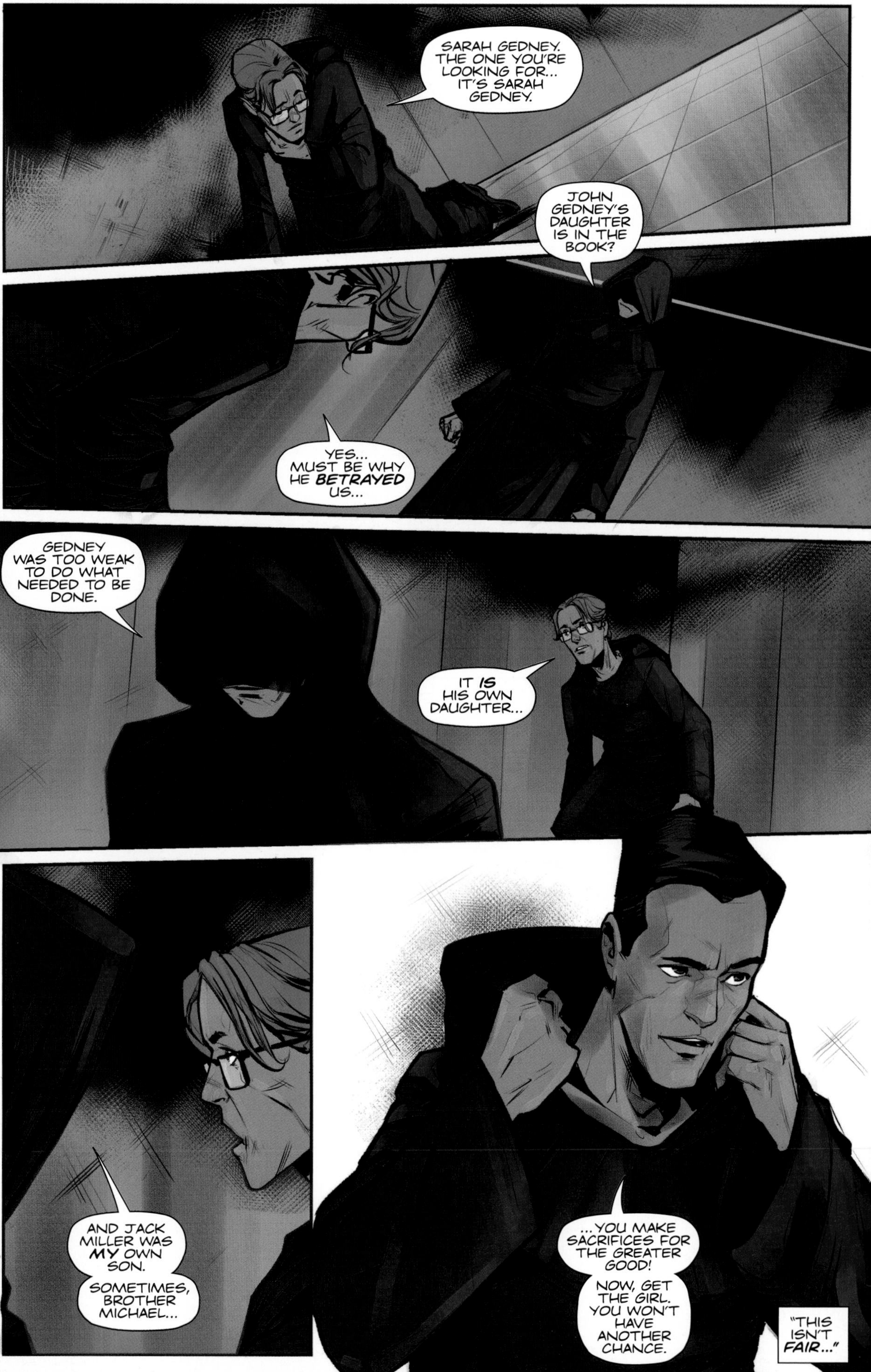
SARAH GEDNEY. THE ONE YOU'RE LOOKING FOR... IT'S SARAH GEDNEY.
JOHN GEDNEY'S DAUGHTER IS IN THE BOOK?
YES... MUST BE WHY HE **BETRAYED** US...
GEDNEY WAS TOO WEAK TO DO WHAT NEEDED TO BE DONE.
IT ***IS*** HIS OWN DAUGHTER...
AND JACK MILLER WAS ***MY*** OWN SON.
SOMETIMES, BROTHER MICHAEL...
...YOU MAKE SACRIFICES FOR THE GREATER GOOD!
NOW, GET THE GIRL. YOU WON'T HAVE ANOTHER CHANCE.
"THIS ISN'T ***FAIR...***"

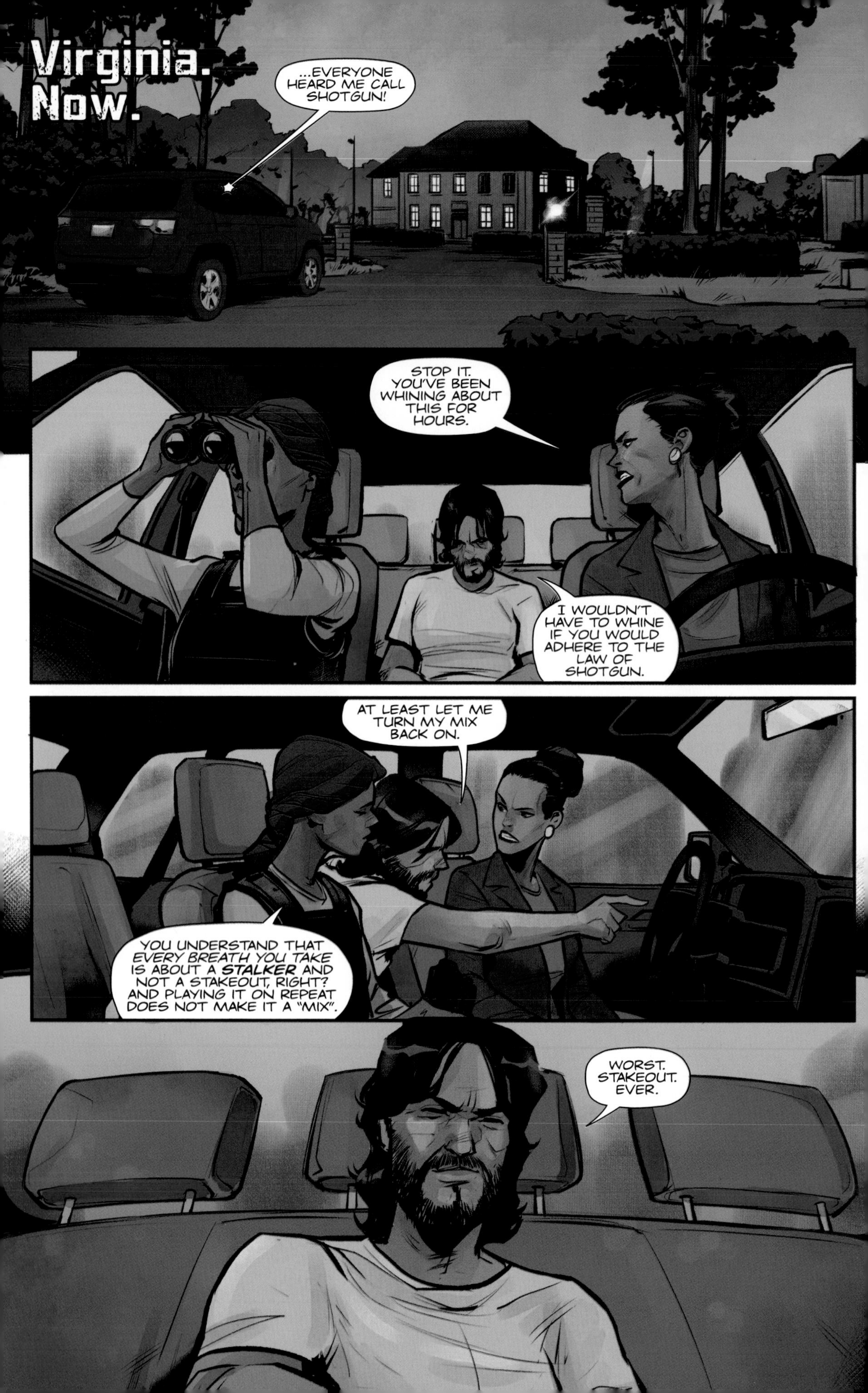
Virginia. Now.
...EVERYONE HEARD ME CALL SHOTGUN!
STOP IT. YOU'VE BEEN WHINING ABOUT THIS FOR HOURS.
I WOULDN'T HAVE TO WHINE IF YOU WOULD ADHERE TO THE LAW OF SHOTGUN.
AT LEAST LET ME TURN MY MIX BACK ON.
YOU UNDERSTAND THAT *EVERY BREATH YOU TAKE* IS ABOUT A **STALKER** AND NOT A STAKEOUT, RIGHT? AND PLAYING IT ON REPEAT DOES NOT MAKE IT A "MIX".
WORST. STAKEOUT. EVER.

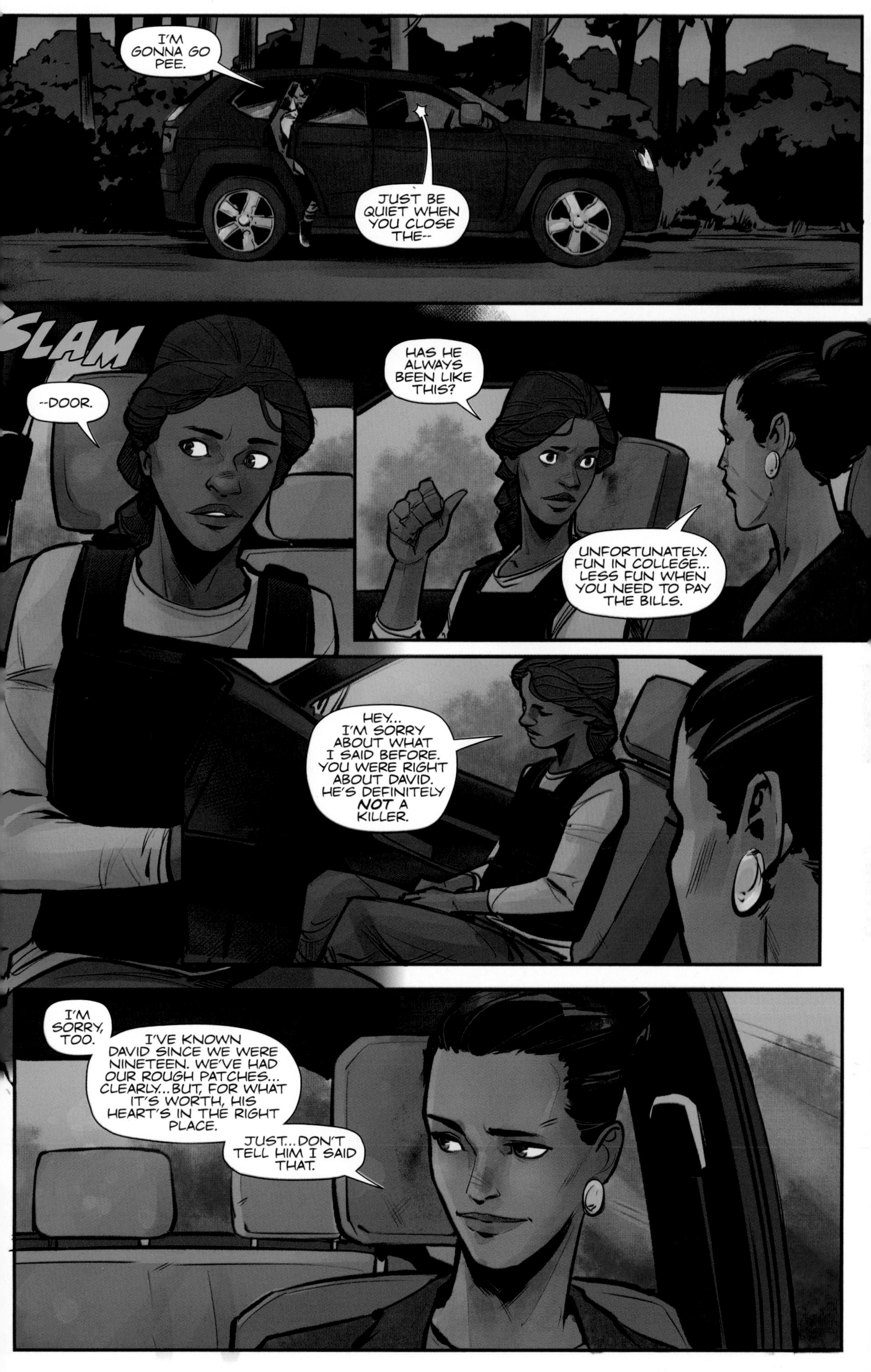
I'M GONNA GO PEE.
JUST BE QUIET WHEN YOU CLOSE THE--
SLAM
--DOOR.
HAS HE ALWAYS BEEN LIKE THIS?
UNFORTUNATELY. FUN IN COLLEGE... LESS FUN WHEN YOU NEED TO PAY THE BILLS.
HEY... I'M SORRY ABOUT WHAT I SAID BEFORE. YOU WERE RIGHT ABOUT DAVID. HE'S DEFINITELY *NOT* A KILLER.
I'M SORRY, TOO.
I'VE KNOWN DAVID SINCE WE WERE NINETEEN. WE'VE HAD OUR ROUGH PATCHES... CLEARLY...BUT, FOR WHAT IT'S WORTH, HIS HEART'S IN THE RIGHT PLACE.
JUST...DON'T TELL HIM I SAID THAT.

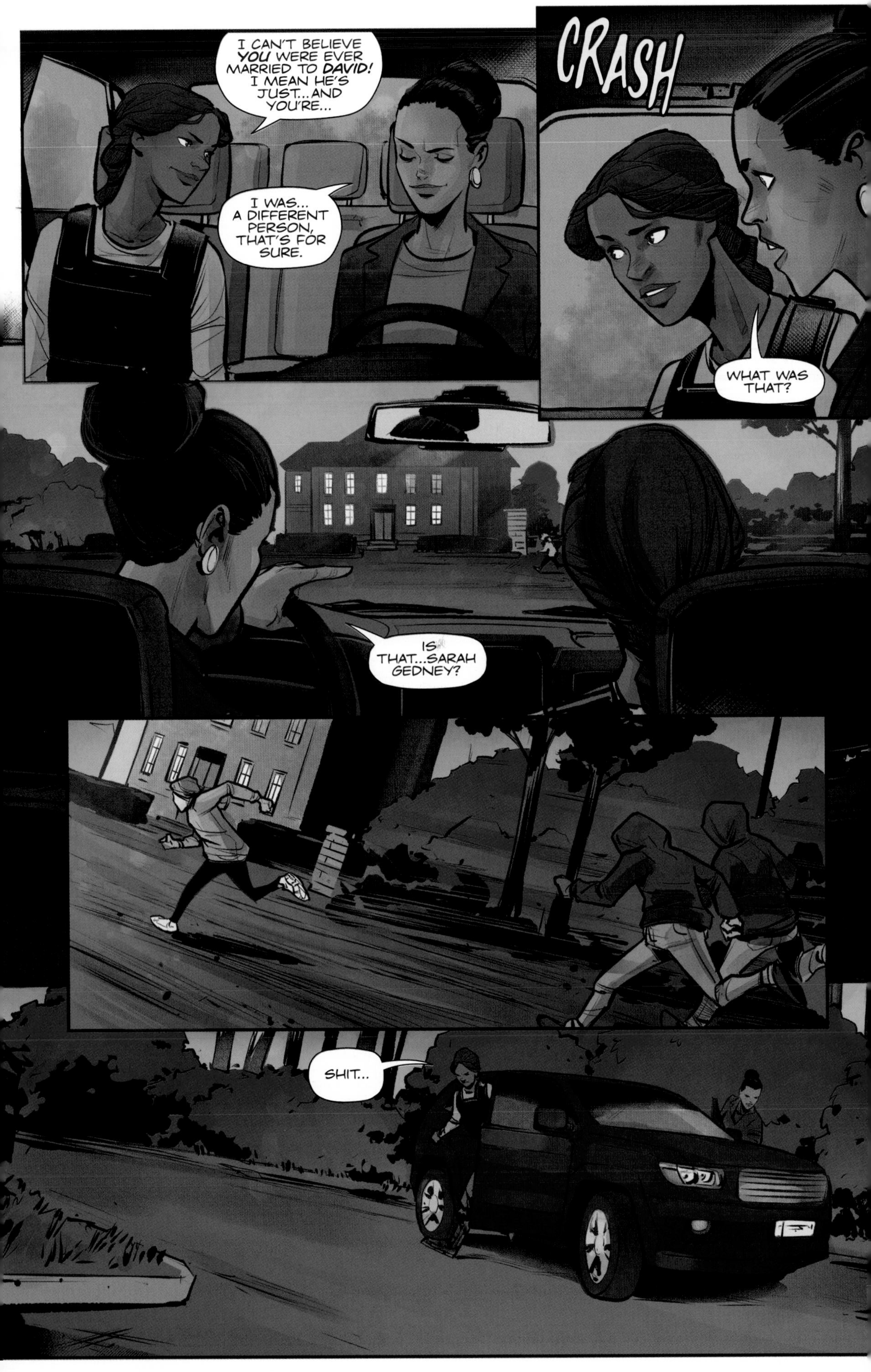
I CAN'T BELIEVE YOU WERE EVER MARRIED TO DAVID! I MEAN HE'S JUST...AND YOU'RE...
I WAS... A DIFFERENT PERSON, THAT'S FOR SURE.
CRASH
WHAT WAS THAT?
IS THAT...SARAH GEDNEY?
SHIT...

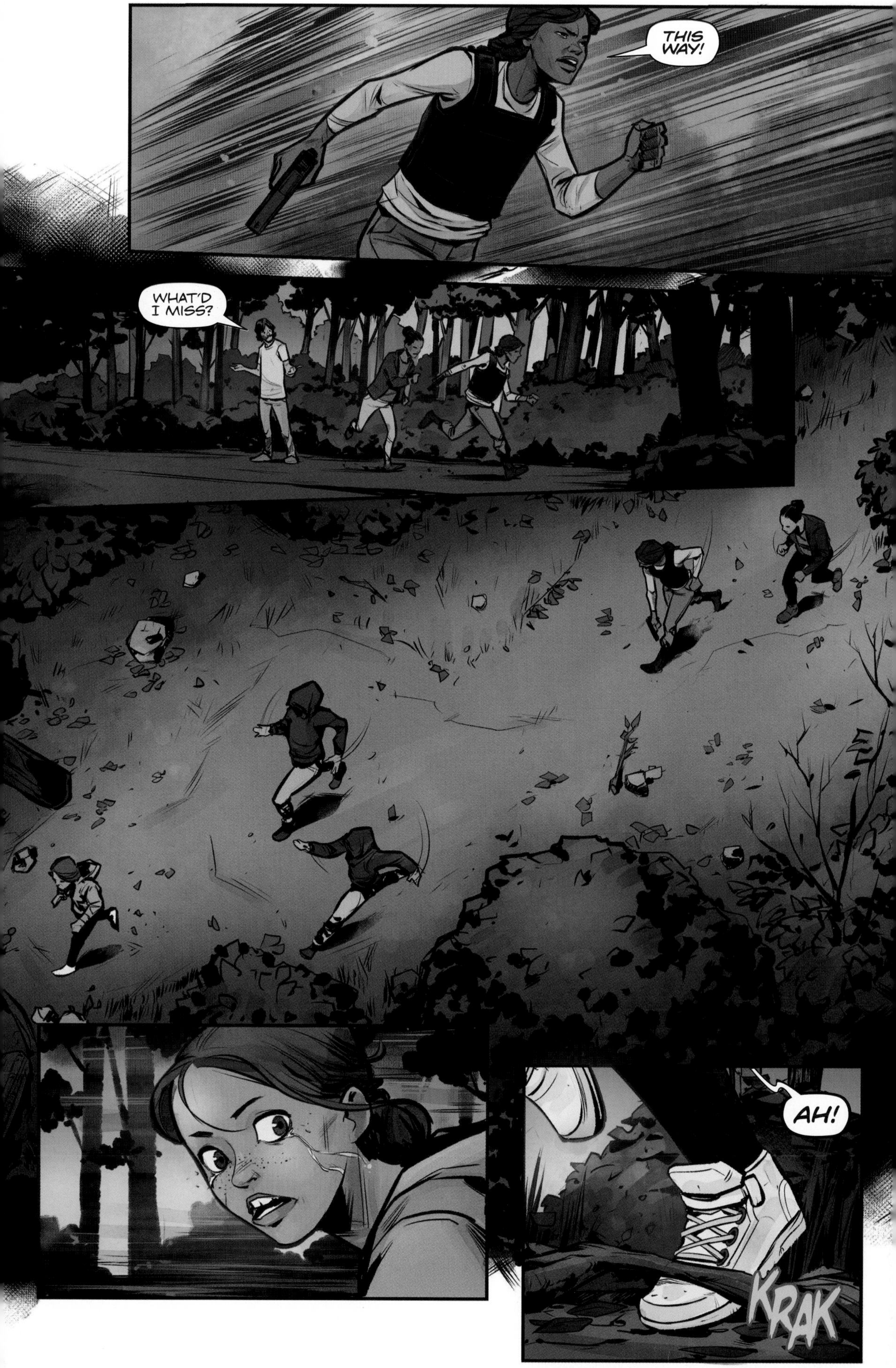
THIS WAY!
WHAT'D I MISS?
AH!
KRAK

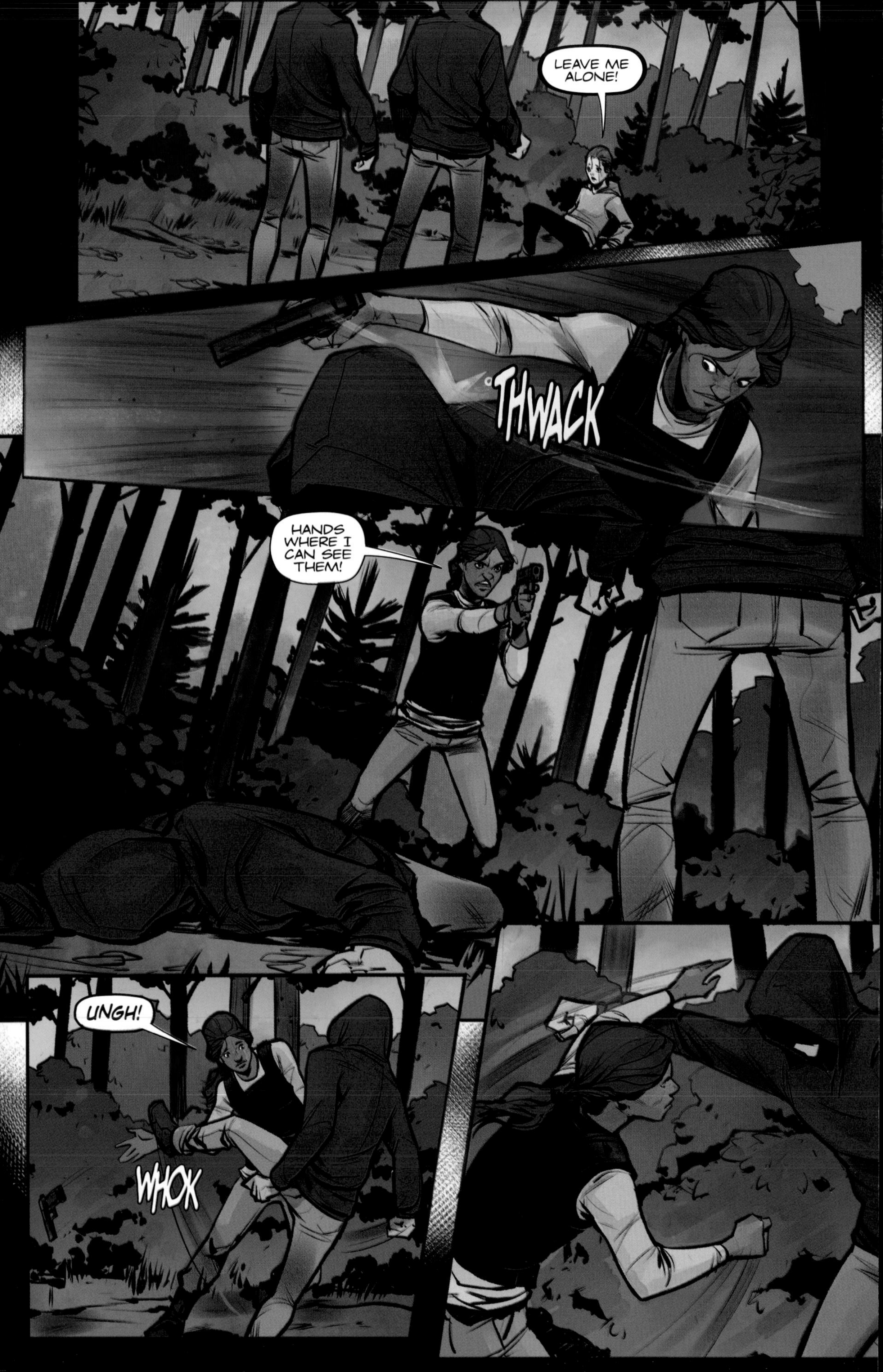
LEAVE ME ALONE!
THWACK
HANDS WHERE I CAN SEE THEM!
UNGH!
WHOK

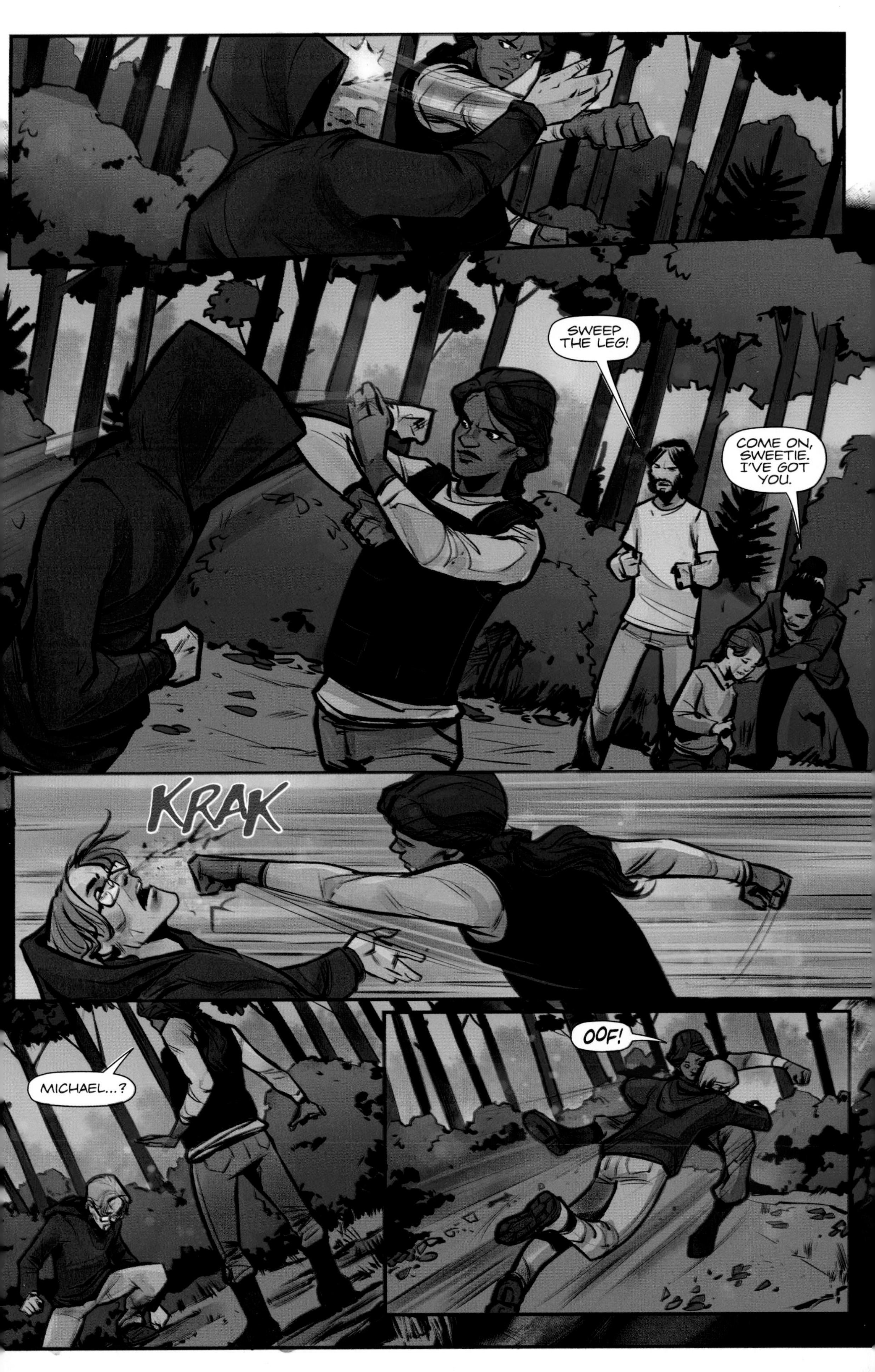
SWEEP THE LEG!
COME ON, SWEETIE. I'VE GOT YOU.
KRAK
MICHAEL...?
OOF!

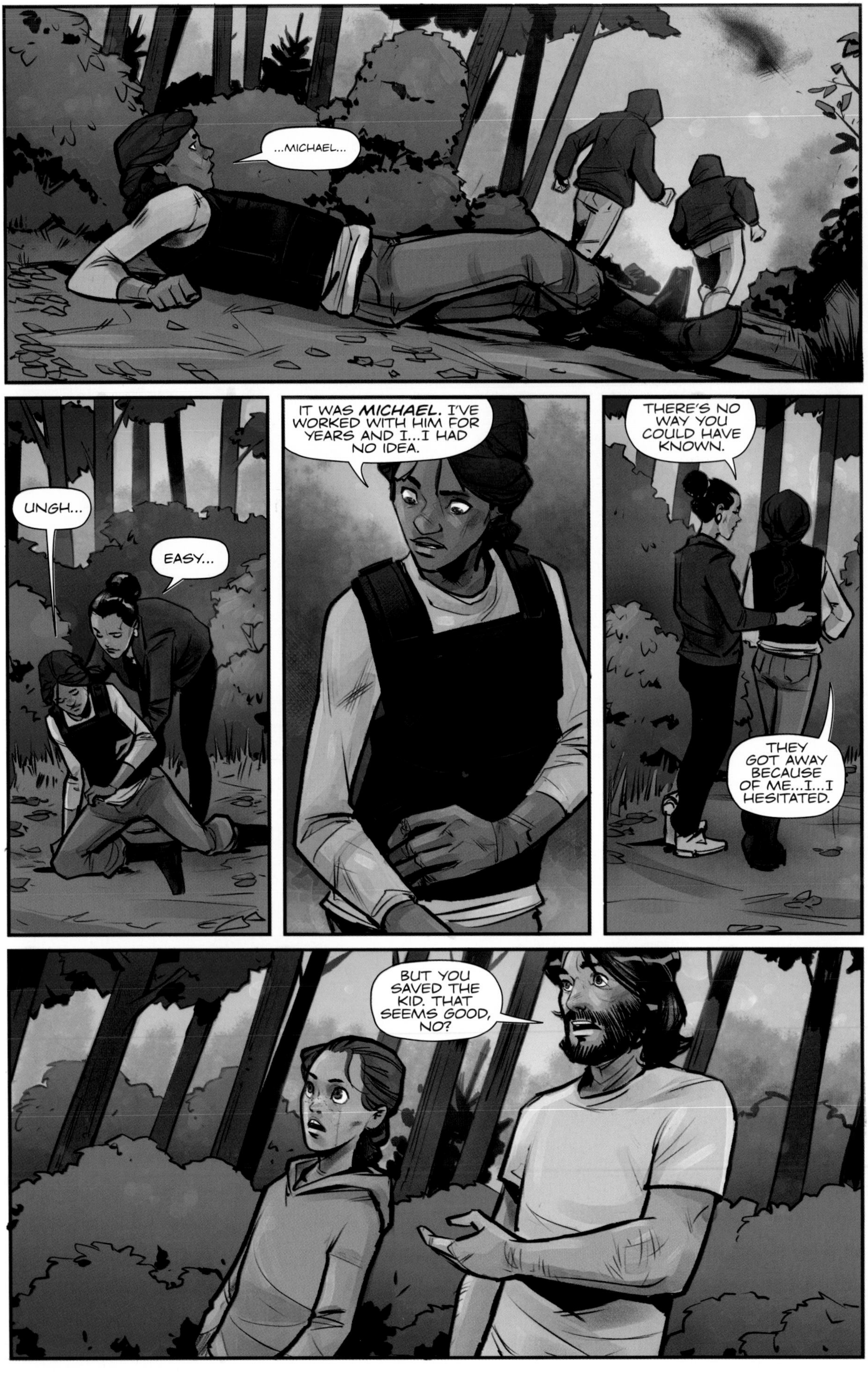
...MICHAEL...
UNGH...
EASY...
IT WAS **MICHAEL.** I'VE WORKED WITH HIM FOR YEARS AND I...I HAD NO IDEA.
THERE'S NO WAY YOU COULD HAVE KNOWN.
THEY GOT AWAY BECAUSE OF ME...I...I HESITATED.
BUT YOU SAVED THE KID. THAT SEEMS GOOD, NO?

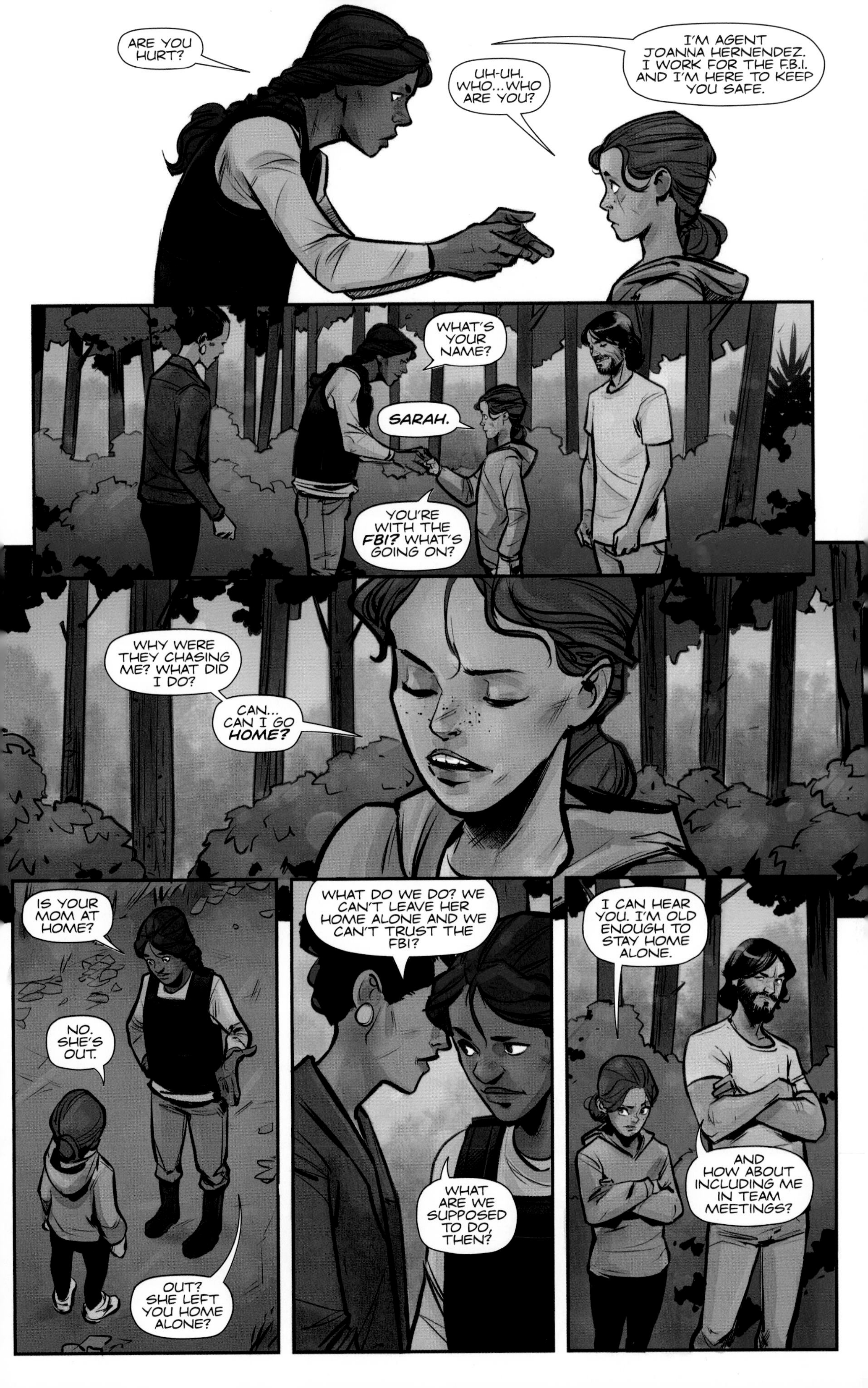

ARE YOU HURT?
UH-UH. WHO...WHO ARE YOU?
I'M AGENT JOANNA HERNENDEZ. I WORK FOR THE F.B.I. AND I'M HERE TO KEEP YOU SAFE.
WHAT'S YOUR NAME?
SARAH.
YOU'RE WITH THE FBI? WHAT'S GOING ON?
WHY WERE THEY CHASING ME? WHAT DID I DO?
CAN... CAN I GO HOME?
IS YOUR MOM AT HOME?
NO. SHE'S OUT.
OUT? SHE LEFT YOU HOME ALONE?
WHAT DO WE DO? WE CAN'T LEAVE HER HOME ALONE AND WE CAN'T TRUST THE FBI?
WHAT ARE WE SUPPOSED TO DO, THEN?
I CAN HEAR YOU. I'M OLD ENOUGH TO STAY HOME ALONE.
AND HOW ABOUT INCLUDING ME IN TEAM MEETINGS?

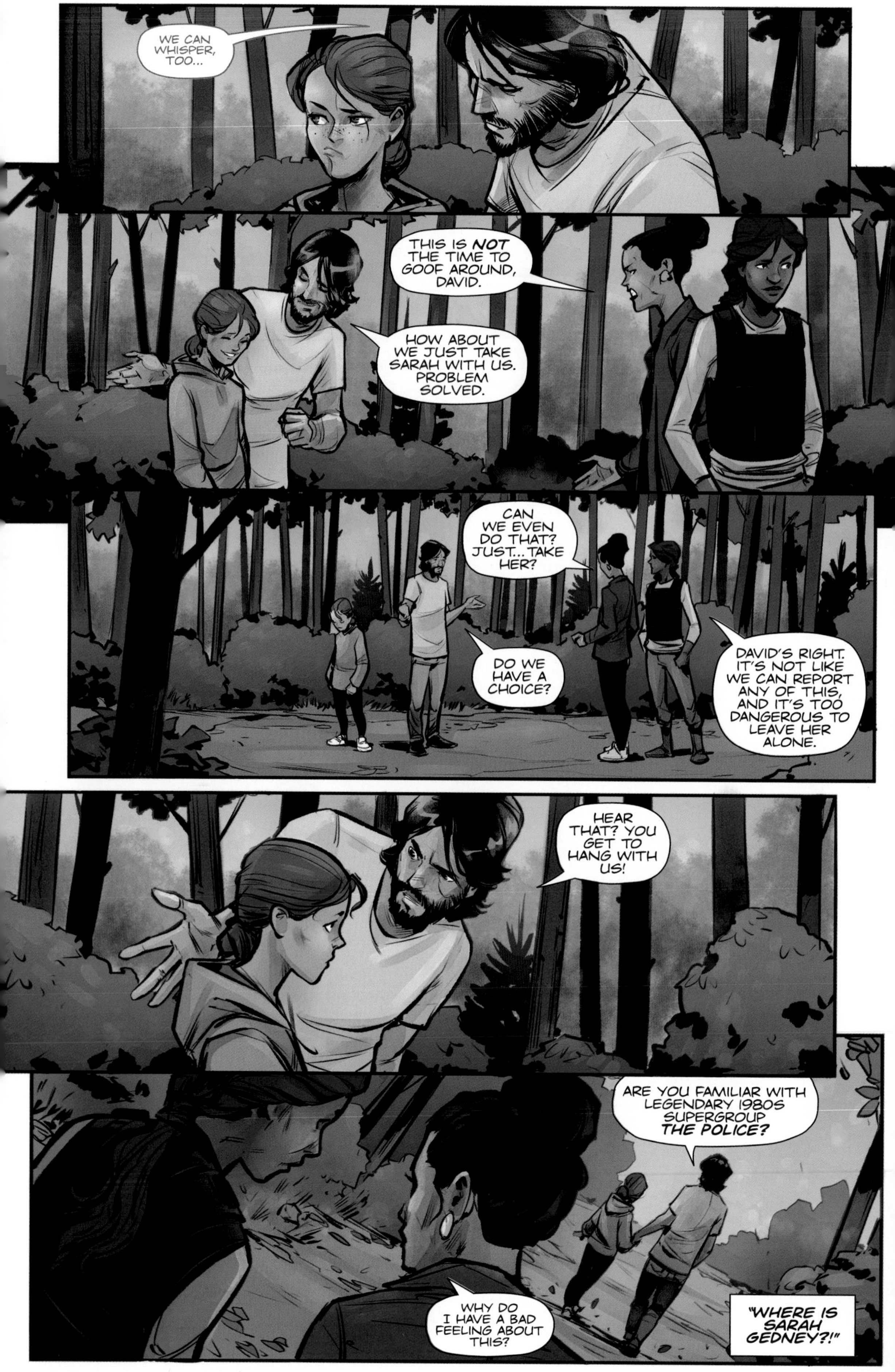
WE CAN WHISPER, TOO...
THIS IS NOT THE TIME TO GOOF AROUND, DAVID.
HOW ABOUT WE JUST TAKE SARAH WITH US. PROBLEM SOLVED.
CAN WE EVEN DO THAT? JUST... TAKE HER?
DO WE HAVE A CHOICE?
DAVID'S RIGHT. IT'S NOT LIKE WE CAN REPORT ANY OF THIS, AND IT'S TOO DANGEROUS TO LEAVE HER ALONE.
HEAR THAT? YOU GET TO HANG WITH US!
ARE YOU FAMILIAR WITH LEGENDARY 1980s SUPERGROUP THE POLICE?
WHY DO I HAVE A BAD FEELING ABOUT THIS?
"WHERE IS SARAH GEDNEY?!"

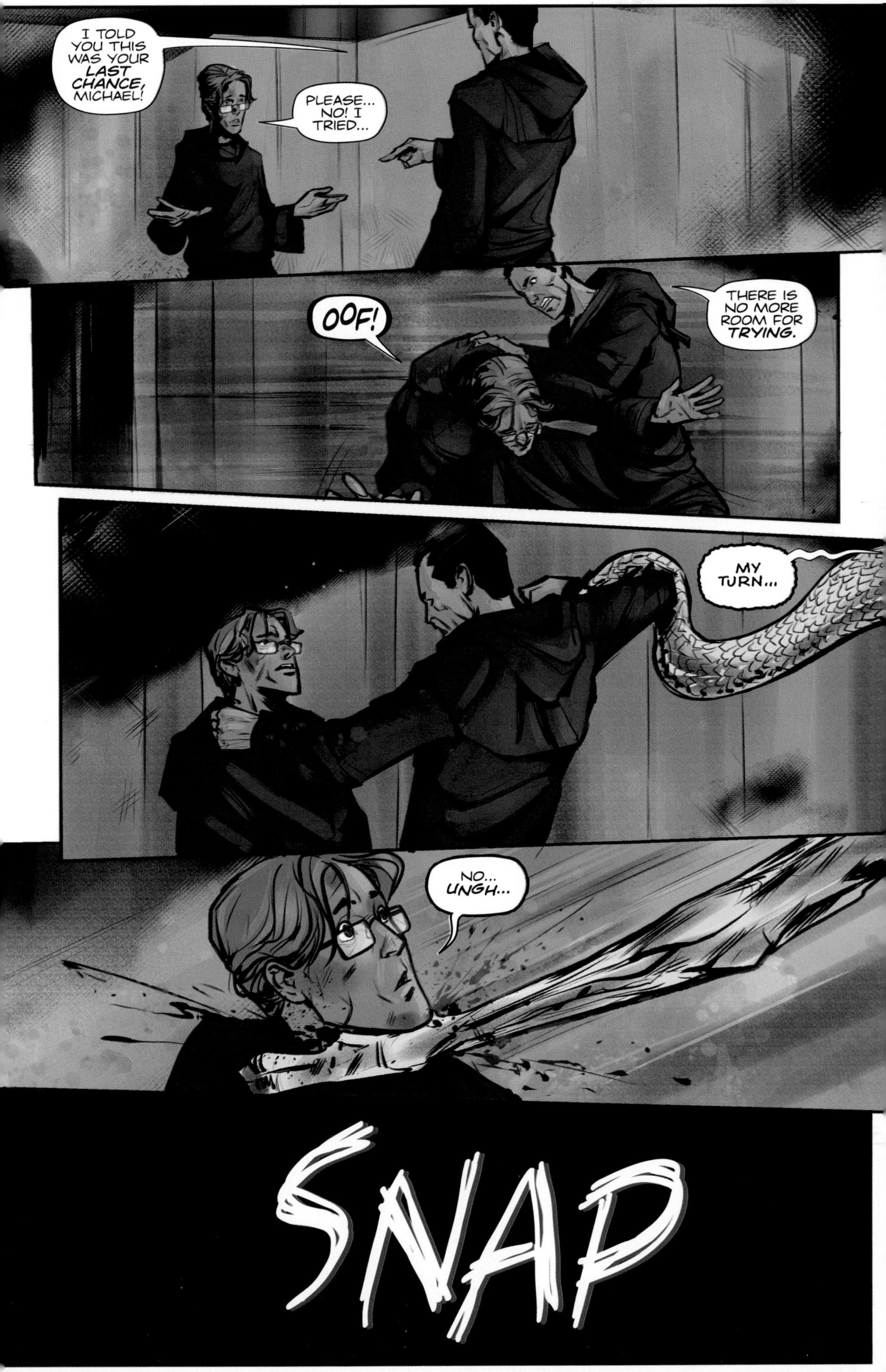
I TOLD YOU THIS WAS YOUR LAST CHANCE, MICHAEL!
PLEASE... NO! I TRIED...
OOF!
THERE IS NO MORE ROOM FOR TRYING.
MY TURN...
NO... UNGH...
SNAP

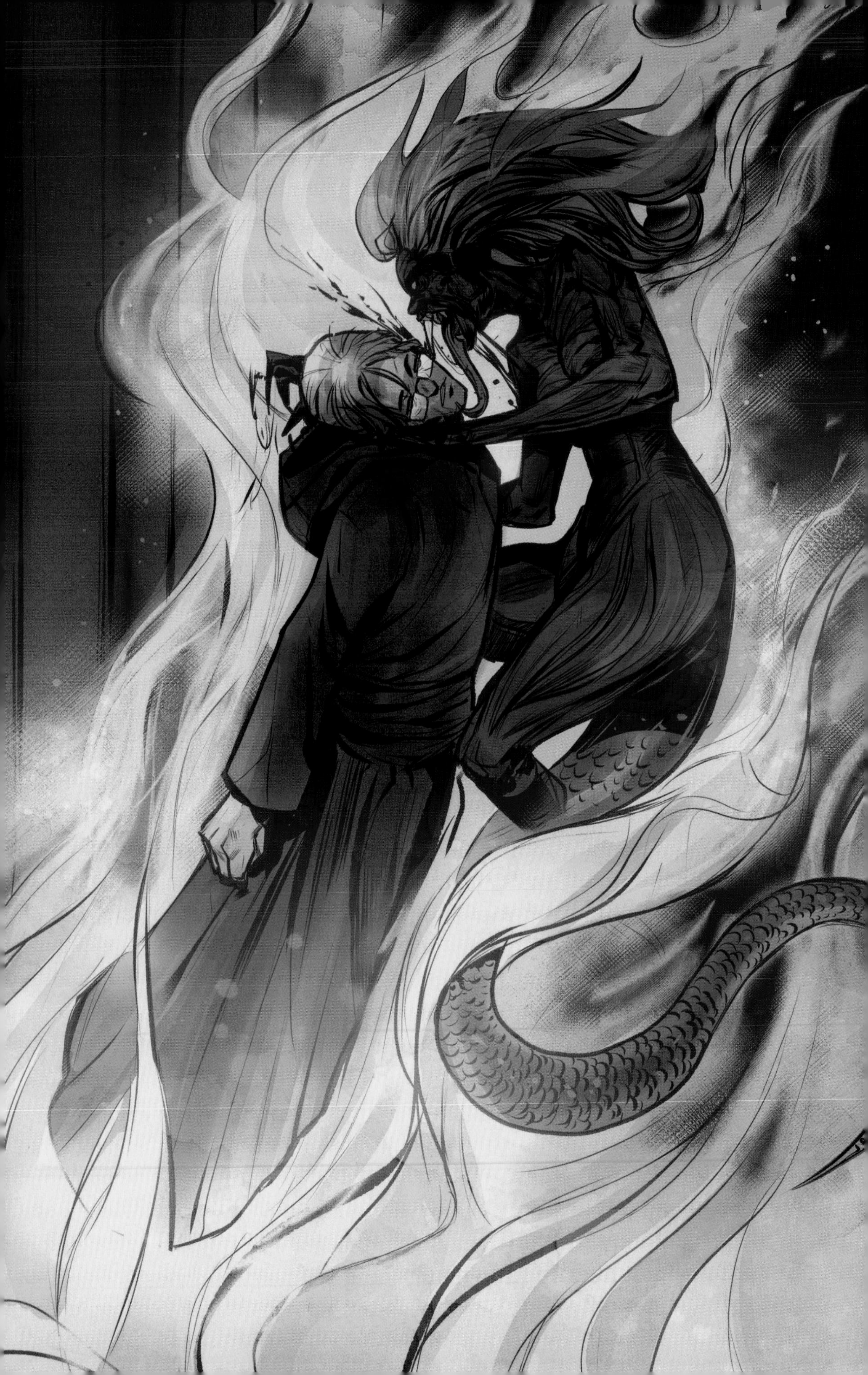

5

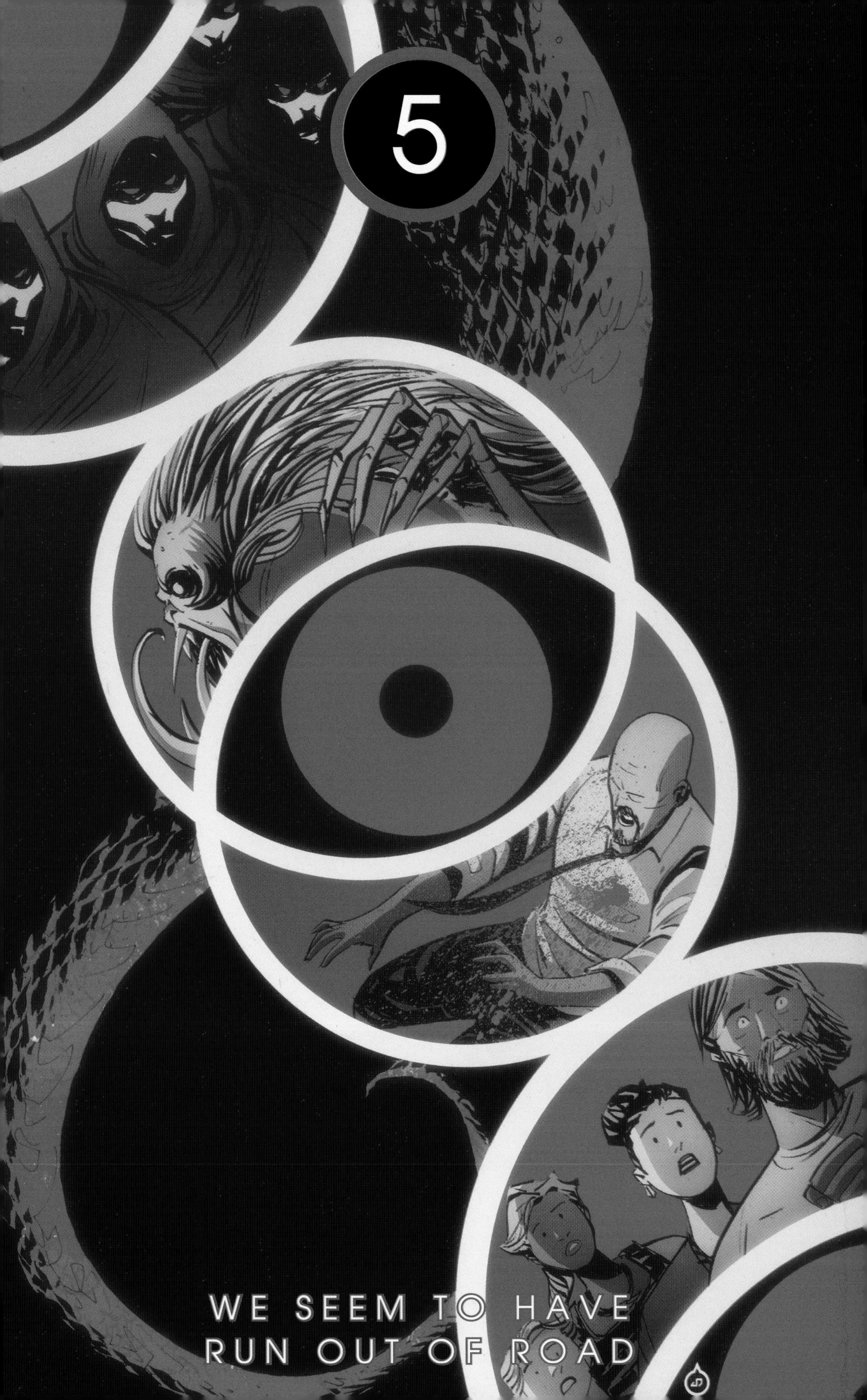

WE SEEM TO HAVE RUN OUT OF ROAD

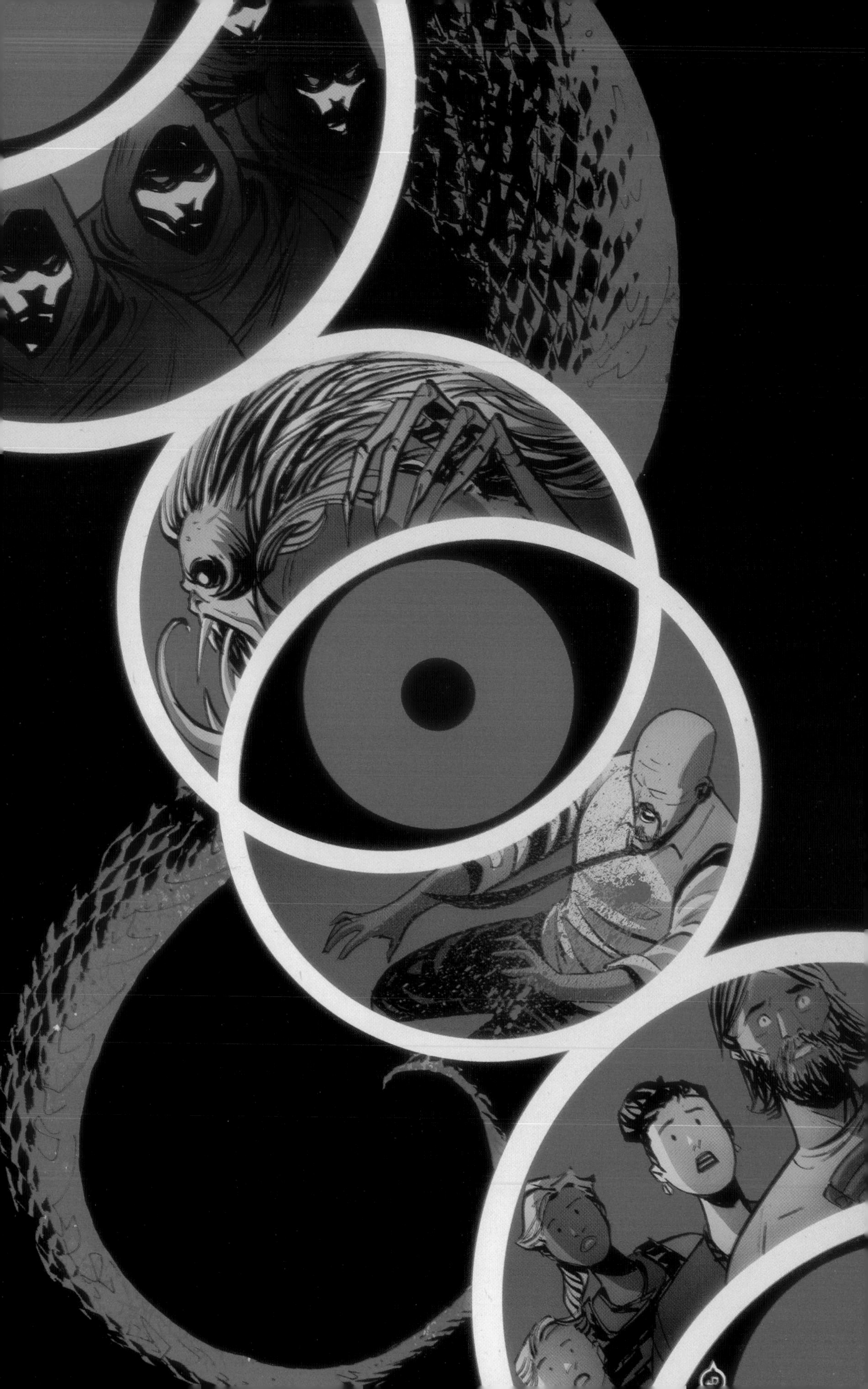

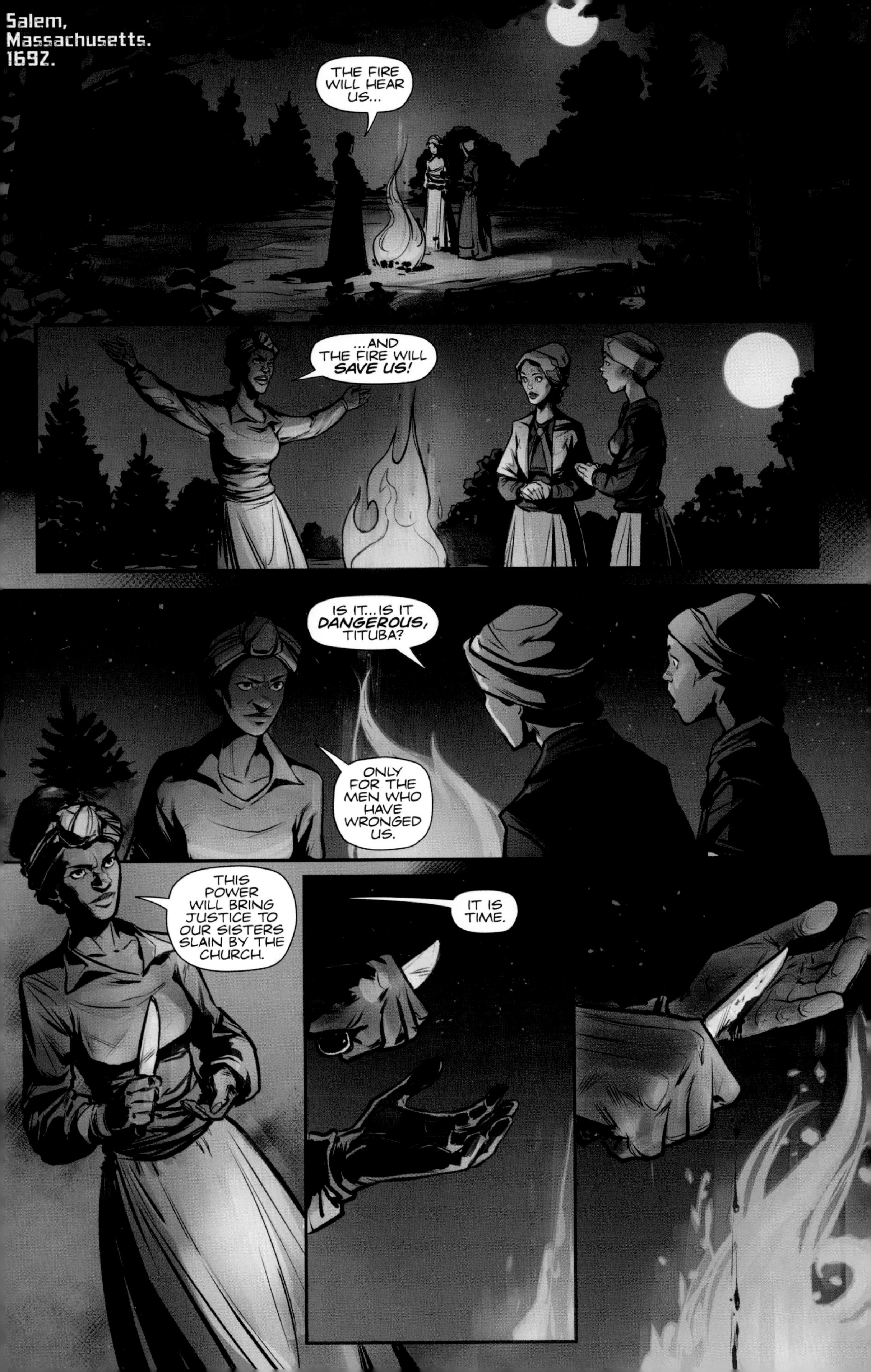

Salem, Massachusetts. 1692.
THE FIRE WILL HEAR US...
...AND THE FIRE WILL SAVE US!
IS IT...IS IT DANGEROUS, TITUBA?
ONLY FOR THE MEN WHO HAVE WRONGED US.
THIS POWER WILL BRING JUSTICE TO OUR SISTERS SLAIN BY THE CHURCH.
IT IS TIME.

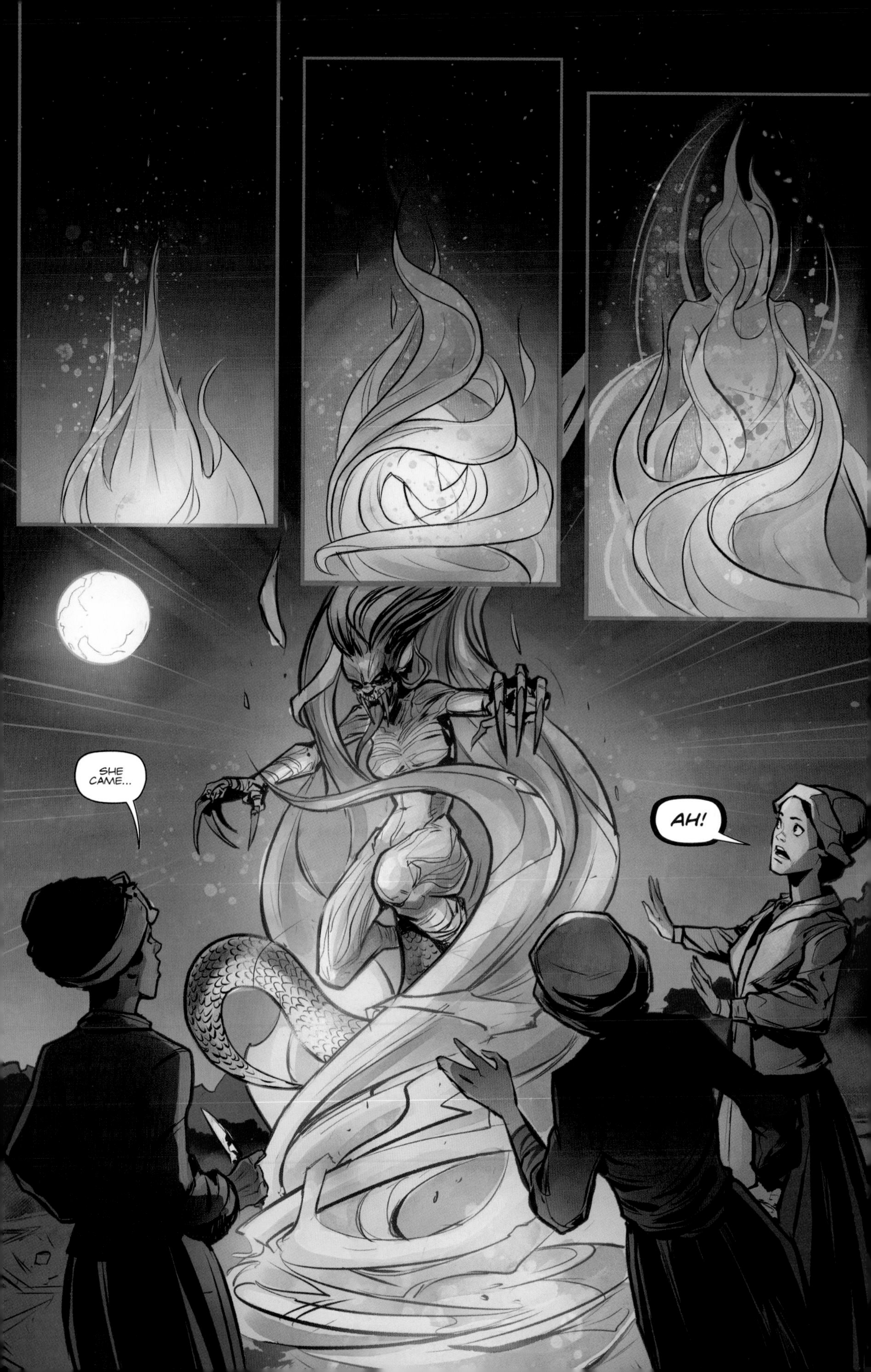
SHE CAME...
AH!

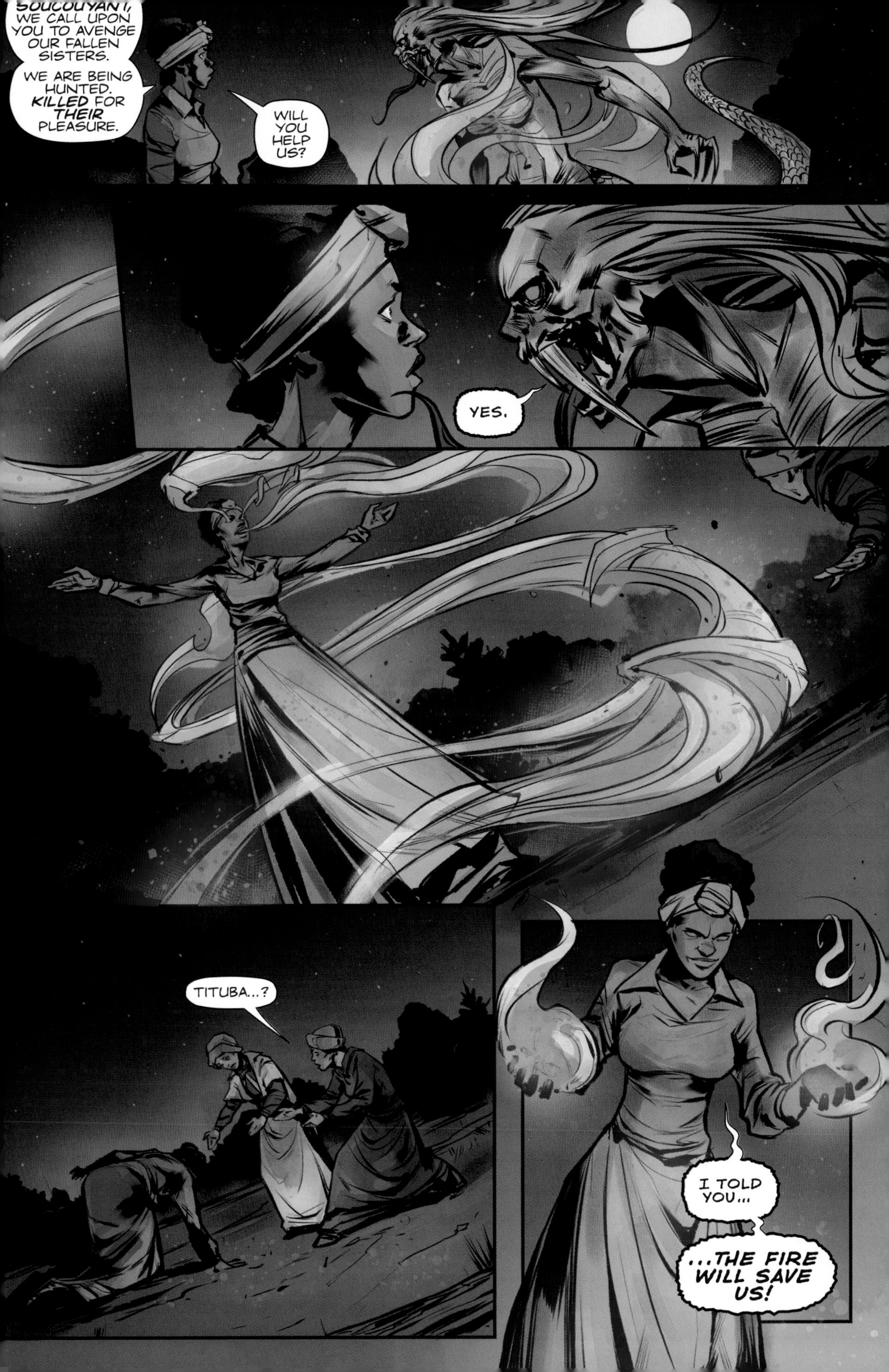
SOUCOUYANT, WE CALL UPON YOU TO AVENGE OUR FALLEN SISTERS.
WE ARE BEING HUNTED. KILLED FOR THEIR PLEASURE.
WILL YOU HELP US?
YES.
TITUBA...?
I TOLD YOU...
...THE FIRE WILL SAVE US!

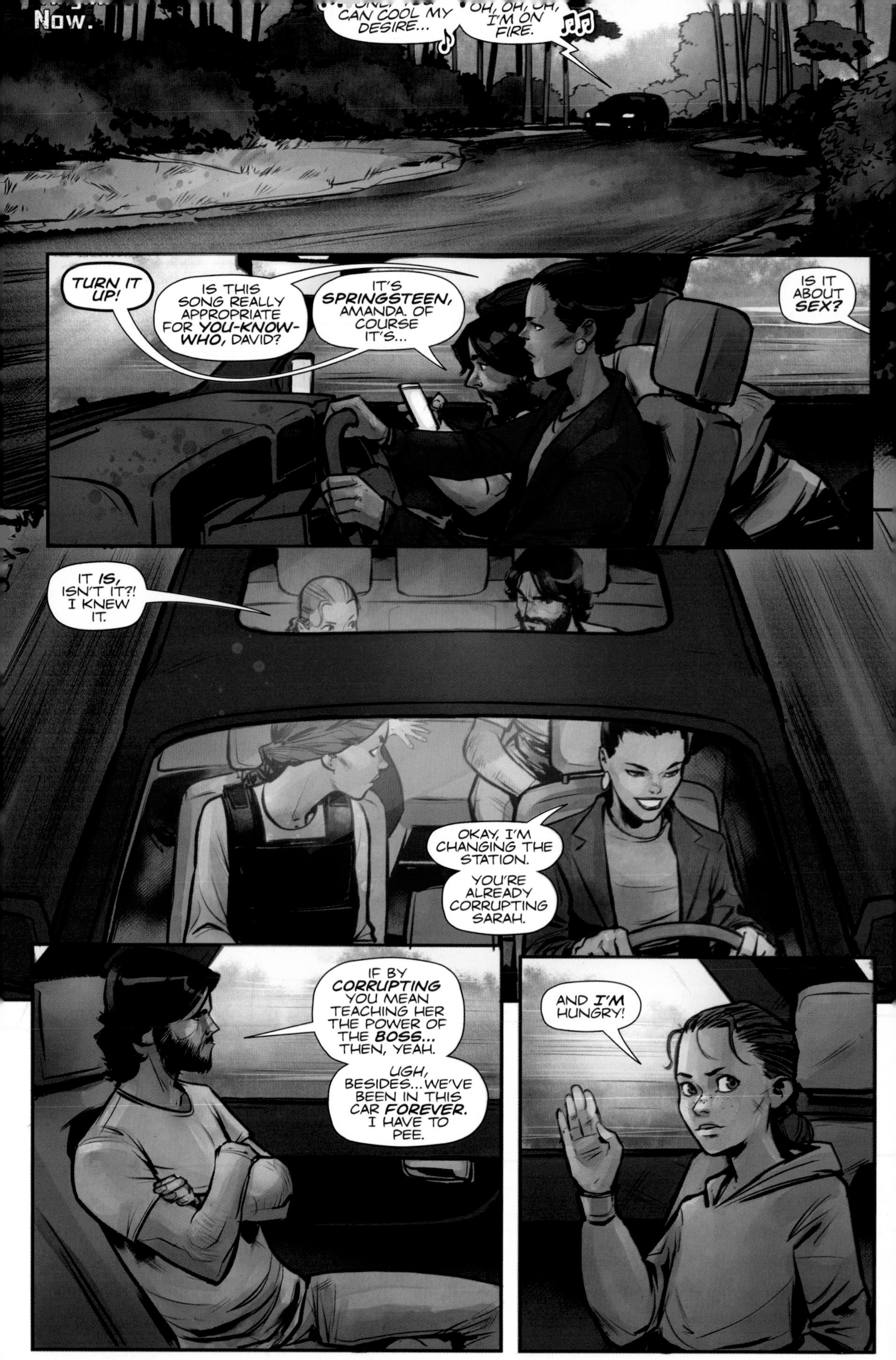
Now.
CAN COOL MY DESIRE...
OH, OH, OH, I'M ON FIRE.
TURN IT UP!
IS THIS SONG REALLY APPROPRIATE FOR YOU-KNOW-WHO, DAVID?
IT'S SPRINGSTEEN, AMANDA. OF COURSE IT'S...
IS IT ABOUT SEX?
IT IS, ISN'T IT?! I KNEW IT.
OKAY, I'M CHANGING THE STATION.
YOU'RE ALREADY CORRUPTING SARAH.
IF BY CORRUPTING YOU MEAN TEACHING HER THE POWER OF THE BOSS... THEN, YEAH.
UGH, BESIDES...WE'VE BEEN IN THIS CAR FOREVER. I HAVE TO PEE.
AND I'M HUNGRY!

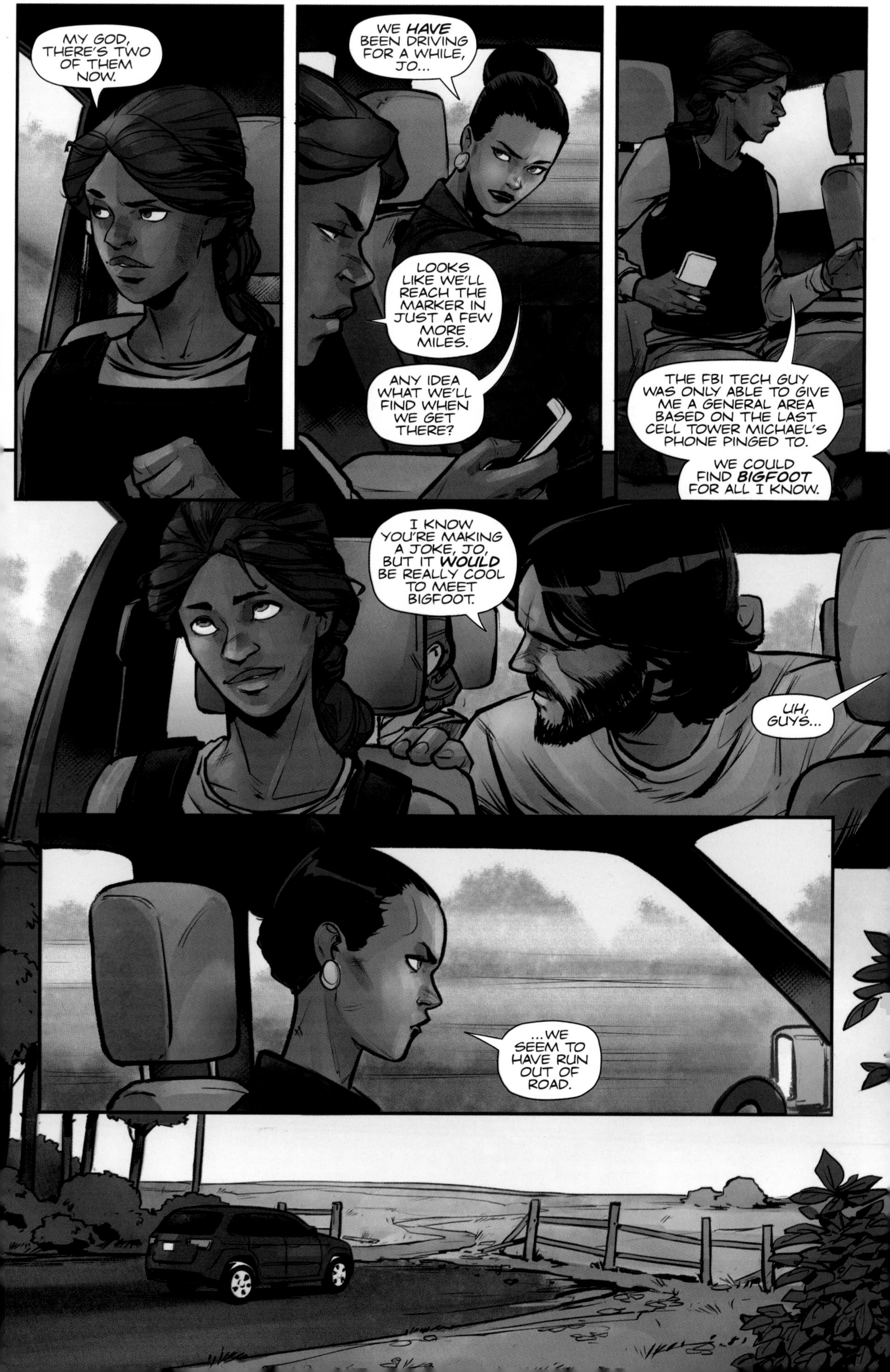
MY GOD, THERE'S TWO OF THEM NOW.
WE **HAVE** BEEN DRIVING FOR A WHILE, JO...
LOOKS LIKE WE'LL REACH THE MARKER IN JUST A FEW MORE MILES.
ANY IDEA WHAT WE'LL FIND WHEN WE GET THERE?
THE FBI TECH GUY WAS ONLY ABLE TO GIVE ME A GENERAL AREA BASED ON THE LAST CELL TOWER MICHAEL'S PHONE PINGED TO.
WE COULD FIND **BIGFOOT** FOR ALL I KNOW.
I KNOW YOU'RE MAKING A JOKE, JO, BUT IT **WOULD** BE REALLY COOL TO MEET BIGFOOT.
UH, GUYS...
...WE SEEM TO HAVE RUN OUT OF ROAD.

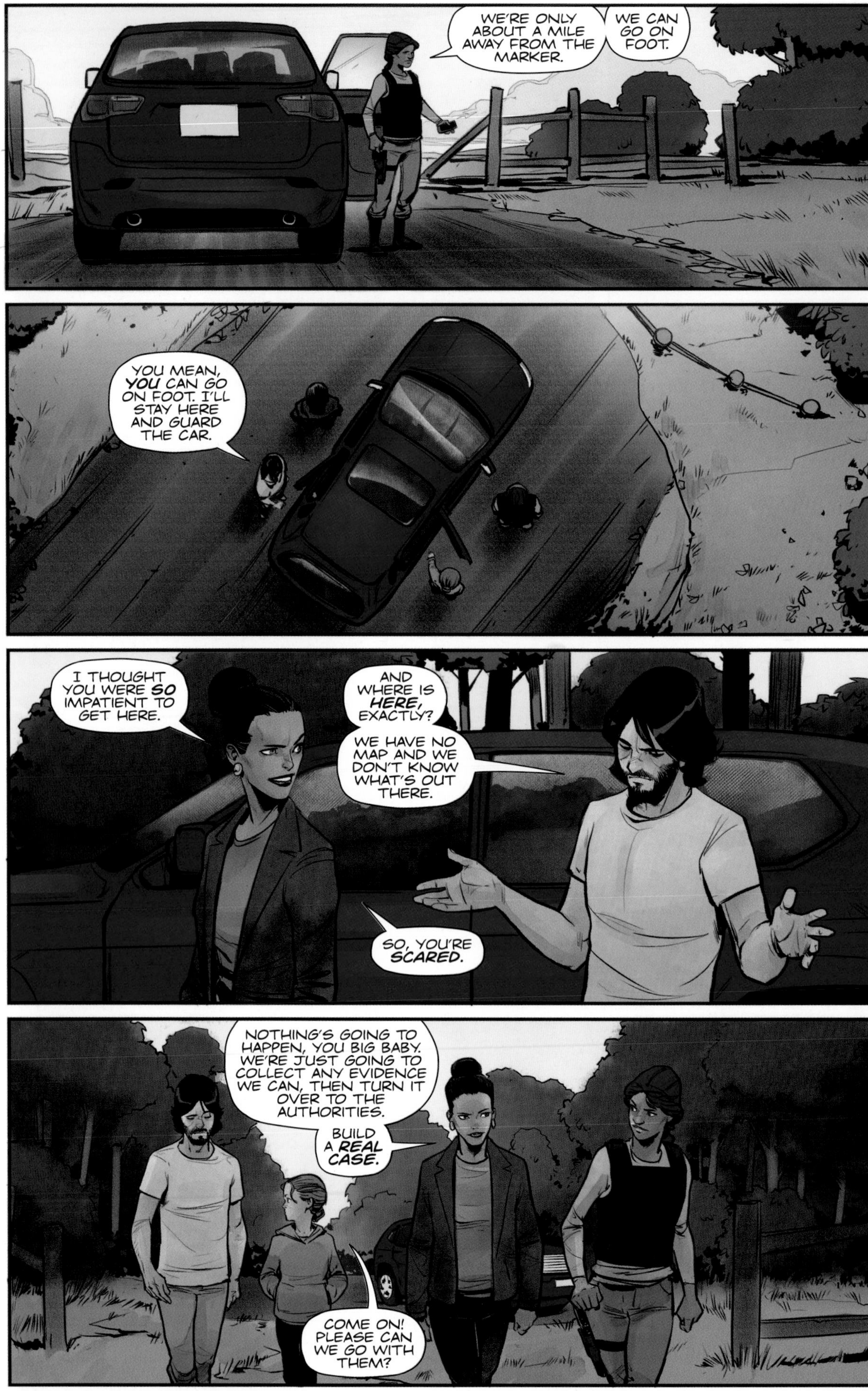
WE'RE ONLY ABOUT A MILE AWAY FROM THE MARKER.
WE CAN GO ON FOOT.
YOU MEAN, YOU CAN GO ON FOOT. I'LL STAY HERE AND GUARD THE CAR.
I THOUGHT YOU WERE SO IMPATIENT TO GET HERE.
AND WHERE IS HERE, EXACTLY?
WE HAVE NO MAP AND WE DON'T KNOW WHAT'S OUT THERE.
SO, YOU'RE SCARED.
NOTHING'S GOING TO HAPPEN, YOU BIG BABY. WE'RE JUST GOING TO COLLECT ANY EVIDENCE WE CAN, THEN TURN IT OVER TO THE AUTHORITIES.
BUILD A REAL CASE.
COME ON! PLEASE CAN WE GO WITH THEM?

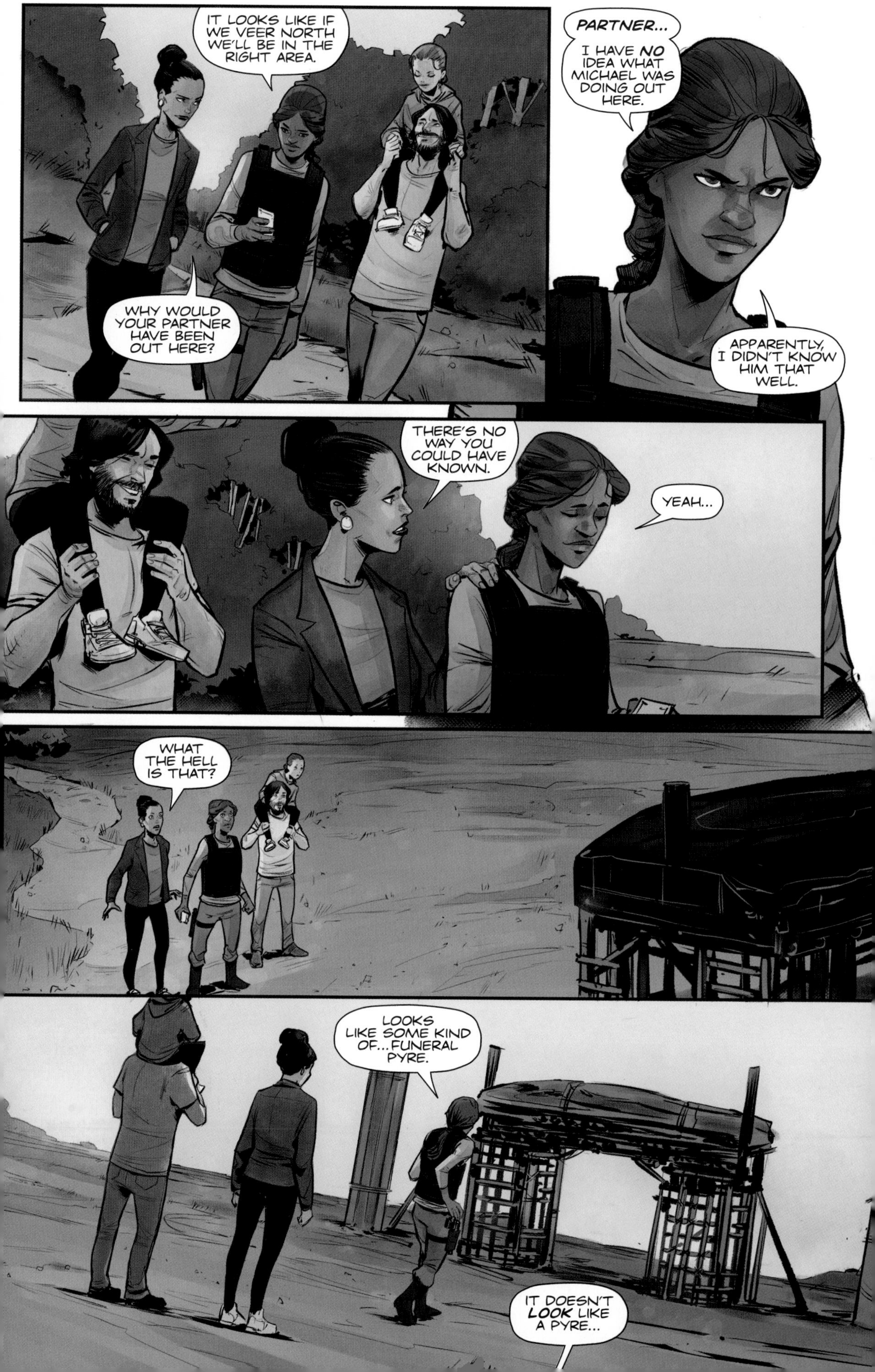
IT LOOKS LIKE IF WE VEER NORTH WE'LL BE IN THE RIGHT AREA.
WHY WOULD YOUR PARTNER HAVE BEEN OUT HERE?
PARTNER... I HAVE NO IDEA WHAT MICHAEL WAS DOING OUT HERE.
APPARENTLY, I DIDN'T KNOW HIM THAT WELL.
THERE'S NO WAY YOU COULD HAVE KNOWN.
YEAH...
WHAT THE HELL IS THAT?
LOOKS LIKE SOME KIND OF...FUNERAL PYRE.
IT DOESN'T LOOK LIKE A PYRE...

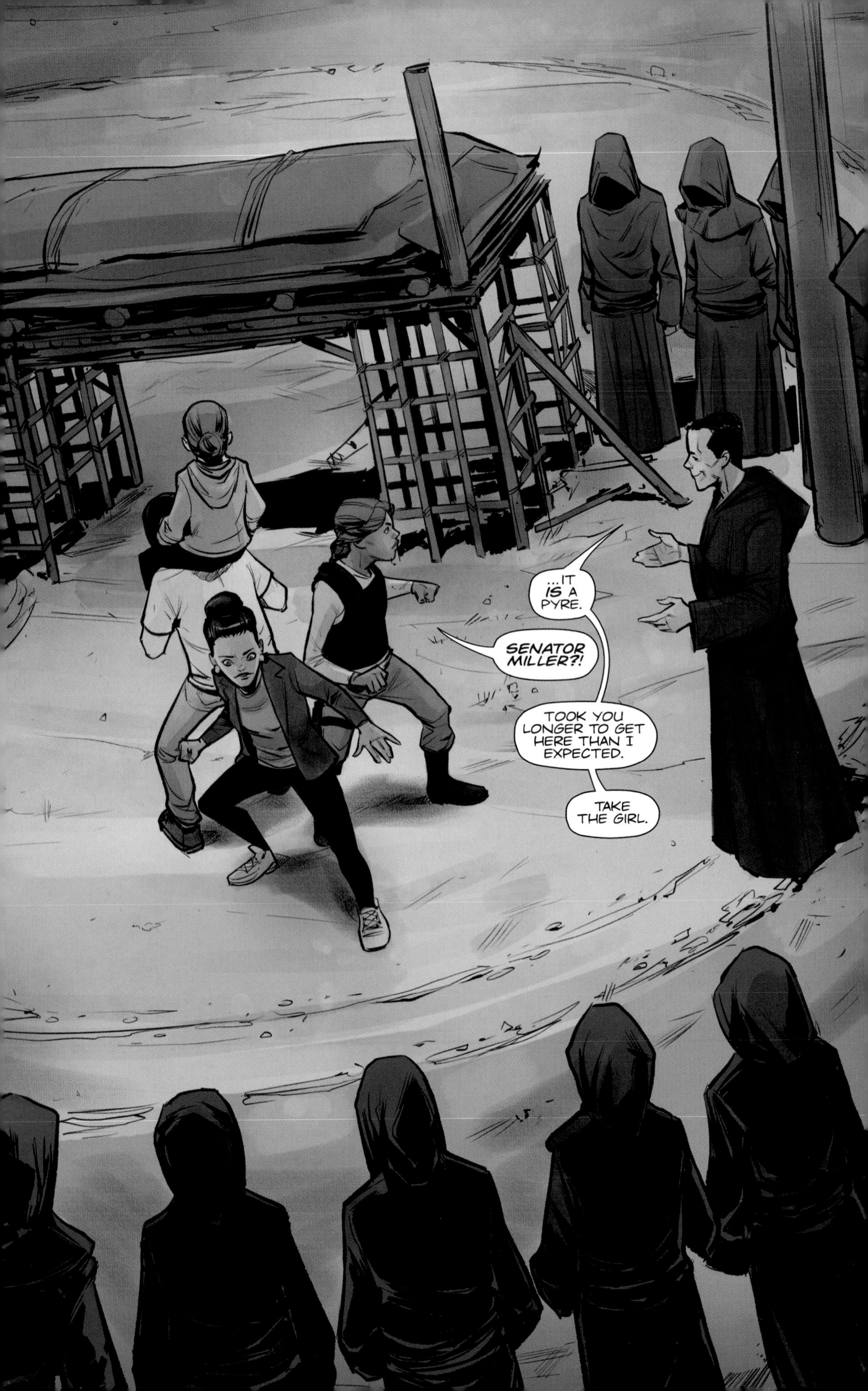
...IT IS A PYRE.
SENATOR MILLER?!
TOOK YOU LONGER TO GET HERE THAN I EXPECTED.
TAKE THE GIRL.

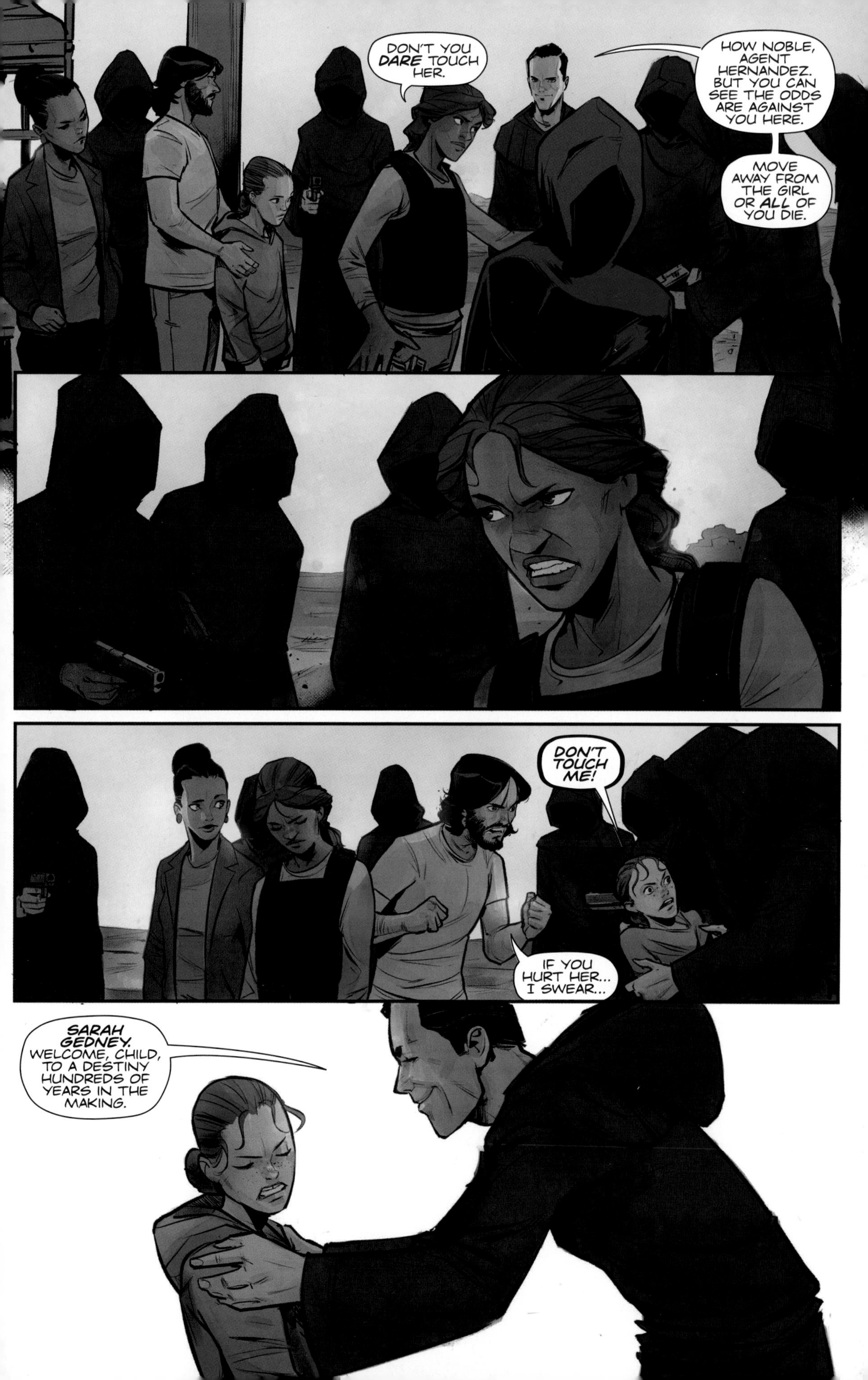
DON'T YOU DARE TOUCH HER.
HOW NOBLE, AGENT HERNANDEZ. BUT YOU CAN SEE THE ODDS ARE AGAINST YOU HERE.
MOVE AWAY FROM THE GIRL OR ALL OF YOU DIE.
DON'T TOUCH ME!
IF YOU HURT HER... I SWEAR...
SARAH GEDNEY. WELCOME, CHILD, TO A DESTINY HUNDREDS OF YEARS IN THE MAKING.

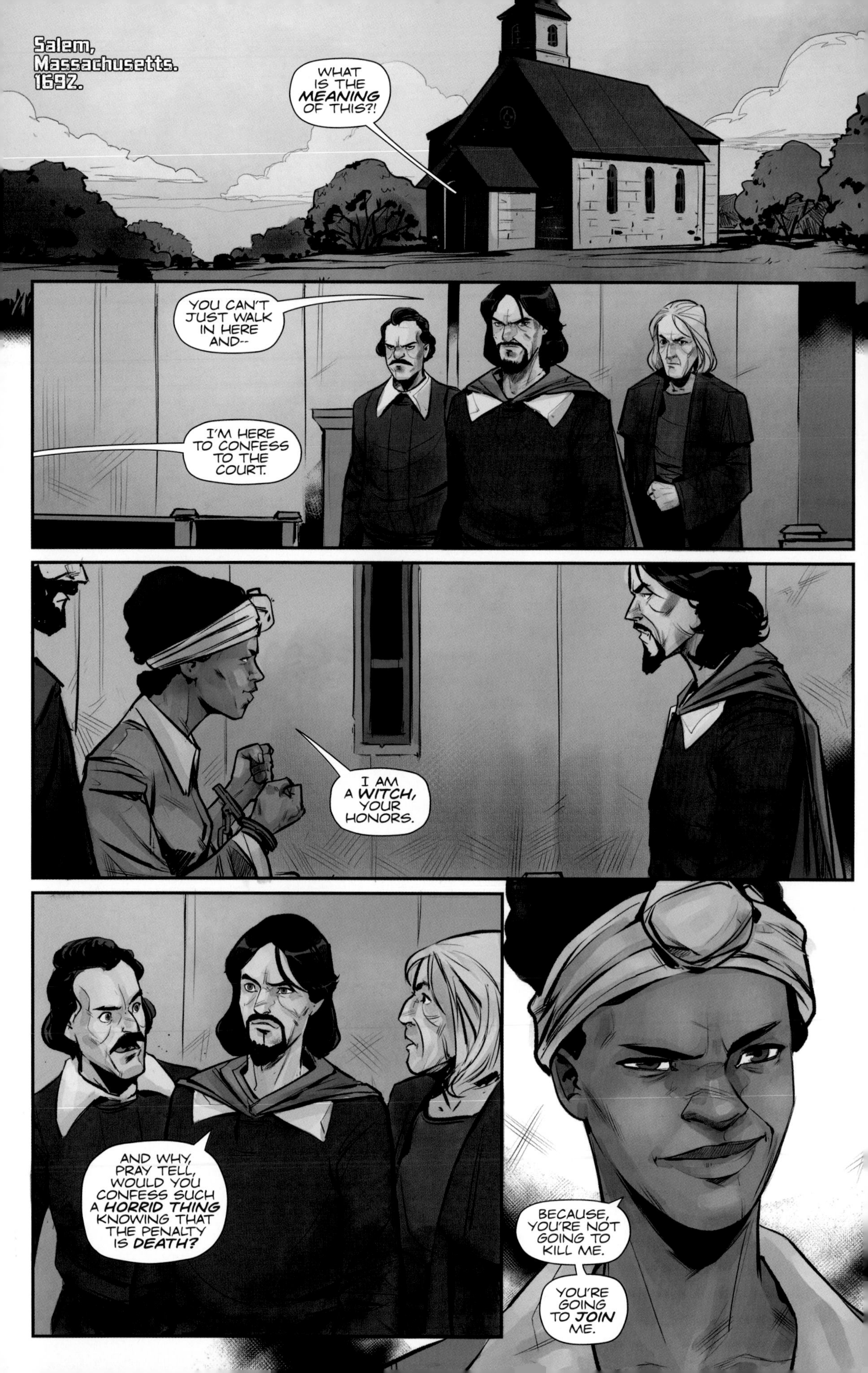
Salem, Massachusetts. 1692.
WHAT IS THE MEANING OF THIS?!
YOU CAN'T JUST WALK IN HERE AND--
I'M HERE TO CONFESS TO THE COURT.
I AM A WITCH, YOUR HONORS.
AND WHY, PRAY TELL, WOULD YOU CONFESS SUCH A HORRID THING KNOWING THAT THE PENALTY IS DEATH?
BECAUSE, YOU'RE NOT GOING TO KILL ME.
YOU'RE GOING TO JOIN ME.

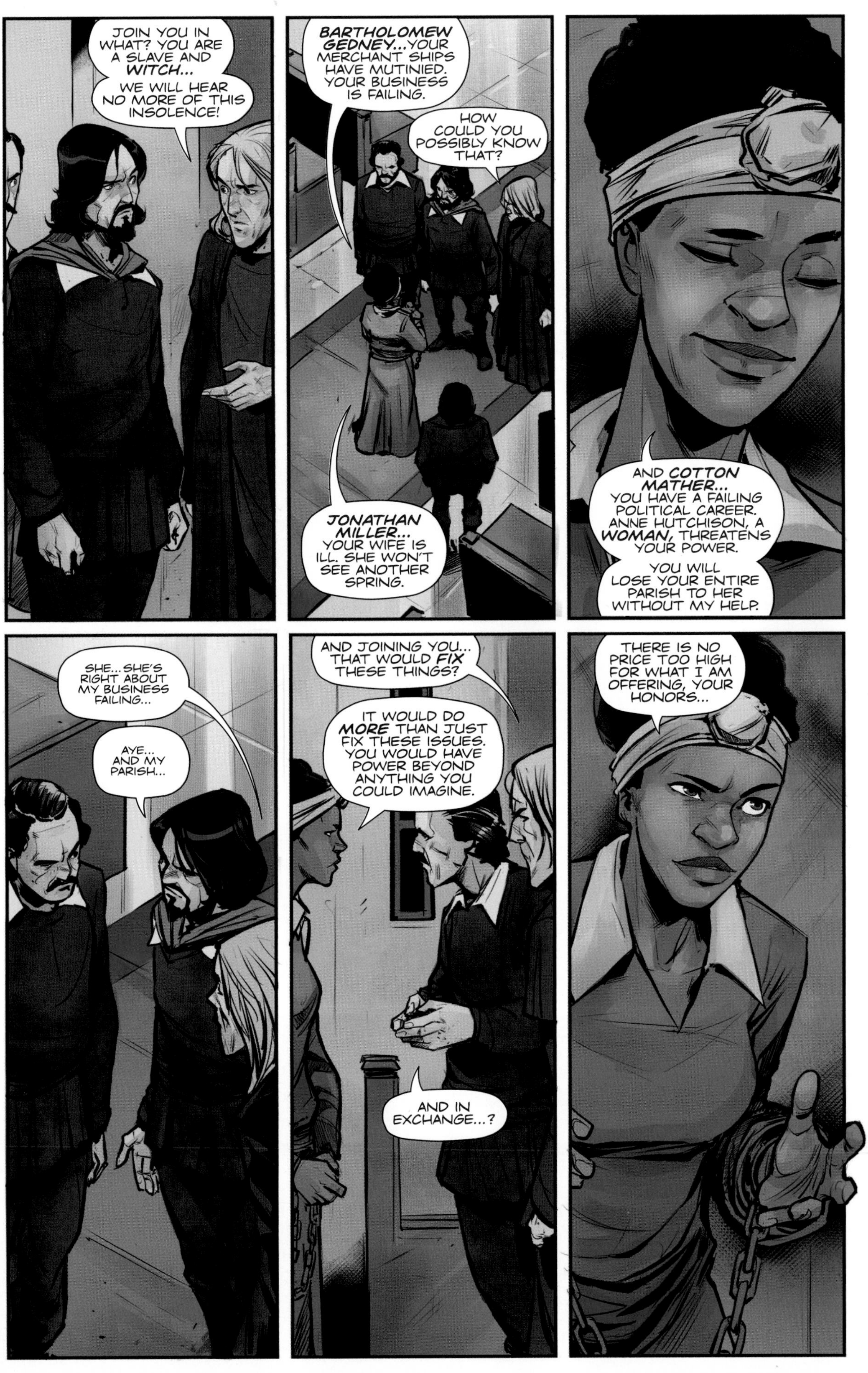

JOIN YOU IN WHAT? YOU ARE A SLAVE AND WITCH...
WE WILL HEAR NO MORE OF THIS INSOLENCE!
BARTHOLOMEW GEDNEY...YOUR MERCHANT SHIPS HAVE MUTINIED. YOUR BUSINESS IS FAILING.
HOW COULD YOU POSSIBLY KNOW THAT?
JONATHAN MILLER... YOUR WIFE IS ILL. SHE WON'T SEE ANOTHER SPRING.
AND COTTON MATHER... YOU HAVE A FAILING POLITICAL CAREER. ANNE HUTCHISON, A WOMAN, THREATENS YOUR POWER.
YOU WILL LOSE YOUR ENTIRE PARISH TO HER WITHOUT MY HELP.
SHE...SHE'S RIGHT ABOUT MY BUSINESS FAILING...
AYE... AND MY PARISH...
AND JOINING YOU... THAT WOULD FIX THESE THINGS?
IT WOULD DO MORE THAN JUST FIX THESE ISSUES. YOU WOULD HAVE POWER BEYOND ANYTHING YOU COULD IMAGINE.
AND IN EXCHANGE...?
THERE IS NO PRICE TOO HIGH FOR WHAT I AM OFFERING, YOUR HONORS...

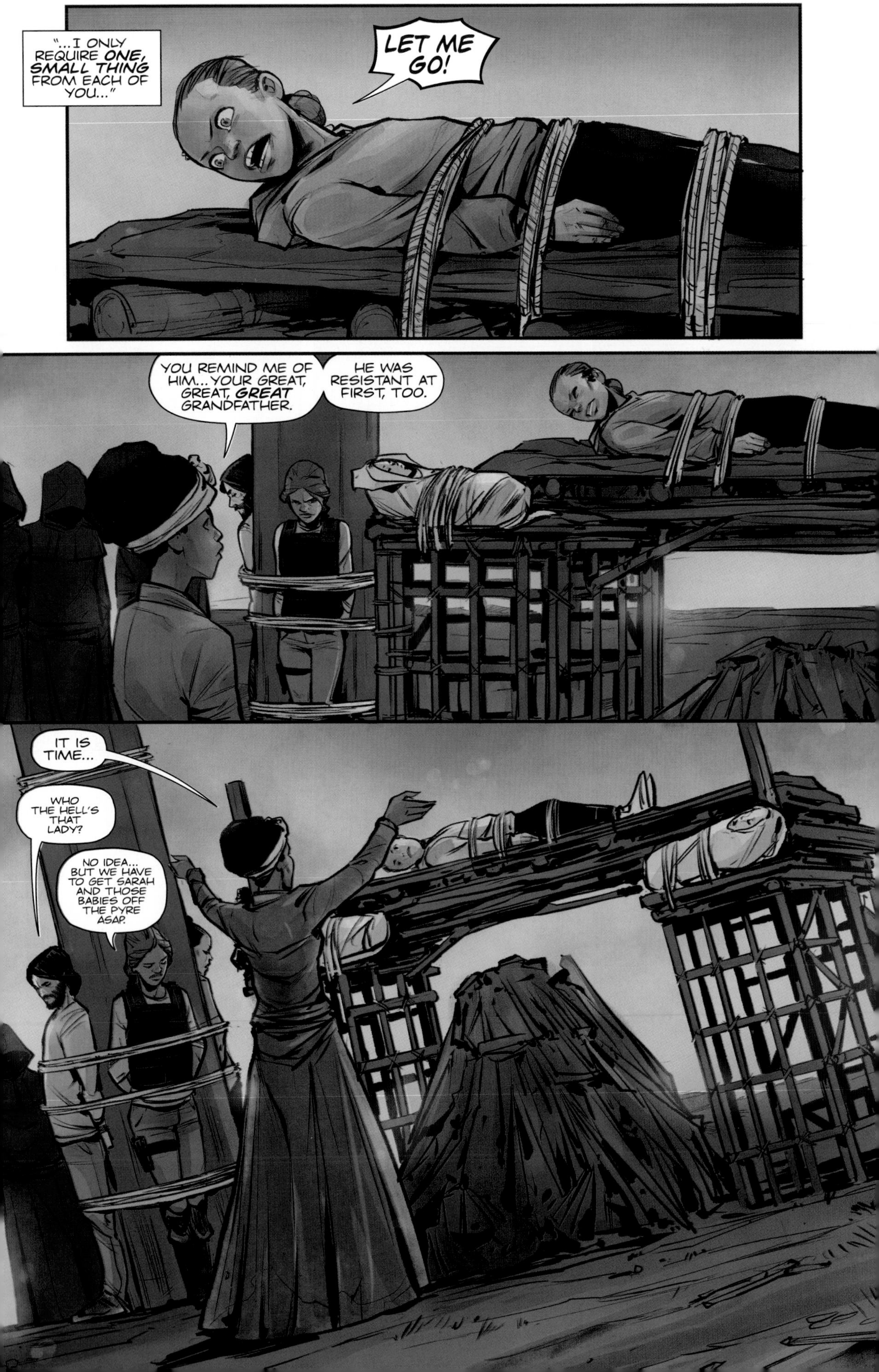
"...I ONLY REQUIRE ONE, SMALL THING FROM EACH OF YOU..."
LET ME GO!
YOU REMIND ME OF HIM... YOUR GREAT, GREAT, GREAT GRANDFATHER.
HE WAS RESISTANT AT FIRST, TOO.
IT IS TIME...
WHO THE HELL'S THAT LADY?
NO IDEA... BUT WE HAVE TO GET SARAH AND THOSE BABIES OFF THE PYRE ASAP.

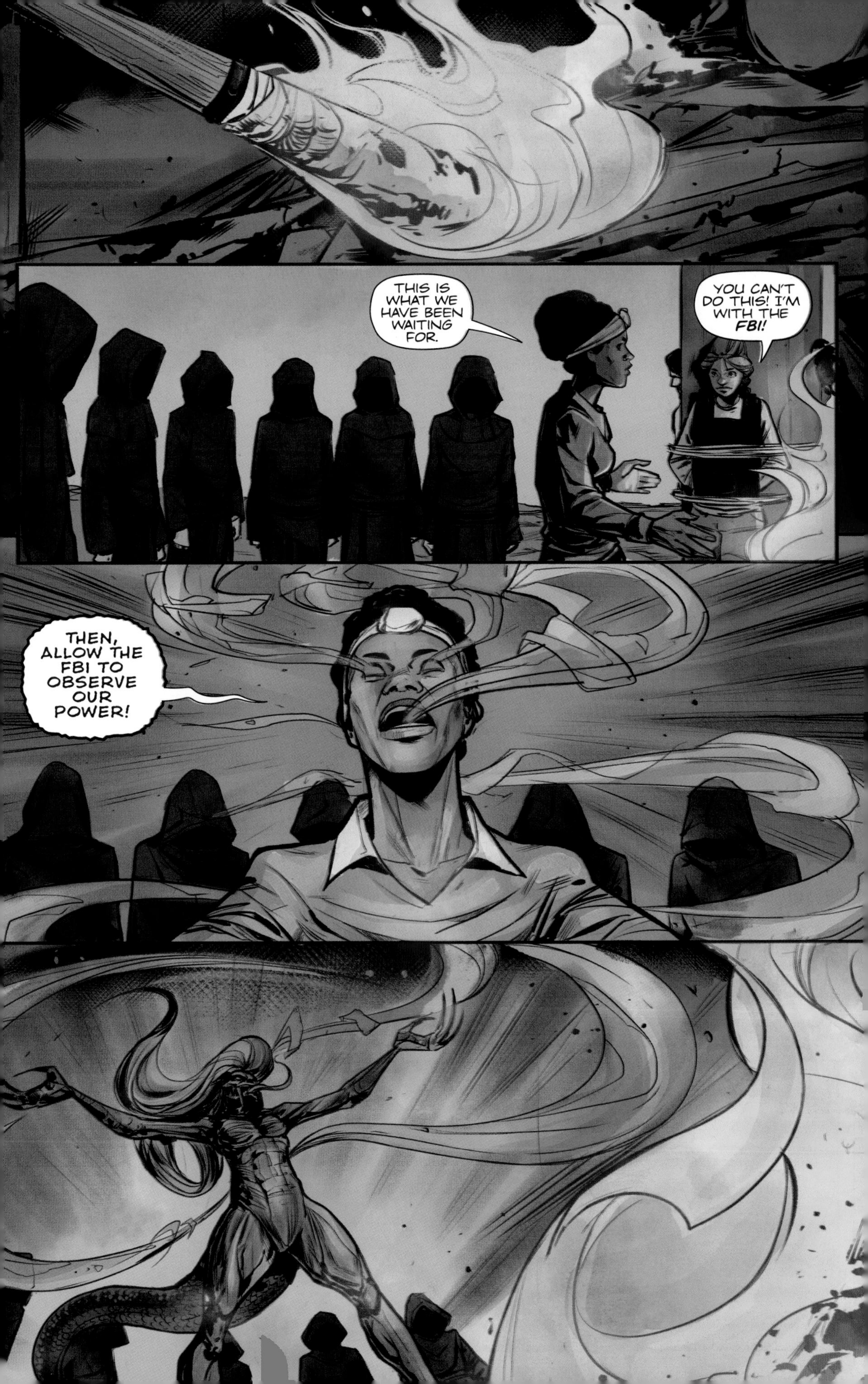
THIS IS WHAT WE HAVE BEEN WAITING FOR.
YOU CAN'T DO THIS! I'M WITH THE FBI!
THEN, ALLOW THE FBI TO OBSERVE OUR POWER!

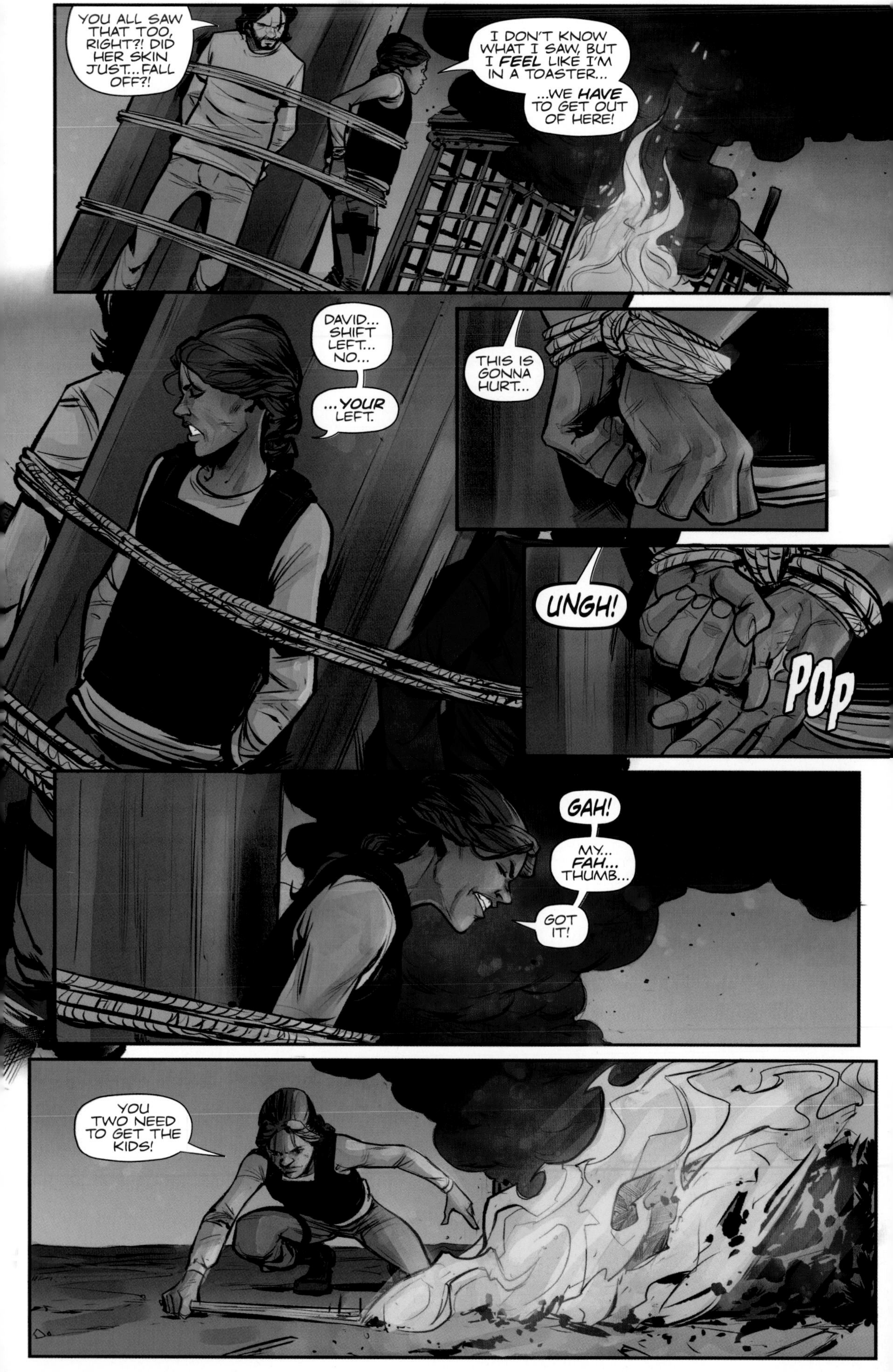
YOU ALL SAW THAT TOO, RIGHT?! DID HER SKIN JUST...FALL OFF?!
I DON'T KNOW WHAT I SAW, BUT I FEEL LIKE I'M IN A TOASTER...
...WE HAVE TO GET OUT OF HERE!
DAVID... SHIFT LEFT... NO...
...YOUR LEFT.
THIS IS GONNA HURT...
UNGH!
POP
GAH!
MY... FAH... THUMB...
GOT IT!
YOU TWO NEED TO GET THE KIDS!

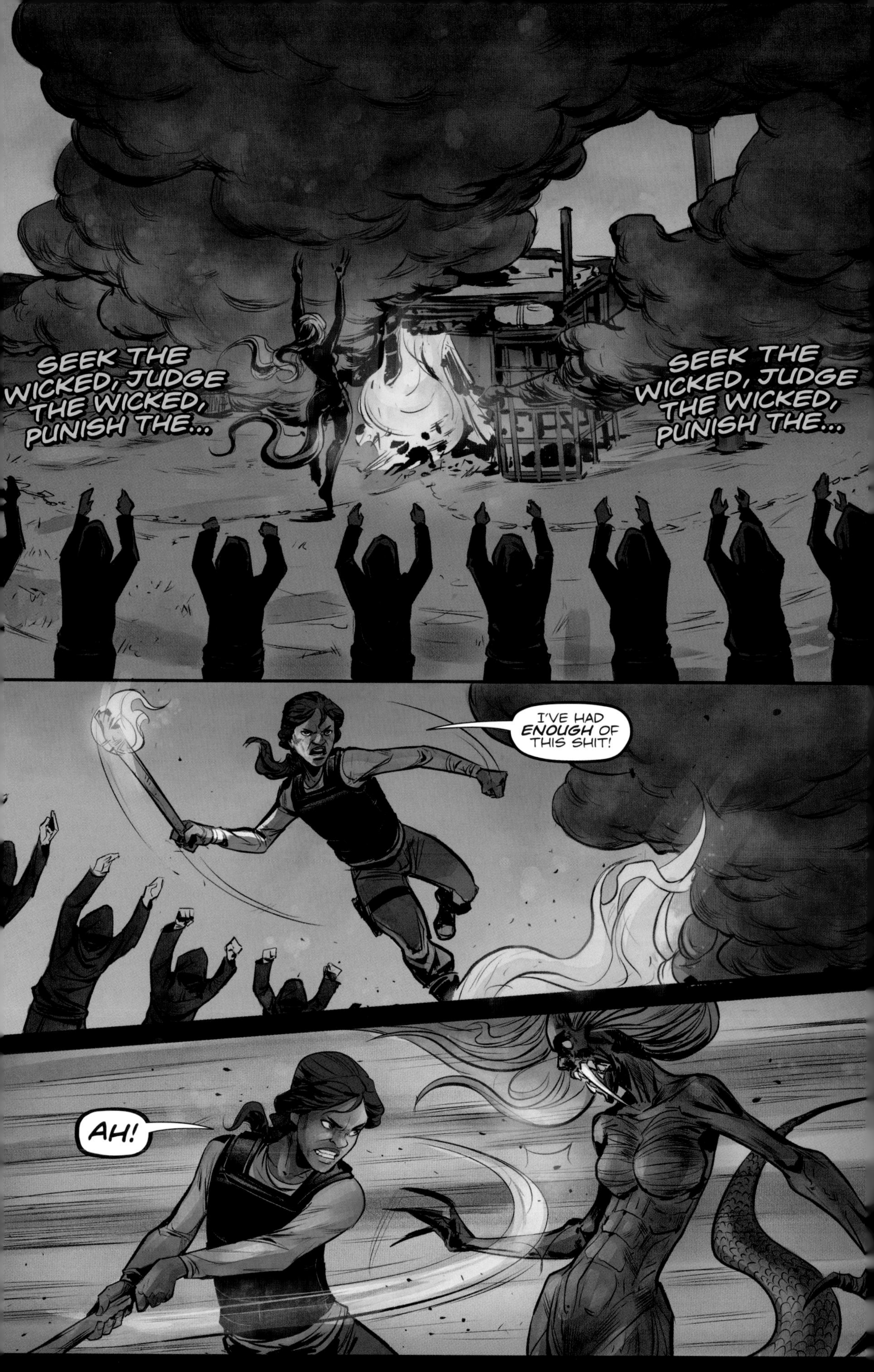
SEEK THE WICKED, JUDGE THE WICKED, PUNISH THE...
SEEK THE WICKED, JUDGE THE WICKED, PUNISH THE...
I'VE HAD ENOUGH OF THIS SHIT!
AH!

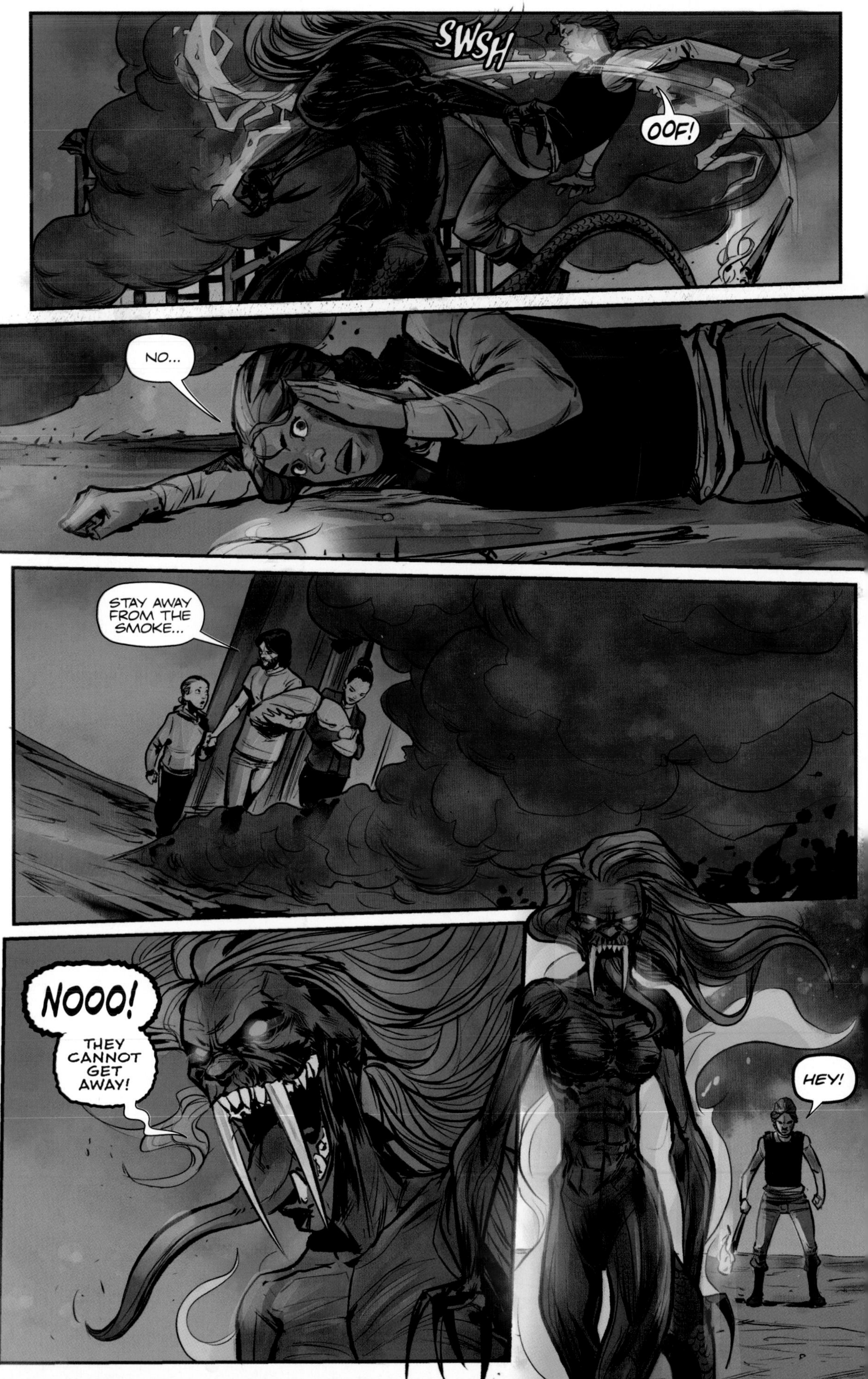
SWSH
OOF!
NO...
STAY AWAY FROM THE SMOKE...
NOOO!
THEY CANNOT GET AWAY!
HEY!

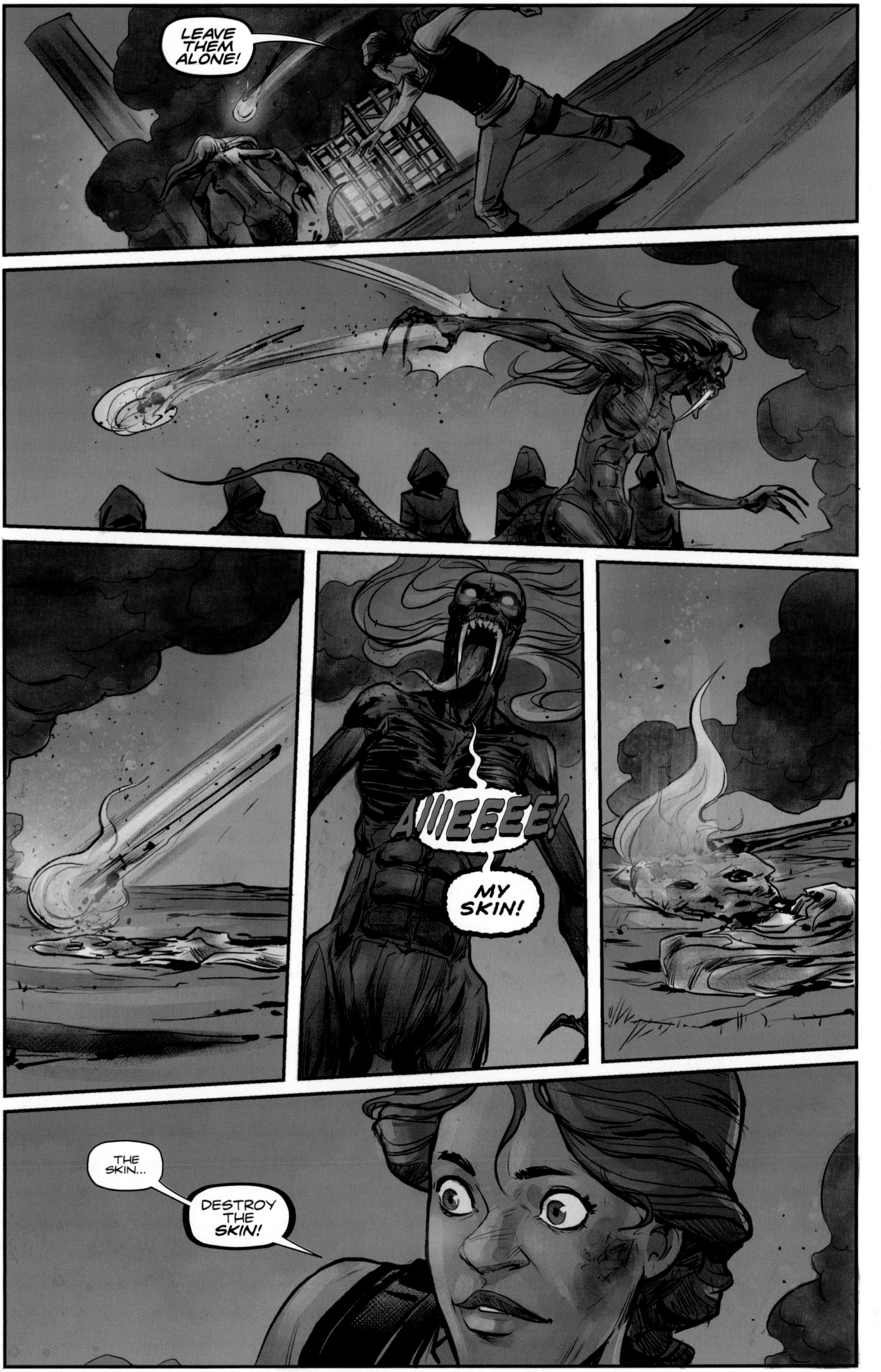
LEAVE THEM ALONE!
AIIIEEEEE!
MY SKIN!
THE SKIN...
DESTROY THE SKIN!

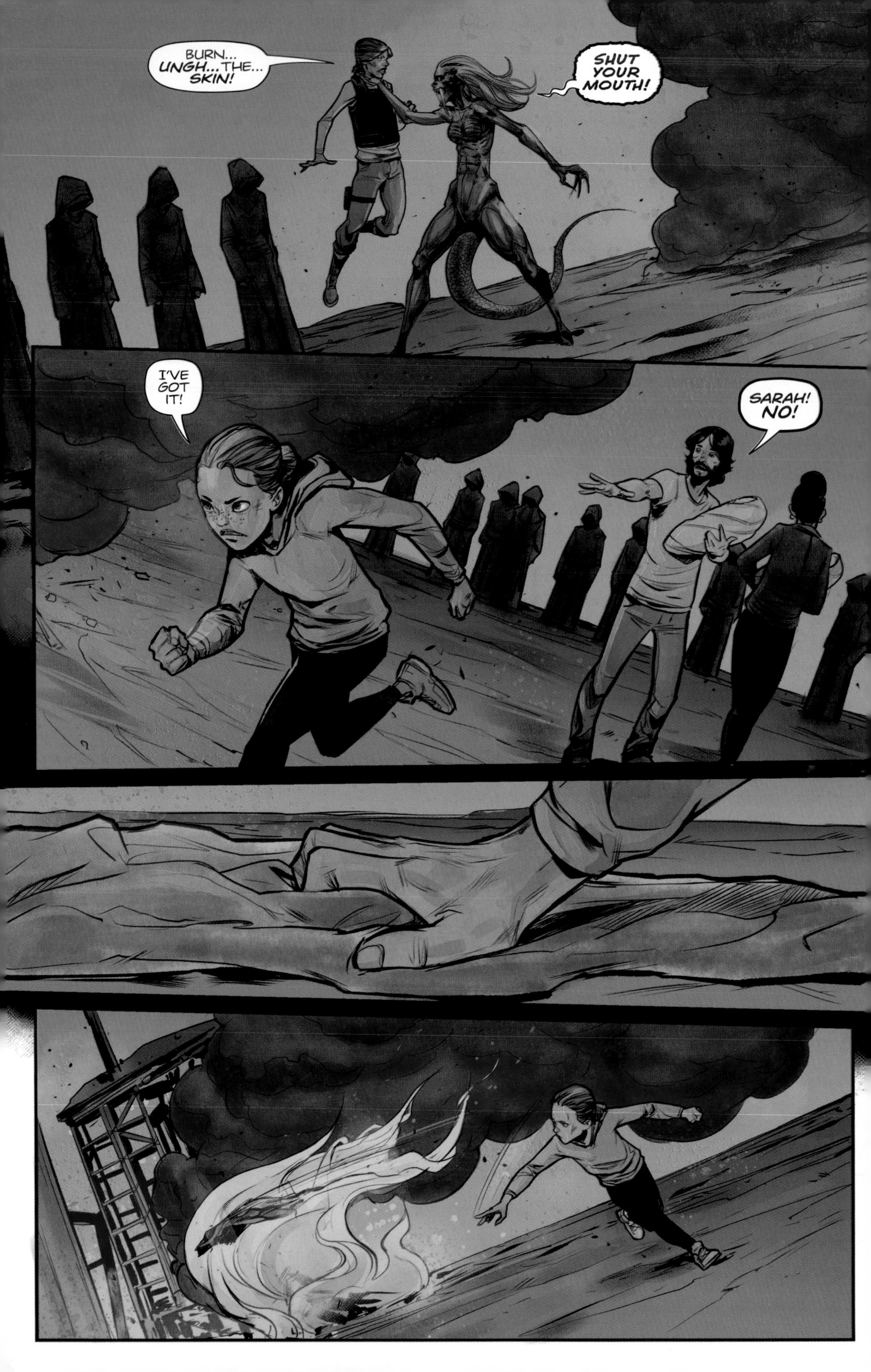
BURN... UNGH... THE... SKIN!
SHUT YOUR MOUTH!
I'VE GOT IT!
SARAH! NO!

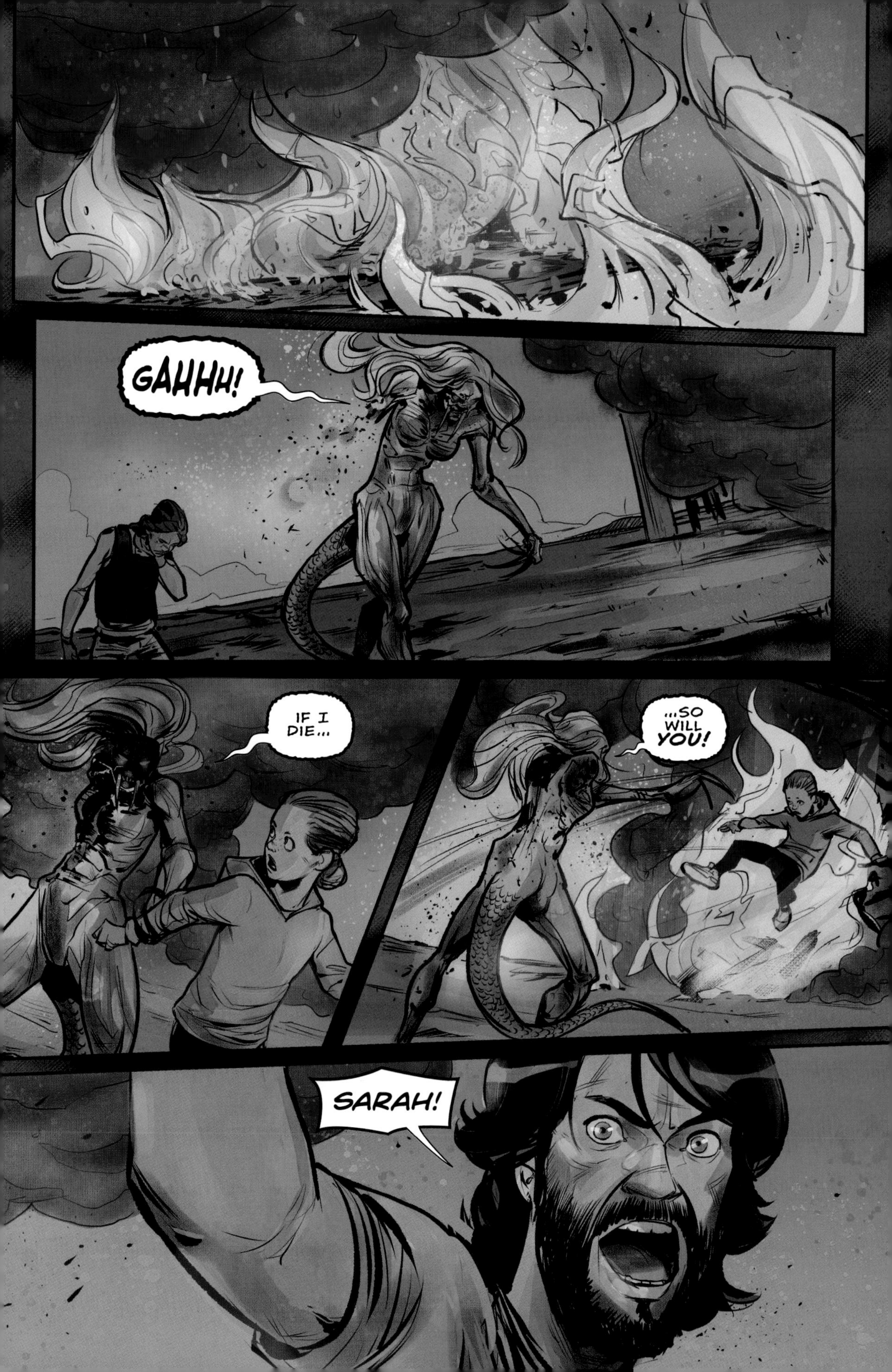
GAHHH!
IF I DIE...
...SO WILL YOU!
SARAH!

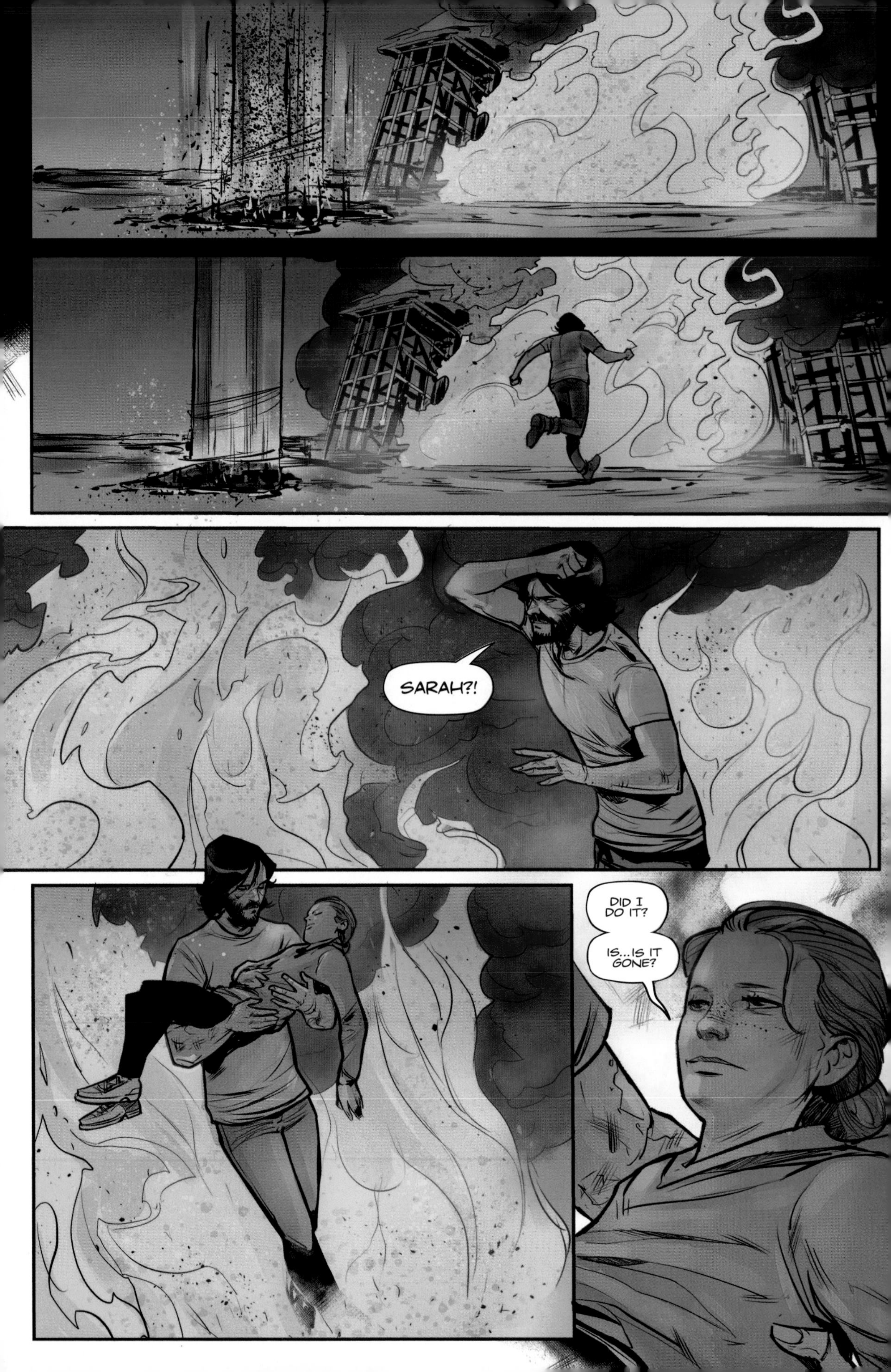
SARAH?!
DID I DO IT?
IS...IS IT GONE?

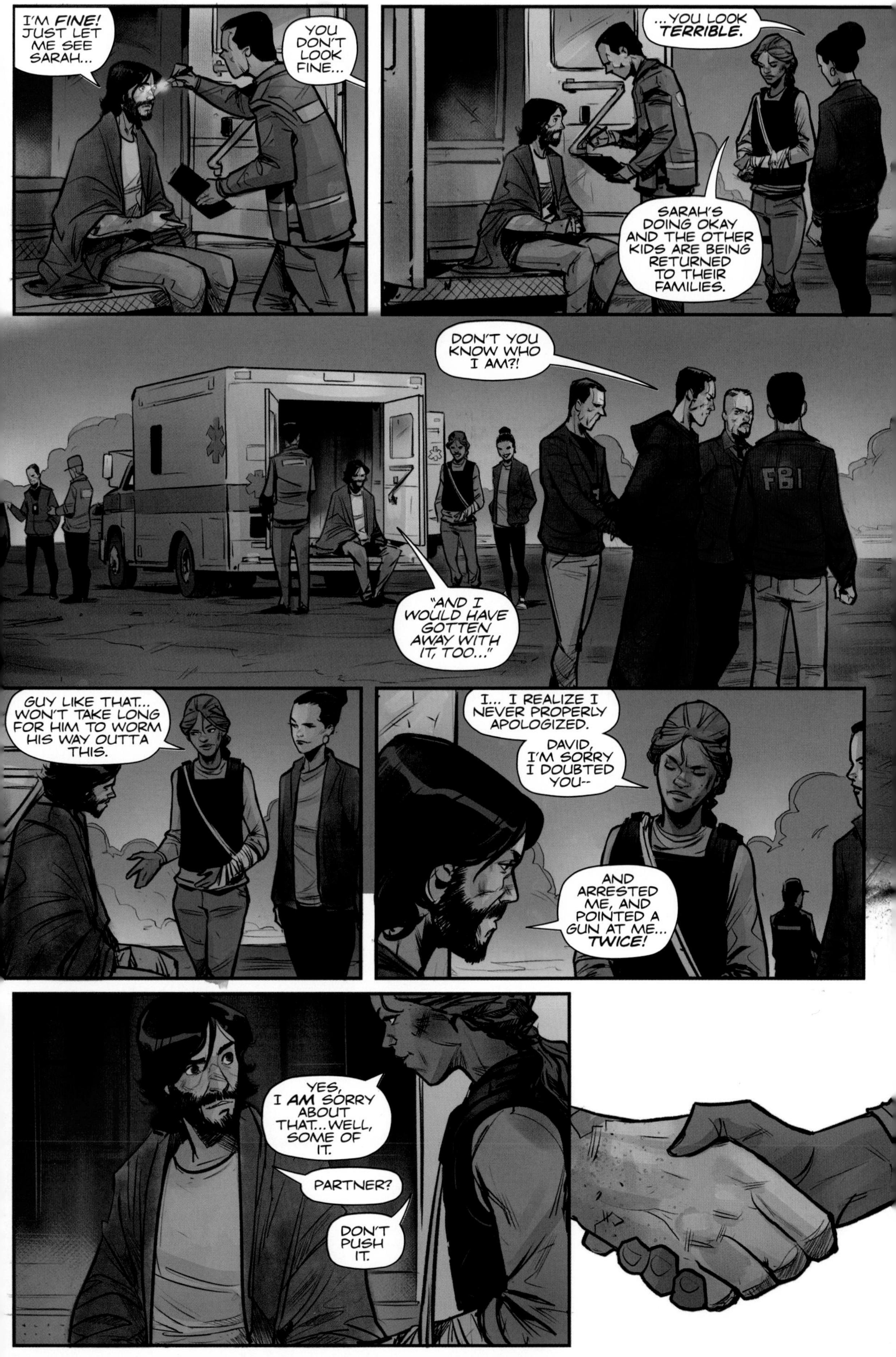
I'M FINE! JUST LET ME SEE SARAH...
YOU DON'T LOOK FINE...
...YOU LOOK TERRIBLE.
SARAH'S DOING OKAY AND THE OTHER KIDS ARE BEING RETURNED TO THEIR FAMILIES.
DON'T YOU KNOW WHO I AM?!
"AND I WOULD HAVE GOTTEN AWAY WITH IT, TOO..."
GUY LIKE THAT... WON'T TAKE LONG FOR HIM TO WORM HIS WAY OUTTA THIS.
I... I REALIZE I NEVER PROPERLY APOLOGIZED.
DAVID, I'M SORRY I DOUBTED YOU--
AND ARRESTED ME, AND POINTED A GUN AT ME... TWICE!
FBI
YES, I AM SORRY ABOUT THAT...WELL, SOME OF IT.
PARTNER?
DON'T PUSH IT.

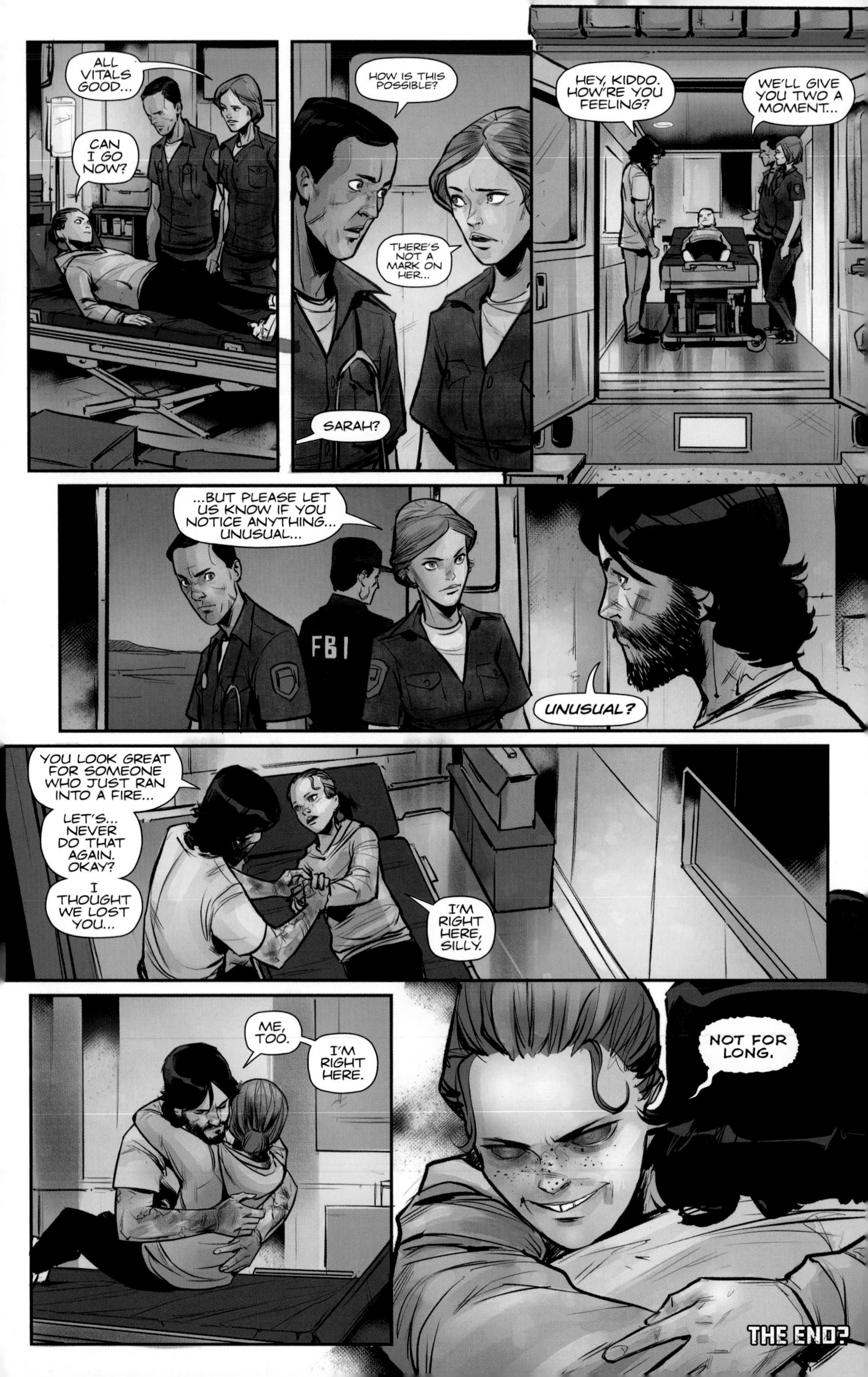
ALL VITALS GOOD...
CAN I GO NOW?
HOW IS THIS POSSIBLE?
THERE'S NOT A MARK ON HER...
SARAH?
HEY, KIDDO. HOW'RE YOU FEELING?
WE'LL GIVE YOU TWO A MOMENT...
...BUT PLEASE LET US KNOW IF YOU NOTICE ANYTHING... UNUSUAL...
FBI
UNUSUAL?
YOU LOOK GREAT FOR SOMEONE WHO JUST RAN INTO A FIRE...
LET'S... NEVER DO THAT AGAIN. OKAY?
I THOUGHT WE LOST YOU...
I'M RIGHT HERE, SILLY.
ME, TOO.
I'M RIGHT HERE.
NOT FOR LONG.
THE END?

DESCENDENT™

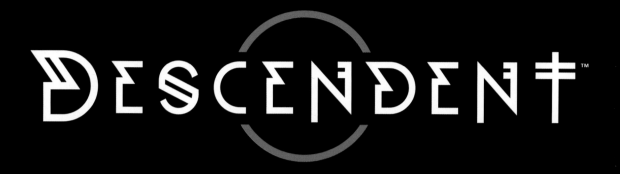

BEHIND THE SCENES

Issue 1
ANDREI BRESSAN
variant cover

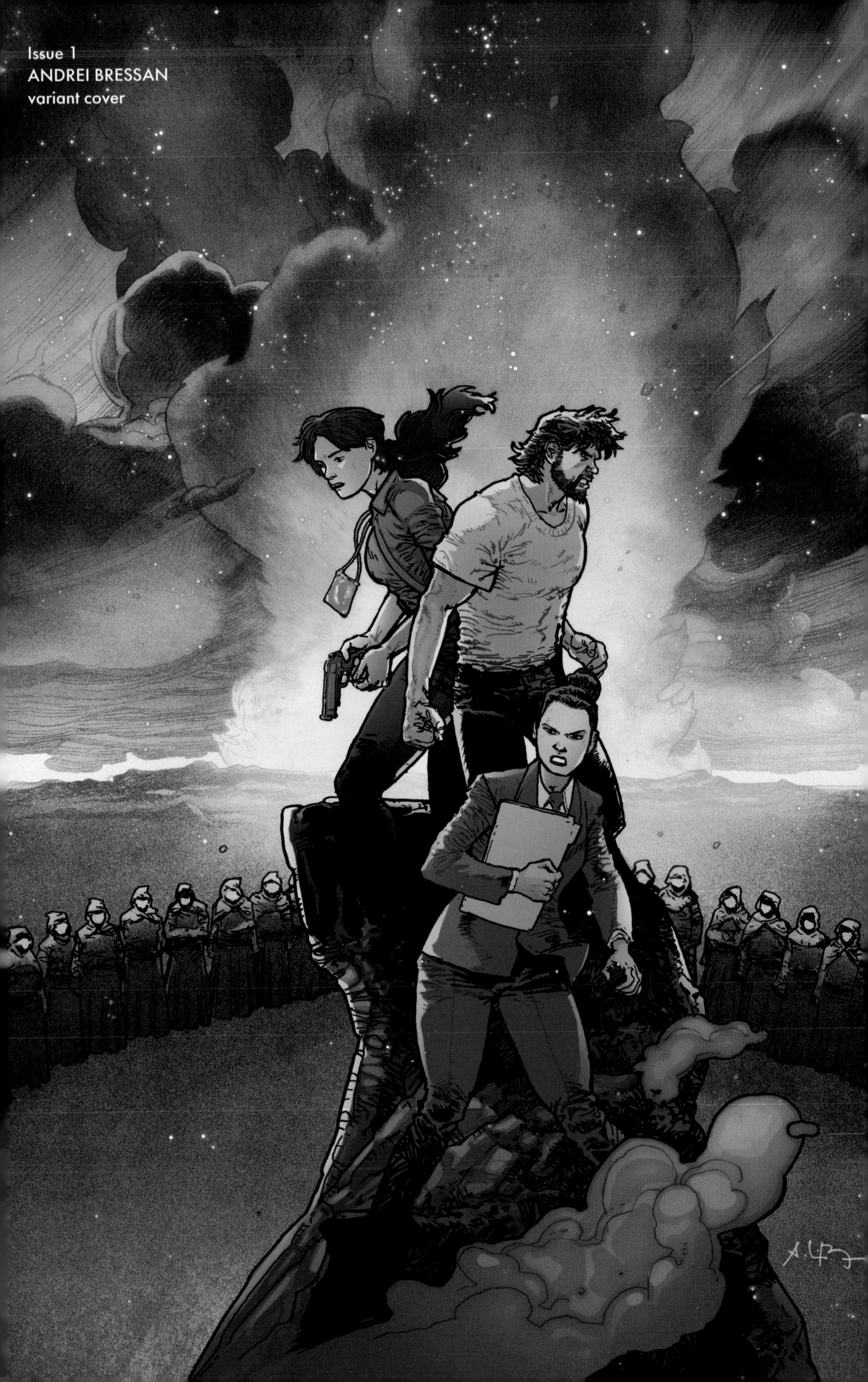

Issue 1
ANDREI BRESSAN
virgin variant cover

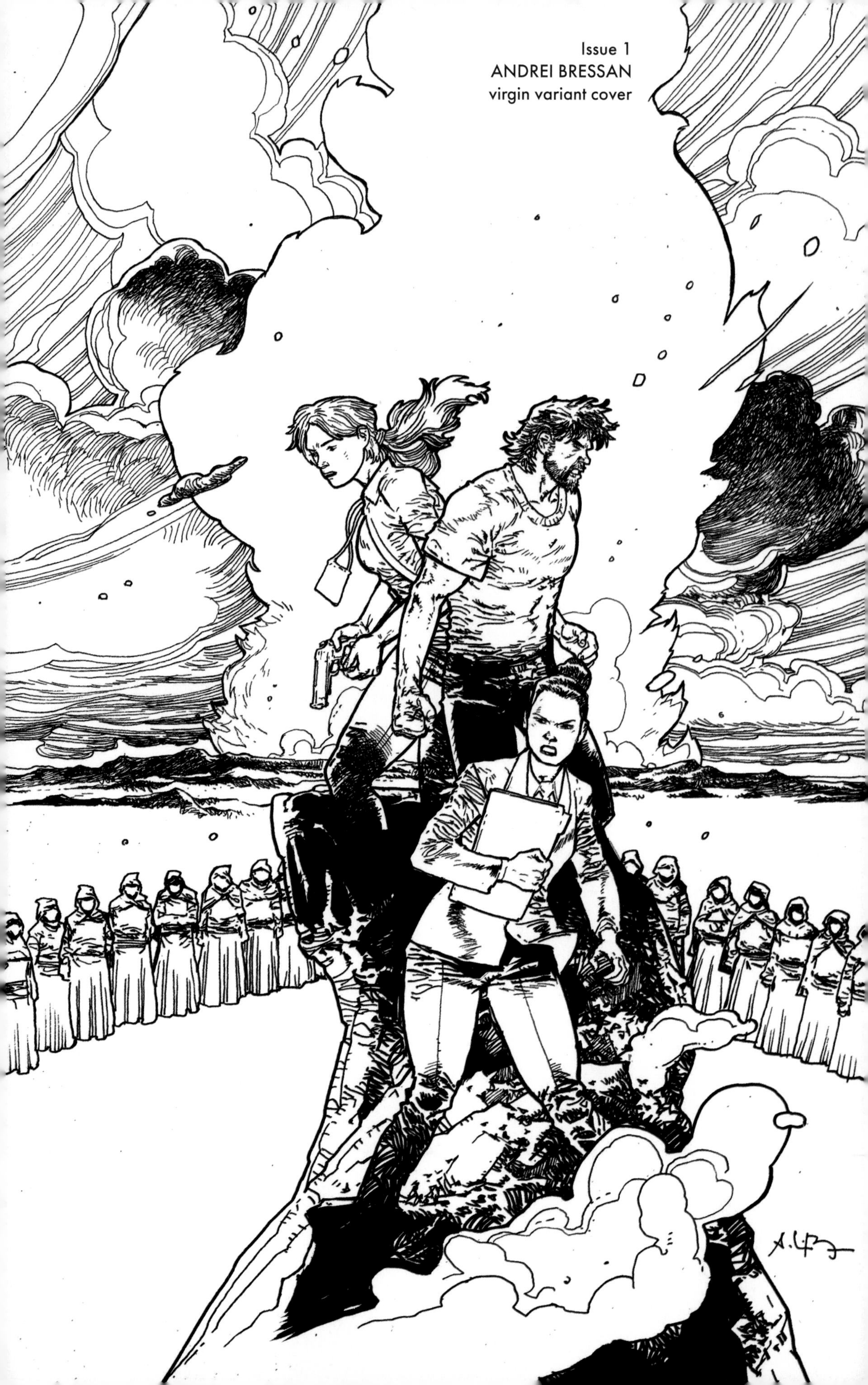

DESCENDENT™

#1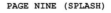

script by
STEPHANIE PHILLIPS

PAGE NINE (SPLASH)

Full-page splash shows DAVID (revealed) on his knees with security forces surrounding him and pointing guns at him. The TRUCK is crashed against a pole behind David. The scene is a bit chaotic as DAVID is about to be arrested. David looks a bit nonchalant as he has his hands behind his head. Perhaps a slight grin on his face.

1 Soldier: On the ground! Hands in the air!

David is our main character, so his look is something I am definitely open to discussing. I have this image of a less good-looking Jeffrey Dean Morgan in my head. I am thinking about 40-45 years old with the shaggy hair, salt and pepper beard. He is not particularly neat, so jeans, t-shirt, and sneakers are a fine look.

layouts by
EVGENIY BORNYAKOV

pencils & inks by
EVGENIY BORNYAKOV

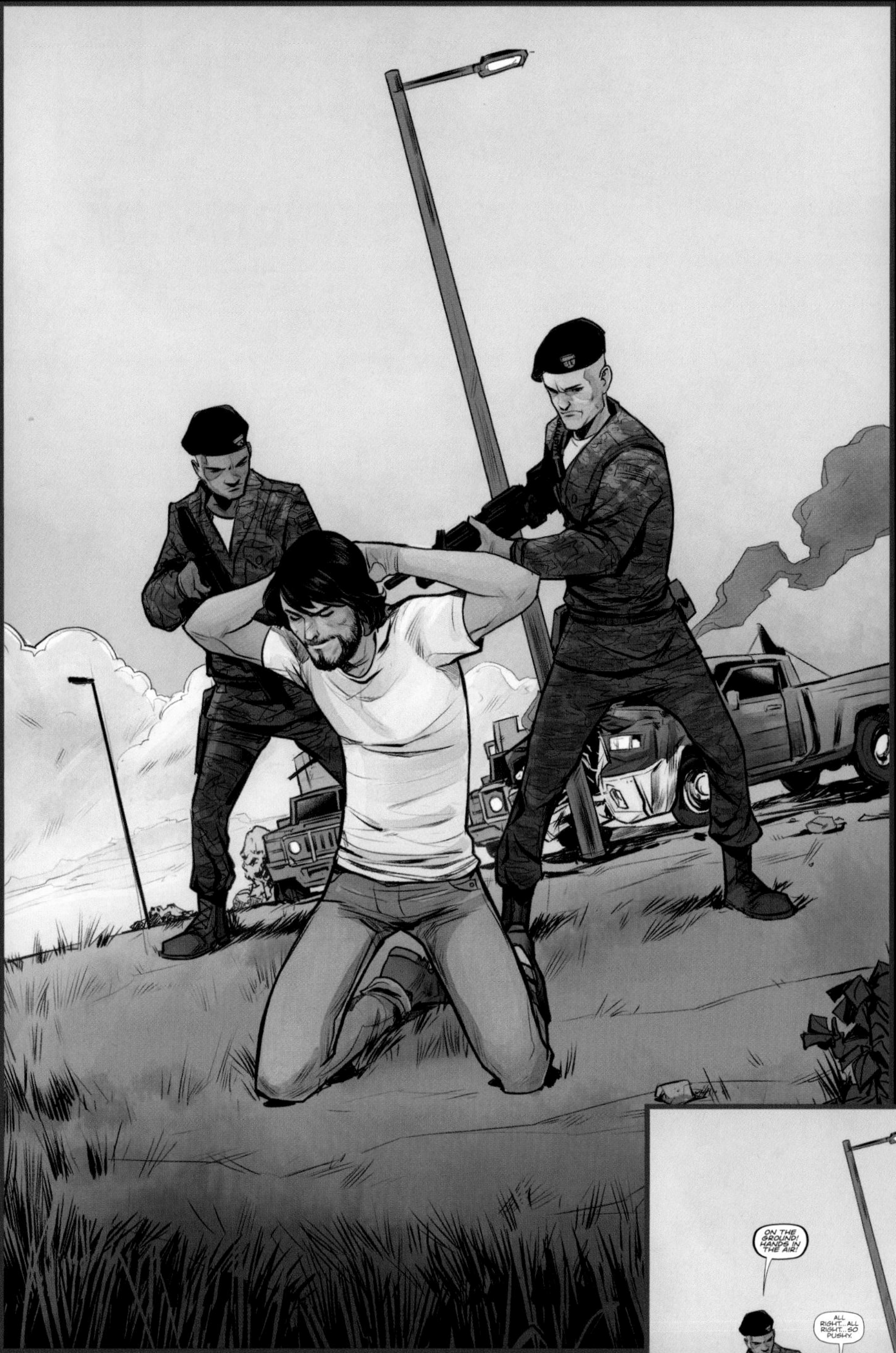

colors by

LAUREN AFFE

PAGE 09 PROCESS

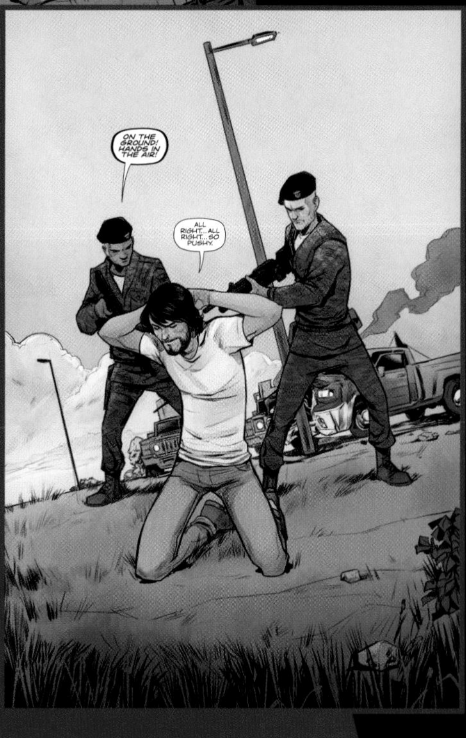

ON THE GROUND! HANDS IN THE AIR!
ALL RIGHT...ALL RIGHT...SO PUSHY.

lettering by

TROY PETERI

DESCENDENT™

sketchbook

art by EVGENIY BORNYAKOV

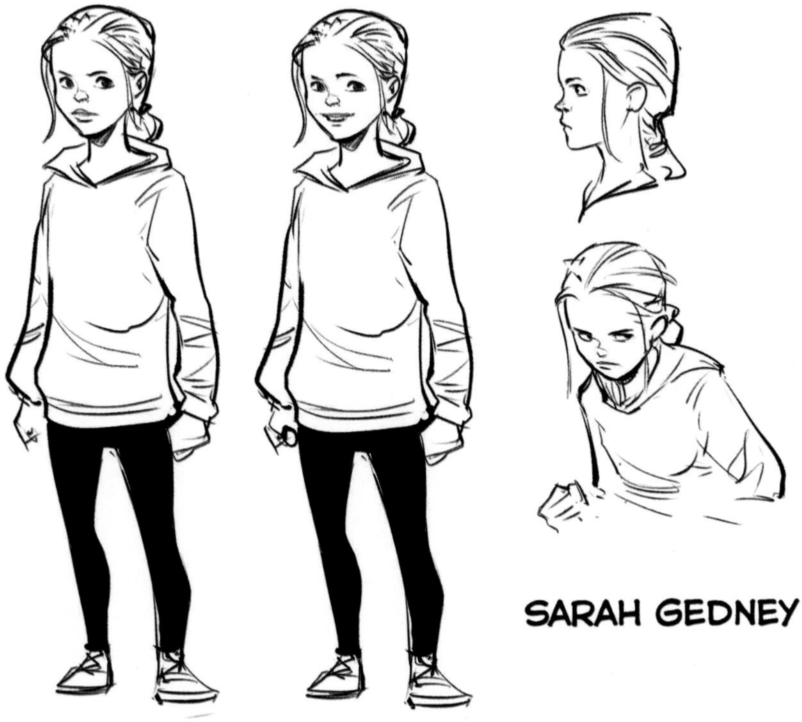
SARAH GEDNEY

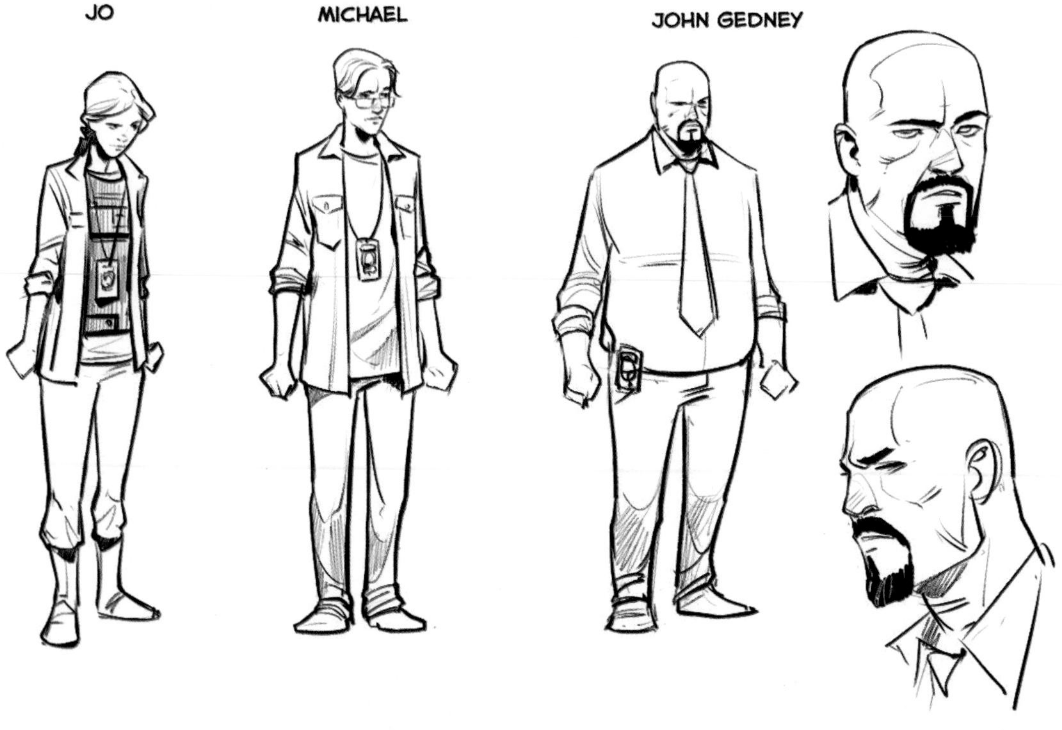
JO
MICHAEL
JOHN GEDNEY

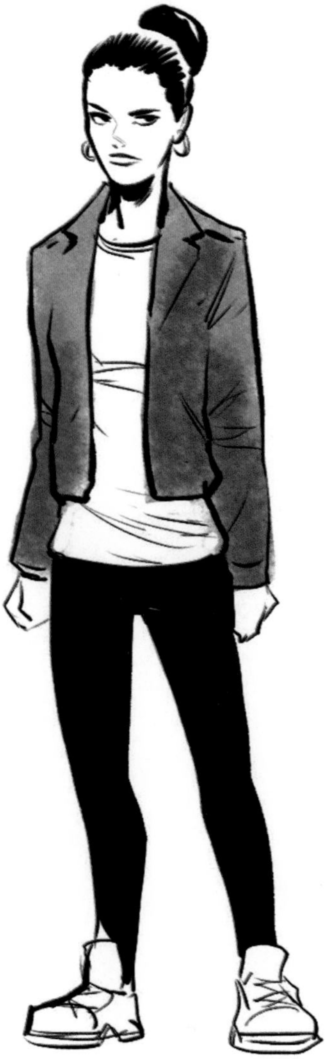

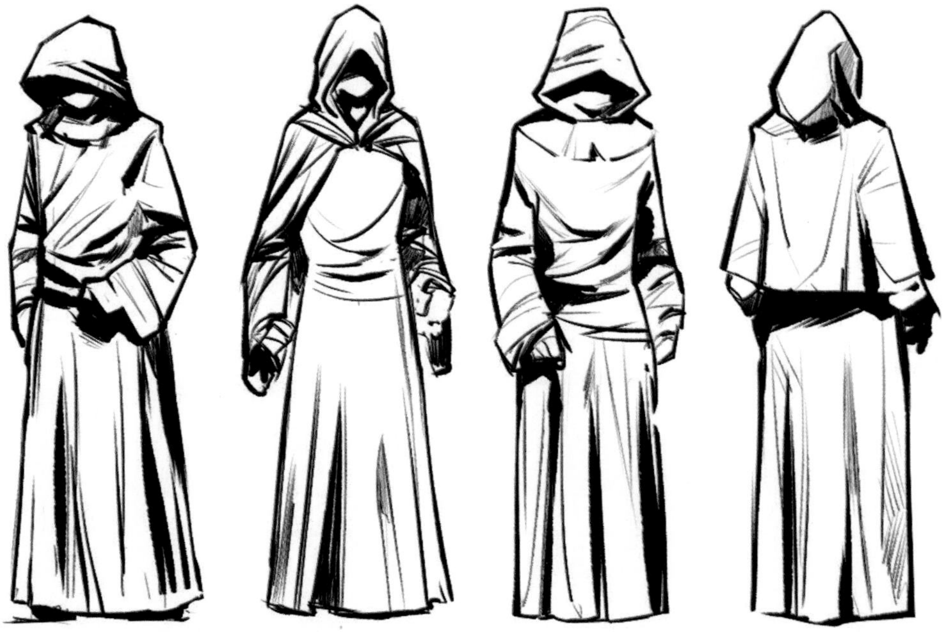

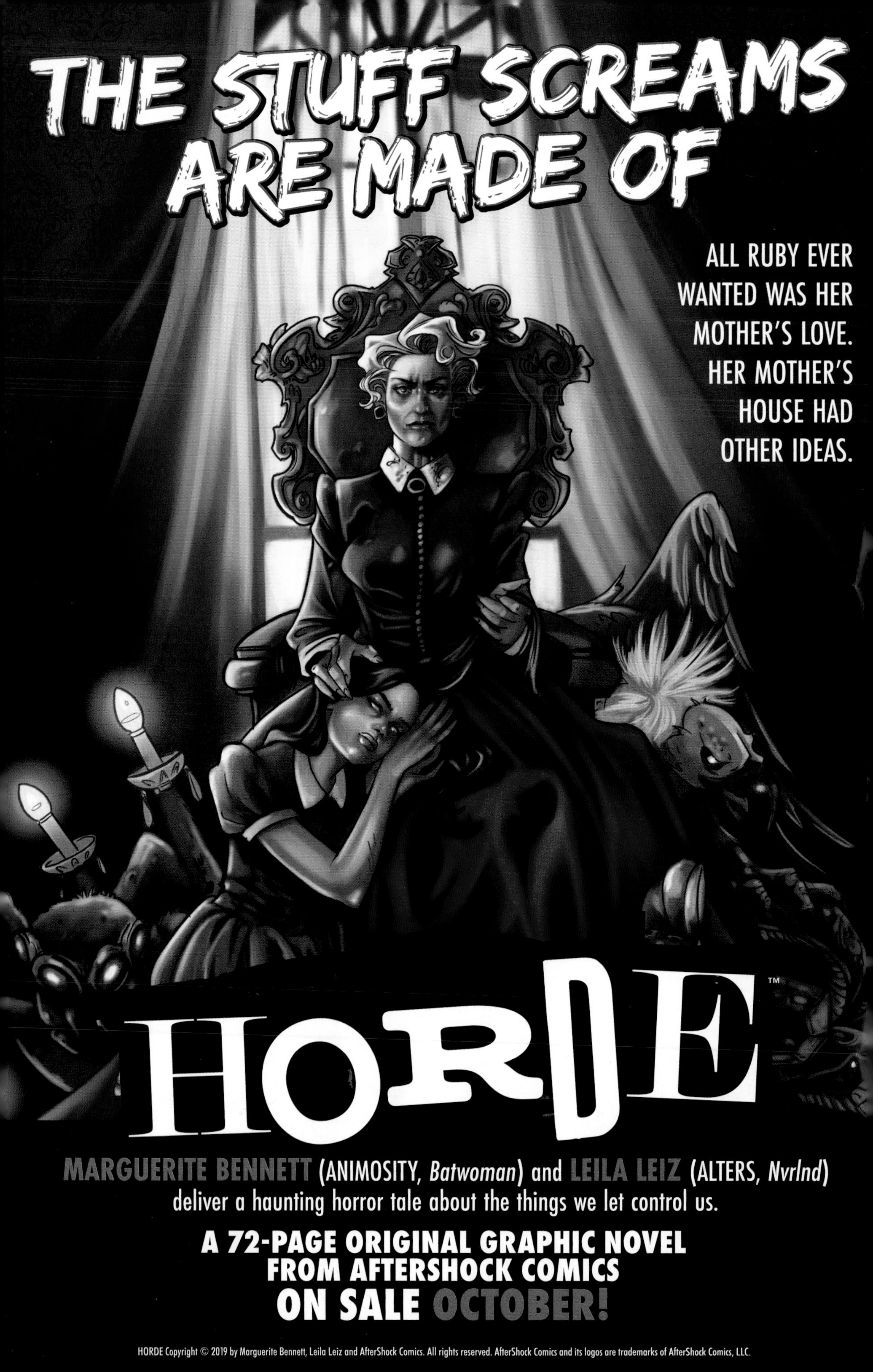

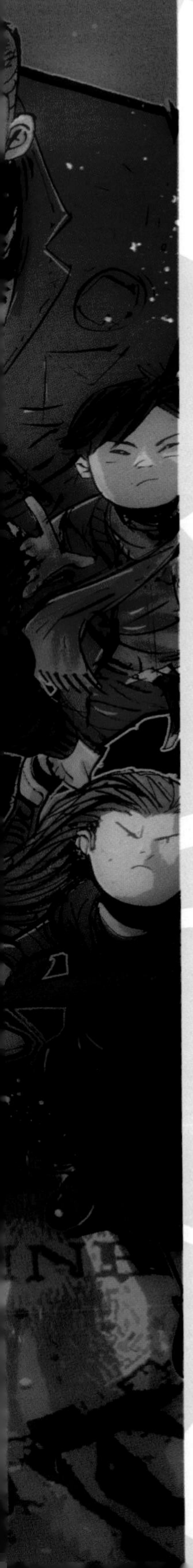

STOCK UP ON THESE GREAT AFTERSHOCK COLLECTIONS!

A WALK THROUGH HELL VOL 1
GARTH ENNIS / GORAN SUDZUKA
SEP181388

ALTERS VOL 1 & VOL 2
PAUL JENKINS / LEILA LEIZ
MAR171244 & APR181239

AMERICAN MONSTER VOL 1
BRIAN AZZARELLO / JUAN DOE
SEP161213

ANIMOSITY YEAR ONE, VOL 1, VOL 2, VOL 3 & VOL 4
MARGUERITE BENNETT / RAFAEL DE LATORRE
FEB181034, JAN171219, AUG171130, MAY181314 & FEB191349

ANIMOSITY: EVOLUTION VOL 1 & VOL 2
MARGUERITE BENNETT / ERIC GAPSTUR
MAR181079 & FEB188089

ANIMOSITY: THE RISE HARDCOVER
MARGUERITE BENNETT / JUAN DOE
AUG178324

ART OF JIM STARLIN HARDCOVER
JIM STARLIN
MAR181077

BABYTEETH YEAR ONE, VOL 1 & VOL 2
DONNY CATES / GARRY BROWN
OCT181328, OCT171087 & APR181225

BETROTHED VOL 1
SEAN LEWIS / STEVE UY
DEC181449161115

BEYONDERS VOL 1
PAUL JENKINS / WESLEY ST. CLAIRE
JAN191468

BLACK-EYED KIDS VOL 1, VOL 2 & VOL 3
JOE PRUETT / SZYMON KUDRANSKI
AUG161115, FEB171100 & JAN181152

BROTHERS DRACUL VOL 1
CULLEN BUNN / MIRKO COLAK
SEP181404

CAPTAIN KID VOL 1
MARK WAID / TOM PEYER / WILFREDO TORRES
APR171231

CLAN KILLERS VOL 1
SEAN LEWIS / ANTONIO FUSO
JAN191469

COLD WAR VOL 1
CHRISTOPHER SEBELA / HAYDEN SHERMAN
JUL181518

DARK ARK VOL 1 & VOL 2
CULLEN BUNN / JUAN DOE
FEB181035 & SEP181394

DREAMING EAGLES HARDCOVER
GARTH ENNIS / SIMON COLEBY
AUG161114

ELEANOR & THE EGRET VOL 1
JOHN LAYMAN / SAM KEITH
DEC171041

FU JITSU VOL 1
JAI NITZ / WESLEY ST. CLAIRE
APR181241

HER INFERNAL DESCENT VOL 1
LONNIE NADLER / ZAC THOMPSON / KYLE CHARLES / EOIN MARRON
OCT181341

HOT LUNCH SPECIAL VOl 1
ELIOT RAHAL / JORGE FORNES
DEC181449

INSEXTS YEAR ONE, VOL 1 & VOL 2
MARGUERITE BENNETT / ARIELA KRISTANTINA
APR181228, JUN161072 & SEP171098

JIMMY'S BASTARDS VOL & VOL 2
GARTH ENNIS / RUSS BRAUN
DEC171040 & JUN181333

LOST CITY EXPLORERS VOL 1
ZACHARY KAPLAN / ALVARO SARRASECA
NOV181434

MONSTRO MECHANICA VOL 1
PAUL ALLOR / CHRIS EVENHUIS
JUL181517

MOTH & WHISPER VOL 1
TED ANDERSON / JEN HICKMAN
FEB191351

NORMALS VOL 1
ADAM GLASS / DENNIS CALERO
SEP181391

OUT OF THE BLUE VOL 1 & VOL 2
GARTH ENNIS / KEITH BURNS
JAN191460 & MAY191310

PATIENCE! CONVICTION! REVENGE! VOL 1
PATRICK KINDLON / MARCO FERRARI
FEB191350

PESTILENCE VOL 1 & VOL 2
FRANK TIERI / OLEG OKUNEV
NOV171154, OCT181340

REPLICA VOL 1
PAUL JENKINS / ANDY CLARKE
MAY161030

ROUGH RIDERS VOL 1, VOL 2 & VOL 3
ADAM GLASS / PATRICK OLLIFFE
OCT161101, SEP171097 & AUG181474

SECOND SIGHT VOL 1
DAVID HINE / ALBERTO PONTICELL
DEC161186

SHIPWRECK VOL 1
WARREN ELLIS / PHIL HESTER
MAR181078

SHOCK VOL 1 HARDCOVER & VOL 2 HARDCOVER
VARIOUS
JAN181139 & APR191300

SUPERZERO VOL 1
AMANDA CONNER / JIMMY PALMIOTTI / RAFAEL DE LATORRE
MAY161029

UNHOLY GRAIL VOL 1
CULLEN BUNN / MIRKO COLAK
JAN181151

WITCH HAMMER OGN
CULLEN BUNN / DALIBOR TALAJIC
SEP181387

WORLD READER VOL 1
JEFF LOVENESS / JUAN DOE
SEP171096

www.aftershockcomics.com/collections

ABOUT THE CREATORS OF

DESCENDENT™

STEPHANIE PHILLIPS writer

@Steph_Smash

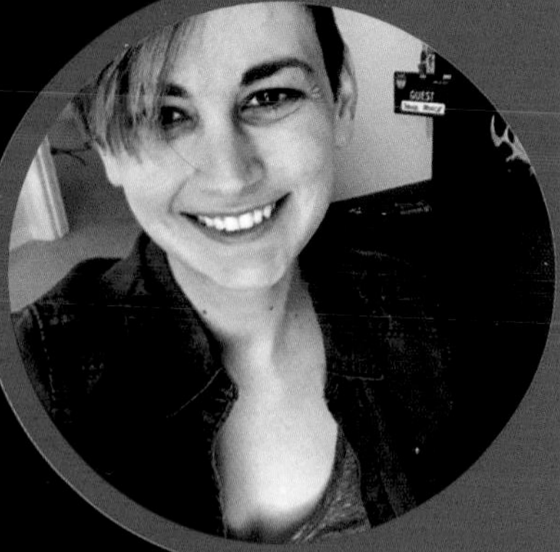

Stephanie Phillips is a comic book writer from Tampa, FL currently living in Buffalo, NY. Her work appears with AfterShock, Top Cow, Black Mask, Ominous Press and more. Along with comics, Stephanie is a writing professor at the University at Buffalo and a PhD candidate for English. She really likes pancakes and one time wore matching socks.

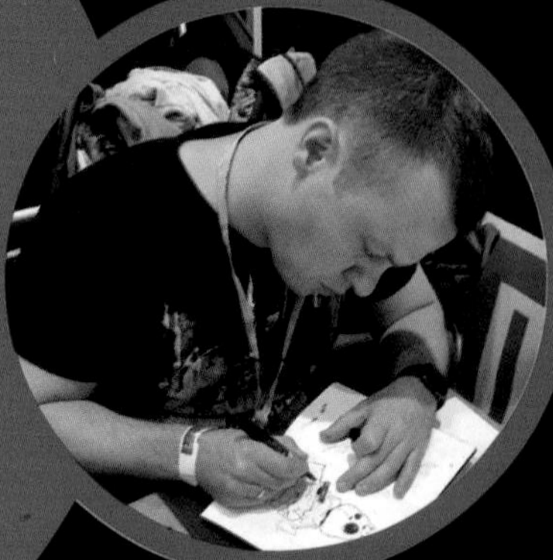

EVGENIY BORNYAKOV artist

@EvgenyBornyakov

Evgeniy Bornyakov is a Russian artist who started his career working as an illustrator for games, storyboarding and animation. But his love for comic books won. As a comic book artist he began his career at the publishing house Bubble. These days he illustrates for AfterShock Comics.

LAUREN AFFE colorist

@laurenaffe

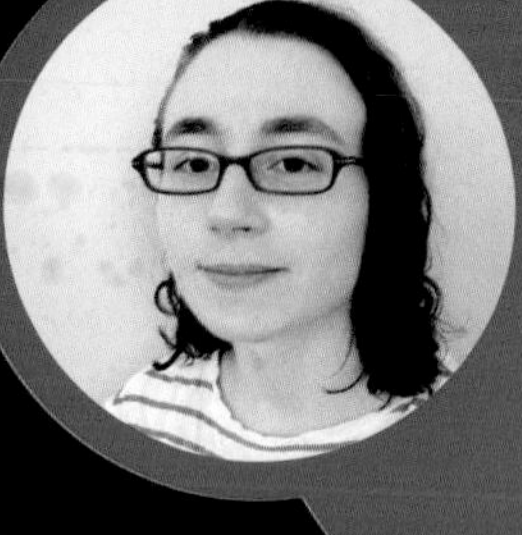

Lauren has been working in comics since graduating from SCAD in 2010. She has operated as color artist on many creator owned titles from Dark Horse Comics (*Buzzkill, The Ghost Fleet, The Paybacks*) and Image Comics (*Five Ghosts*). This has led to work on Dynamite Entertainment's *Turok: Dinosaur Hunter* relaunch as well as projects for Marvel Comics. In addition to THE REVISIONIST and DEAD KINGS for AfterShock, she is currently working on new projects for Stela, Random House and Image Comics.

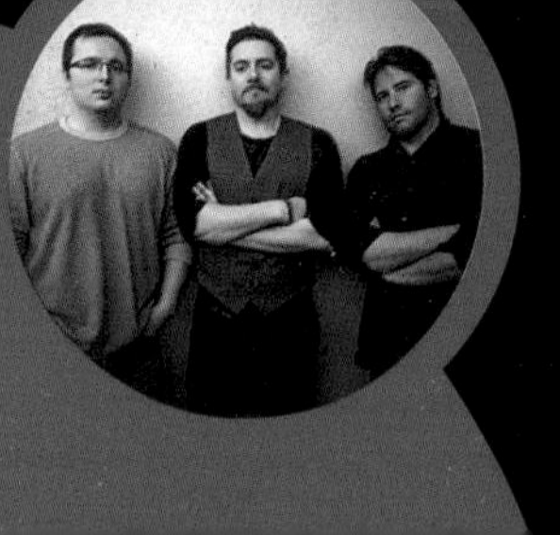

TROY PETERI letterer

@A_Larger_World

Troy Peteri, Dave Lanphear and Joshua Cozine are collectively known as A Larger World Studios. They've lettered everything from *The Avengers, Iron Man, Wolverine, Amazing Spider-Man* and *X-Men* to more recent titles like *The Spirit, Batman & Robin Eternal* and *Pacific Rim*. They can be reached at studio@largerworld.com for your lettering and design needs.